THE WEST
THAT NEVER WAS

THE WEST

BOOKS BY TONY THOMAS

The Films of Errol Flynn (with Rudy Behlmer and Cliff McCarty)
The Busby Berkeley Book
Ustinov in Focus
Music for the Movies
Cads and Cavaliers
The Films of Kirk Douglas
Song and Dance: The Films of Gene Kelly
The Films of Marlon Brando
The Films of the Forties
The Great Adventure Films
Hollywood's Hollywood (with Rudy Behlmer)
Burt Lancaster
Gregory Peck
Sam Wood: Hollywood Professional

From a Life of Adventure
Film Score
Harry Warren and the Hollywood Musical
Ronald Reagan: The Hollywood Years
The Films of 20th Century-Fox (with Aubrey Solomon)
Hollywood and the American Image
The Films of Olivia de Havilland
Queen Mary and the Spruce Goose
The Films of Henry Fonda
That's Dancing
Howard Hughes in Hollywood
The Cinema of the Sea
A Wonderful Life: The Films and Career of James Stewart

THAT NEVER WAS

BY TONY THOMAS

A CITADEL PRESS BOOK
Published by Carol Communications

ACKNOWLEDGMENTS

As with my other books dealing with film my basic point of research has been the library of The Academy of Motion Picture Arts and Sciences (Los Angeles), for which I am again grateful to Linda Mehr and her staff. I am also grateful to Packy Smith for his help and encouragement, and in the difficult business of collecting the photographs I owe thanks to Eddie Brandt, Bob Colman, Mark Haggard and Mark Willoughby of Collectors Bookshop (Hollywood).

Designed by A. Christopher Simon

Manufactured in the United States of America
ISBN 0-8065-1121-4

To the Memory of
Colonel Timothy J. McCoy, U.S.A.

CONTENTS

FOREWORD: WESTWARD

How many westerns have there been? No one seems to know the exact number. The first one of any substance, *The Great Train Robbery,* made in 1903, was one reel in length—about ten minutes—and it was followed by hundreds and hundreds of others of that size over the next ten years, until Cecil B. DeMille came along and made the first western feature, *The Squaw Man,* which ran to six reels. In the teen years of the 20th century, most westerns ran to two reels, with the five reeler coming into general service with the '20s. In 1923 came the first western epic, *The Covered Wagon,* followed by John Ford's *The Iron Horse* the following year, both of which brought some respectability to a form of film that was mostly an offshoot of the dime novel. *In Old Arizona,* released in January of 1929, became the first sound western and signaled even greater success for the genre, thereby laying to rest the fears that sound would kill off the appeal of the western.

While it is impossible to come up with an exact listing of silent westerns, most of which have long vanished or decomposed, much better records have been kept since the arrival of sound. To date the number of sound westerns is close to 3500—and this does not include the vast amount of product made for television. It is an astonishing body of work, especially in view of its narrow focus.

We have now had westerns for many more years than there was a Wild West. Almost all westerns are set in the years between the Civil War and the ending of the 19th century, with the volume of stories told about that period far exceeding the amount of history upon which is it supposedly based. More six-shooters have been fired, more cattle rustled, more banks and stagecoaches held up, more cowboys have brawled in saloons, more wagons have rumbled westward, more Indians have been shot from their ponies and more cavalry have ridden to the rescue in the movies than the real West ever knew.

Of all the depictions of American life put on film, the western is the least accurate and the most romanticized. The fabric is largely woven from fiction, which is not in itself surprising. What is perhaps surprising is that everybody knows it is fiction, with only the driest of historians raising any protest. Westerns are made for profit and pleasure, and being aware of that need has little bearing upon any appreciation for the real West. Hollywood created a West that never really was but it is possible to enjoy it alongside the West that really is. At least, that has been my experience.

My fascination with the West began as a child seeing westerns. Starting at about the age of nine, I became dazzled with the sight of men riding around on horses amid vast landscapes of deserts and mountains in what seemed like perpetual summer. The values were simplistic. The good guys were solidly so and the bad guys were the opposite. Buck Jones, Tim McCoy, Ken Maynard, George O'Brien, Bill "Hopalong Cassidy" Boyd, Tex Ritter, John Wayne and Johnny Mack Brown became my supermen. This hardly made me unique—I was merely one of millions of boys in the late '30s and early '40s who made Saturday matinees a ritualistic den of vicarious pleasure. It was a pleasure most of us eventually put aside, except that in my case it left me with a great curiosity about the lands in which all these adventures took place, not knowing at the time that most of these pictures were shot within 50 miles of Los Angeles.

In time, I traveled through all of the states west of the Mississippi and the western provinces of Canada. I began my career as a broadcaster and writer at the age of 20 and I have had the great good fortune to combine my work with my interests. In the summer of 1948, I even had a fling at being a cowboy. I worked on a ranch in the beautiful foothills of the Rockies in Alberta, a little to the west of Cochrane, where I quickly learned that I was not cut out for such a life. Up at six, out on the range at seven, all day in the saddle—it seemed little like the movies. After a month or so, I was ready to go back to sitting behind microphones, reading newscasts and commercials.

In 1956, I was hired by the Canadian Broadcasting Corporation as a radio producer at the network headquarters in Toronto. Gradually, I talked my bosses into letting me do programs about Hollywood, its people and the picture business. Over the next ten years, I went back and forth between Toronto and Los Angeles, after which I made it my home, and interviewed every actor, director, producer, writer and composer I could get to. I also indulged myself by seeking out some of the western heroes I had idolized as a boy. It was not always the pleasure I had hoped for. I found Ken Maynard living in a rundown trailer park in San Fernando and I visited Hoot Gibson in Las Vegas shortly before he died, when he was a shell of his former robust self. On the other hand, it was a comfort to visit Randolph Scott in his Beverly Hills home, which backed onto a golf course, and to meet the affable Joel McCrea on his ranch in Camarillo.

I soon found that talking about making westerns was a limited subject. I once asked Johnny Mack Brown if he had enjoyed making westerns and that courtly southern gentleman looked at me as if I had asked a silly question, which I had. He said he had enjoyed playing cowboys as a child, "Didn't you?" and that getting well paid to do it as an adult was sheer luck. All the cowboy stars said the same thing. With Richard Boone, I was able to dig a little deeper into the mystique of the western. I interviewed him at the time he was appearing as Paladin in the television series *Have Gun, Will Travel*. "The western is like the Commedia Dell'Arte or the Greek plays, in that there's a certain formula pre-established, with a hero and villain and little ambiguity. I think the simple line has a lot to do with the success of the western, that plus the action and the scenic scope that lends itself so well to photography." What about the vicarious pleasure of watching gunfights and brawls and riding horses through the wide open spaces? "Well, ever since men began enjoying art in any form we've always liked to identify with heroes. The hero well done is a pleasure to watch. We like to ride alongside him. We'd all like to be able to lead cavalry charges and outdraw villains in saloons. I've played the character many times—and I'd like to live as he does."

Asking directors like Delmer Daves, Howard Hawks and Sam Peckinpah why they made so many westerns provoked the same kind of responses as asking a man why he likes to eat or to make love. Feeling foolish, I would turn to other questions, although one day hoping I could put the question to John Ford. The crusty old master did not suffer interviewers very kindly and I was warned that if I ever did get to talk to him I should tred softly. Finally, through the considerable offices of John Wayne, I got to meet Ford. I placed my question. He stared at me for a moment and I expected to be tossed out. Instead, "The western is the *real* picture. It's full of action and character. It moves. The people move. You see the outdoors, the exteriors—nature—horses, rivers, valleys." I pressed my luck. Why do you love making westerns? Another stare. "I *like* cowboys. I like stunt men. They're a wonderful, kindly group of gentlemen. Easy to work with. Besides, it gives me a chance to get out of southern California and go to Arizona, where I breathe fresh air. It gives you a different view on life. I relax. I sleep better at night. That's why I like to do westerns. I have no obsession about them, but I do love the West. I punched cows for a while when I was young. Twelve dollars a month. The food was very good. Also, I have a family background of western cavalry. Two of my uncles who fought in the Civil War later fought against the Indians. I was brought up on stories about the West. That's about all there is to it." After Ford had said that, I knew I would be an idiot to lean on him any further.

The most interesting westerner I ever knew was Tim McCoy, who was also the finest authority on the West I ever had the pleasure to meet. While it is unwise to become acquainted with film actors one has worshipped—disappointment is virtually guaranteed—McCoy was the exception. He was in fact a far more erudite and well spoken man than his image as a movie cowboy would have led most people to believe. I met him first in 1961 when I went to record a radio series for the CBC, which later resulted in being able to bring him to Toronto on two occasions for radio and television appearances. This in turn led to a friendship which resulted in my being his guest at his home in Nogales, Arizona, on several visits. He had built himself a small hacienda, which he called Los Arcos, in which he lived with his Danish-born wife Inga and sons Ronald (named after his close friend Ronald Colman) and Tim. After supper we would go to his study and talk, or rather in my case, listen. McCoy had explored the West and its history, particularly the military history, and it was from him I learned in detail about the Custer campaigns. He had even spoken with Indians who had taken part in the famed Last Stand. But aside from the real West, I also wanted to know about his years in Hollywood.

THOMAS: Tim, did you enjoy making western pictures?

McCOY: Of course, I did. It was a lot of fun and damned remunerative. I liked the income and the life it brought. I certainly don't regret having gone into pictures.

THOMAS: So many of the characters in these films, even the heroes, seemed semi-illiterate, and yet here you were, an educated man, an army colonel, riding around with them.

McCOY: Well, I maintained my ranch in Wyoming all during the Hollywood years and I always felt that if I played an illiterate cowboy I'd have an awful lot of explaining to do to my Wyoming friends. I used to tell newspapermen who interviewed me, who didn't think I talked down-to-earth enough for them, that they were thinking of the Bret Harte characters and the days of the gold rush. It was hard to convince them that people had been going to school in the West for generations.

THOMAS: How does the real thing compare with the stuff you did in pictures?

McCOY: It doesn't, really. They always twisted the truth to fit the picture. You must always remember that these films were never meant to be historical documents. They're entertainment, and if you entertain the customers they will go away happy. However, I always maintained that it did no harm to mix a little authenticity with the entertainment.

THOMAS: But such a definite form of entertainment—like a living, breathing American myth.

McCOY: That's exactly what it is. Unfortunately, it also became a stereotype, ending up with all the westerns looking as if they'd been cut with the same cookie cutter.

THOMAS: Was there any truth in it?

McCOY: Oh, yes. For example, in Wyoming. We had what was known as the invasion, when the rustlers got so bad—and there's no question about it—that the cattlemen brought in gunmen to round up the rustlers and kill them off.

THOMAS: This is historical fact?

McCOY: This is historical fact. They did this, and they got rid of the fellows who were stealing them blind. There you have one of the patterns for your western stories. Then there's the one dealing with the cattle drives coming up from Texas into Kansas, with a lot of the young cowboys fresh out of the Confederate Army and still pretty wild.

THOMAS: Which gives us the town marshals trying to tame them.

McCOY: Yes, of course. These were fellows who went for their guns rather than their fists, and since they were often drunk, they didn't stand up too well to a sober marshal. They were killed. But there was seldom any such thing as men challenging each other to meet at high noon or to shoot it out in the middle of the street.

THOMAS: They didn't blast away from the hip?

McCOY: No, that hip-shooting is the most exaggerated thing. How can you hit anything unless you're five feet away from it? Any man who's handled firearms knows it takes all you can do to lay your sights, take a deep breath and give a slow triggered squeeze to hit anything with a pistol.

THOMAS: How about those fist fights in westerns?

McCOY: There weren't many fist fights in the West. That was the kind of thing that happened more in the lumber camps. Cowboys weren't fistfighters.

THOMAS: But in the movies they scrap away for ten minutes at a time, fighting like mad.

McCOY: I know, but look at the thrill it gives the picture. The audiences love it, just as they do at prize fights. It's always the little inoffensive fellow who has never hit anyone in his life, who is at the ringside yelling 'Kill the bum!' Come to think of it, that's also the appeal of the western—experiencing something second hand that you think you might like to experience at first hand, with hardly any chance that you ever will.

THOMAS: In your case you had it both ways.

McCOY: I was very lucky, and luck always has a lot to do with timing. I went to Wyoming as a teenager and got in on the tail end of the Old West, and met many ranchers, soldiers and Indians who had been involved in the conflicts of a few years previously. I joined the Army just before they phased out the cavalry, and I arrived in Hollywood as an advisor for the first western epic, *The Covered Wagon*. I was in on many of the best years of western film. I have nothing to complain about.

It was not my lot in life to be another Tim McCoy, but short of that I also have little to complain about.

The fascination with the West, which began as a wide-eyed schoolboy gazing at movies, has led to much enjoyment in travel and in meeting many interesting people. In this book, which is an extension of that enjoyment, I have focused on 40 films, with no claim that they are the greatest of their kind. They are simply films for which I feel a lasting affection and admiration. This is one man's view of Hollywood's view of the West.

PART ONE:

THE WEST IN B MINOR

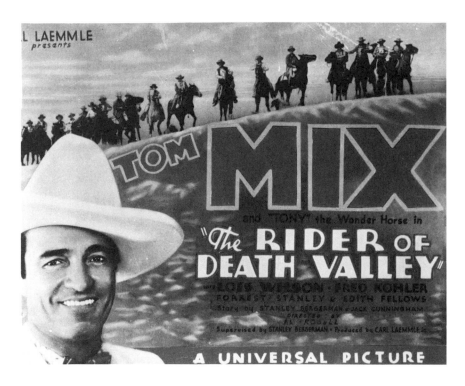

RIDER OF DEATH VALLEY

UNIVERSAL, 1932

Produced by Carl Laemmle, Jr. Directed by Albert Rogell. Written by Jack Cunningham. Photographed by Daniel B. Clark. 78 minutes.

CAST:

(*Tom Rigby*) Tom Mix; (*Helen Joyce*) Lois Wilson; (*Lew Grant*) Fred Kohler; (*Dr. Larabee*) Forrest Stanley; (*Beth Joyce*) Edith Fellows; (*Bill Joyce*) Willard Robertson; (*Tillie*) Mae Busch; (*Peck*) Otis Harlan; (*Gabe Dillon*) Francis Ford.

The image of the cowboy as an international movie star began with Tom Mix. Film historians rightly credit William S. Hart as the man who rescued the western from all the nonsense that had flooded the screen in the first dozen years or so, but it was Mix who caught the public imagination with his breezy personality and his flamboyant stunts. Hart, who made some 40 westerns between 1915 and 1925, wanted to show the nobility of the West, along with its gritty reality. Mix astutely seized upon the western as an entertainment and as a means of becoming rich and famous. Hart was appalled at the western garb of the early films, describing the cowboys as being dressed somewhere between a Wisconsin woodchopper and a Gloucester fisherman. Mix was the man who sported tight breeches with piped edging, fancy shirts and expensively tooled gunbelts. By the mid-'20s, Hart's career was over and Mix was earning $17,000 a week, the most any cowboy star has ever hauled out of a film studio.

Mix not only gave the public good entertainment in his movies, he also allowed publicity about himself that was part of the entertainment. He was said to have been born in a log cabin in Texas, that he served with Teddy Roosevelt's Rough Riders in Cuba, that he fought in the Phillipines and in Mexico, that he was a Texas Ranger and an Oklahoma sheriff, in addition to being a rodeo champion. The public swallowed it without a question. The Mix attitude was, "Tell 'em what they want to hear." The truth did not emerge until 1972, when Paul Mix, a distant and very curious relative, published his book *The Life and Legend of Tom Mix,* on which he had spent years of research.

15

Mix was born in Mix Run, Pennsylvania, on January 6, 1880. He attended a fairground showing of Buffalo Bill's Wild West Show when he was ten and from then on he became smitten with western lore. He learned to ride and rope, and at 18, he joined the Army (Battery M, 4th Artillery Regiment) when the Spanish-American War was declared. His regiment was not involved in either the campaign in Cuba or the one against the insurgents in the Phillipines. He married in 1902—the first of four marriages—and left the Army without permission. The fact that he was a deserter did not come up until his death, by which time he was such an American legend that the Army had to hold its tongue and provide him with military honors at his funeral.

Guthrie, Oklahoma, was the first western town in Mix's life. There he became a physical training instructor, which led him to part-time work as a ranch hand, with occasional excitement as a volunteer law enforcement officer. In 1905, he joined a group called the Cowboy Brigade, which was organized to celebrate the election of President Theodore Roosevelt. This led to Mix being spotted by Colonel Joe Miller, the owner of the 101 Ranch, who hired Mix as a cowboy at 15 dollars a month. This in turn led to him becoming involved in rodeos, at which he proved so adept that the next logical step was the more profitable arena of the Wild West show.

It was while Mix was employed by the Circle D Ranch Wild West Show in 1909 that he made his entry into the world of motion pictures. The Selig Polyscope Company used the show for a film and Mix was hired to handle horses. It was not long before he persuaded his new employers that he would look good in front of the cameras rather than behind them, and in 1910, he was one of the featured players in *Ranch Life in the Great South West,* in which he was billed not only as an expert roper and broncho buster but also an ex-United States Marshal. The legend had begun.

The publicity may have been fanciful but Mix was in truth an expert horseman and a fine marksman. In his early films, he did all his own stunts and because of that, he sustained, as he had in rodeos and shows, many injuries. And despite the silly stories, the Selig pictures were shot in actual settings in all parts of the West, and those that survive are a valuable record of western ranches and range activities of that period. Mix grew and grew in popularity and, in 1918, he was offered a substantial contract by Fox Films. It was now that he soared into the Hollywood firmament, with immense wealth and an extravagant lifestyle. He dressed like a cowboy god, he roared around the country in custom-built sports cars, and his Beverly Hills mansion spelled out his name in neon lights. No one enjoyed being a star more than Tom Mix.

By the end of the silent era, Mix decided his movie career was over. He was nearing 50 and his body was tired. He claimed that he had sustained some 80 injuries in his life on horseback. He accepted an offer to tour as the star of the Sells-Floto Wild West Show at $10,000 per week. This went on until 1932 when Universal enticed him back to Hollywood with a contract that would pay him a similar salary in a series of films to be budgeted at $100,000, the most money that had ever been allocated to B westerns. Mix made nine of these pictures for Universal, all of them above average in their class and one of them, *Rider of Death Valley,* a film of genuine value.

In accepting the Universal offer, Mix made one demand, and that was the choice of cameraman. He wanted Daniel B. Clark, with whom he had worked on most of his best Fox westerns. Universal readily agreed, and Clark is almost as much the star of *Rider of Death Valley* as Mix. Much of the film was shot in the valley and Clark captured the strange beauty of the undulating sand dunes and cliff formations. In one remarkable episode, he devised a mirage of water in the desert, which recedes as a thirst-crazed man tries to reach it. Another sequence, with 30 or so riders galloping over the dunes in coming to the rescue of Mix is photography of exceptional imagery.

In *Rider of Death Valley,* Mix is Tom Rigby, a ranch owner who comes into the gold-fever town of Rome to see that none of his cowboys are tempted to leave in search of the yellow lure. While there, he befriends a six-year-old girl, Beth Joyce (Edith Fellows), whose widower father, Bill (Willard Robertson), is roaming around in a drunken stupor. Tom raises his stetson to her, "How do you do, young lady?" She snorts, "I'm not a lady," to which he replies, "You're the first female I've ever heard admit it." Her father is celebrating because he has found a goldmine in the desert, a fact overheard by a roughneck, Lew Grant (Fred Kohler), and a doctor named Larabee (Forrest Stanley). When Tom visits the father and daughter in their shack outside the town, he finds the man is dying from a gunshot wound. He also discovers Grant and Larabee at the shack, claiming that they heard a shot and came to find out what had happened. Before Bill dies, he hands over a map giving the location of his mine, with the instruction that it should go to his sister, Helen (Lois Wilson). To keep Grant and Larabee in line, Tom tears the map into three pieces, one for himself and the other pieces to them.

Tom takes Beth to his ranch and virtually adopts her, much to the joy of the little girl, who now acquires pretty dresses and much attention. As one observer puts it, "He's gone plumb crazy about that kid." When Helen arrives, Tom agrees to guide her to the mine,

Tom Mix.

Tom Mix, Lois Wilson, Fred Kohler and Forrest Stanley.

Edith Fellows and Tom Mix.

17

along with Grant and Larabee. As the trek proves more and more arduous, the friction among the men grows. Grant attacks Tom and, as a shot is fired, the horses pulling the buggy bolt, carrying Helen. Tom rides after her and pulls her from the dynamite-laden buggy before it sallies over a cliff and explodes in a gully. Lost in the explosion are the supplies, most importantly the water. With only three canisters, the party is now in dire straits. The group finds the mine but soon the cry is not for gold but for water. Grant wanders into the desert and dies following a mirage. Tom sends his horse back to his ranch with a note pinned to its mane. The note falls off but the horse manages to get across to the cowboys that it wants them to follow, which they do, and just in time. Larrabee finds a stick of dynamite and blows up the mine trying to find a source of water, and dies in the attempt. Tom and Helen manage to escape the explosion by jumping behind a sand dune, and their parched throats are now soothed by the water of the rescuers.

Aside from the splendid photography of Clark, *Riders of Death Valley* benefits from the fine script by Jack Cunningham, an expert writer of western films. His dialogue is far ahead of the usual quality in B westerns. As the heroine looks out over the awesome dunes, she muses, "Death Valley—fills you with terror, doesn't it?" Tom replies, "All according to the way you look at it. I kind of like it myself. It doesn't pretend to be anything it isn't." The film also contains some lines highly unusual in a western. When Tom takes the nattily dressed little girl into a bar and sits her on the counter, someone asks him how it feels to be a mother, and the girl not only embarrasses him by letting it be known that he ironed her dress but she adds, "Last night, he washed me all over and put me to bed." Aside from this strange twist, the film is also notable for the veracity of the scenes showing its actors suffering from the lack of water. There is an acute feeling of how dire this situation really is.

Mix was never an actor but he had a sense of confidence and authority in front of the cameras. It was more than adequate for the roles he played, and whenever he had to deal with horses, there was no question of his mastery. His principal horse was Tony, a chestnut he bought in 1912 when the animal was two and which shared star billing—Tom Mix and Tony. Ironically, the

Tom Mix, Fred Kohler and Lois Wilson.

18

Director Albert Rogell instructs Tom Mix on location, with most of the crew wearing masks and goggles to protect them from the heat and glare of sunny Death Valley.

horse would live two years beyond its master, dying in 1942 at 32, an advanced age for a horse. In *Rider of Death Valley,* Mix rode Tony Jr., an Arabian unrelated to the chestnut. The film required a lot of the horse, galloping across the dunes by itself, smashing its way out of a stall and prancing around to get the interest of the cowboys who ride to the rescue. Especially interesting is the scene where Mix has to force the horse to leave him; clearly there was an unusual and touching rapport between the man and his mount.

After finishing the last of the Universal westerns, *The Rustler's Round-Up* in early 1933, Mix again decided it was time to call it quits with film. A showman at heart, he bought an interest in a circus and renamed in The Tom Mix Circus. In 1935, he accepted an offer by movie producer Nat Levine to star in a serial titled *The Miracle Rider,* with fully half the budget going to the star. It was an offer he should have refused. There

was nothing miraculous about the rider of this serial. This was a battered, tired 55-year-old with most of the flair and spirit gone. Anyone seeing *The Miracle Rider* and nothing else of the star would have little understanding of the Mix magic.

It all came to an end on October 12, 1940. Mix was driving his expensive convertible at a high speed along a road near Florence, Arizona. He swerved to miss a detour sign, lost control of his car and crashed in a gully. A suitcase in the back seat shot forward and snapped his neck. A monument, topped by a statue of a horse, was erected on the spot and the inscription reads, "In memory of Tom Mix, whose spirit left his body on this spot, and whose characterizations and portrayals in life served better to fix memories of the Old West in the minds of living men." The sentiment is perhaps a little overdrawn, but what else would have been appropriate for such a man?

Lafe McKee, Wheeler Oakman
and Tim McCoy.

END OF THE TRAIL

COLUMBIA, 1932

Produced by Irving Briskin. Directed by D. Ross Lederman. Written by Stuart Anthony. Photographed by Benjamin Kline. 61 minutes.

CAST:

(*Capt. Tim Travers*) Tim McCoy; (*Luana*) Luana Walter; (*Major Jenkins*) Wheeler Oakman; (*Timmy*) Wally Albright; (*Colonel Burke*) Lafe McKee; (*Sergeant O'Brien*) Wade Boteler; (*Arapahoe Chief*) Chief White Eagle.

When Mike Todd was casting *Around the World in 80 Days,* he had only one man in mind for the officer in charge of the US Cavalry unit that rides to the rescue of Phineas Fogg from an Indian attack. John Wayne offered to play the cameo role but Todd wanted and got Colonel Tim McCoy. His choice was a tribute to the veteran soldier-actor, and Todd's personal gift to him for appearing in the film was a set of gold miniatures of McCoy's 13 campaign medals and victory decorations.

McCoy was the rare cowboy star who was also an acknowledged authority on the West, in particular, on Indian history and affairs. And no one else in Hollywood ever spoke up more forcefully for the Indians. As a film actor, McCoy was in a class of his own. Although he had never set out with the idea of being a performer, he had about him an innate theatricalism. Articulate and well-spoken, he performed with a natural dignity, always very much the Army officer, and his style set him apart from the more roughneck cowboy actors. McCoy seldom brawled in his pictures and never did any trick riding. He was, however, lightning fast on the draw and when he walked into a saloon, ramrod straight, his cool stare sent shivers through the villains. They knew from his very presence that there was trouble brewing.

He was not born to the West. Saginaw, Michigan, was his birthplace (April 10, 1891), where his father, who had been a soldier in his native Ireland, was the chief of police. He instilled in his son a respect for the military and encouraged his interest in the West. At 16, McCoy took a train westward and got off in the town of Lander, Wyoming. His first job was pitching hay on a ranch, but he was soon given a horse and sent out to

Wheeler Oakman and Tim McCoy.

round-up stray cattle. He worked in the Wind River country, where he came into contact with the Arapahoes and the Shoshones, from whom he learned the Indian sign language. Years later, he was given the name High Eagle by the Arapahoes and made a blood brother.

By the time America entered the war in 1917, McCoy had chalked up ten years of ranch life and had gathered a vast amount of research about western history. He applied for officer training with the Army and, because of his offer to organize a regiment of cavalry from among the cowboys of Wyoming and Montana, he was commissioned a captain of cavalry. The plan never went into affect because the Army decided that cavalry would be of no use in the war at this point, and McCoy was transferred to the horse artillery. McCoy liked the Army and decided to make it his profession. He was a colonel by age 30, and since his knowledge of the West and of the Indians was now a matter of record, he was appointed the Adjutant General of Wyoming, giving him the brevet rank of brigadier general. The post also put him in charge of the state's Indian affairs and allowed him to indulge his interest in visiting the actual sites of the Indian Wars and interviewing survivors. McCoy was the first man to research the Custer massacre of 1876

Lafe McKee, Wheeler Oakman and Tim McCoy.

from the Indian side, which material he turned over to Colonel W. A. Graham for use in the latter's book *The Custer Myth.*

It was while serving as the Adjutant General of Wyoming that McCoy came to the attention of Hollywood. In 1923, Paramount contracted him to advise on the gathering of Indians in an epic western they had in preparation, *The Covered Wagon.* He not only got together 500 long-haired Indians but also brought them to Hollywood in two train loads, along with their squaws, papooses, teepees and dogs. Paramount was so impressed that it offered McCoy the job of technical advisor for the film. He resigned his Army commission and accepted. Part of his job was to devise a prologue and appear with the Indians at Grauman's Chinese Theater in Hollywood. The prologue was such a success that, when *The Covered Wagon* opened in London, McCoy and his Indians were sent to repeat their show. The Londoners loved it and McCoy appeared at the London Pavilion for almost one year.

After spending two years publicizing *The Covered Wagon,* it was obvious to both McCoy and others that he had a flair for this kind of thing. In 1926, Irving Thalberg, the head of production at MGM, offered him a contract as the star of a series of westerns, all of which would stress history and some of which would deal with the Indians. The first was *War Paint,* which took McCoy back to his old stamping grounds in Wyoming and again required him to recruit his Indian friends.

In 1929, MGM decided not to renew McCoy's contract, feeling that the coming of sound-on-film made the western a risky venture. He was about to resume his life in Wyoming when Universal offered him the lead in the first sound serial, *The Indians Are Coming,* the success of which led to a Columbia contract for a series. McCoy made 32 films for Columbia over a four year period, the most interesting of which is *End of the Trail.* It is arguably the most extraordinary B western ever made. No film before or since has ever spoken up more forcefully about the tragic fate of the Indians as the white migration overran their lands. That the film was made was entirely due to Tim McCoy.

Columbia was no more interested in Indian history than any other studio but, by 1932, McCoy was enough of a winner for them that they could indulge his ambition to make a film about something dear to him. McCoy persuaded the studio to more than double the usual budget and to let him take a small cast and crew to Wyoming, there to film near Lander and to use the Wind River Reservation, the home of the Arapahoe, and through which the Powder River flowed. *End of the Trail* may have made no more profit than the usual B western of its time, but Columbia did very well with the footage cameraman Benjamin Kline shot of the Wyoming landscape and Indian scenes, which became a primary source of stock shots in countless westerns for years thereafter.

McCoy appears as cavalry captain Tim Travers, who is ordered by his commanding officer, Colonel Burke (Lafe McKee), to ride with 20 men to the protection of a white settlement. En route, the column is attacked and only Travers and two others survive. At the inquiry, Travers complains that the Indians were armed with government rifles and carbines, and that someone in the service must be responsible. Later, the second in command, Major Jenkins (Wheeler Oakman), suggests to Burke that Travers himself is probably the culprit. He is known to be an Indian sympathizer. Actually, the culprit is Jenkins, who causes a court martial for Travers by planting false evidence. Travers takes his adopted son, Timmy (Wally Albright), and leaves the fort. He is soon overtaken by his loyal sergeant, O'Brien (Wade Boteler), who admits he has deserted. This results in Travers and O'Brien being pursued by an Army patrol, and during the course of the chase, Timmy is hit by a bullet. After burying the boy, Travers and O'Brien proceed to the Arapahoe reservation, there to make their home.

News arrives that an Army command under General Webber has been wiped out and that measures must now be taken to control the Arapahoe, who respond by preparing for war. Travers tries to dissuade them and offers to go to Washington on their behalf. As he, O'Brien and a group of Indians move across the country on the way to the train, a unit under Major Jenkins attacks. O'Brien and most of the Indians are killed and Travers is arrested and taken back to the fort. Soon the fort is attacked by the Arapahoe in order to rescue Travers, but after many deaths on either side, he persuades the colonel to let him proceed under a white flag to facilitate a cease fire. As Travers negotiates with the Indians, the dying Jenkins admits to Burke that he and not Travers was responsible for selling government arms to the Indians. The Arapahoe accept Travers' plea to stop the fight, but as he makes his way back to the fort, a demented soldier fires and mortally wounds him. He dies in Burke's arms, giving a weak salute and saying, "Once an Army man, always an Army man."

This was the way McCoy wanted *End of the Trail* to end, but in this Columbia was not about to agree. This was not the kind of a finale that would please the Saturday matinee fans. Back at the studio, McCoy was required to shoot a new ending, which finds him, his arm in a sling, promoted and given charge of Wyoming's Indian affairs, and with an inference that Luana (Luana Walter), the pretty Indian girl he befriended on the reservation, might be a possible future love.

Lafe McKee and Tim McCoy.

The ending is soft but it did not alter the force of the film. McCoy was able to get his points across without censorship. He worked closely with scripter Stuart Anthony on the story but the monologues are plainly the words of McCoy.

After being cashiered, this is what Captain Travers tells his colonel: "From the time this government began dealing with the Indians it has never kept a single treaty it has made with them. The Harney-Sanborn Treaty ceded all of this country to the Sioux and the Arapahoe and the Cheyenne. That treaty specified that all the land north of the North Platte River to the Yellowstone, from the Black Hills west to the Big Horn River, should be the Indian—ceded to them in a scared treaty. When the white men made that treaty, they were very glad to get all the rest of the country and leave the Indians this little plot of land. The Indians, on the other hand, realized that the white man was going to sooner or later to smother them under, and they thought that if they could only protect their hunting grounds, where the elk, the deer, the antelope and the buffalo were—the country in which were buried the bones of their fathers—they were satisfied, too—if the white man would live up to that treaty—and they expected him to.

Luana Walter and Tim McCoy.

"Now, some white fool has discovered gold in Montana. Settlers are pouring into that territory and pleading with the government to send troops out to protect them, that they can take a short cut across the Indian country to the gold fields—and that is what we are here for—to protect white men seeking gold. We've never kept a single treaty with them. That's why I'm for the Indians, because in every instance the white man has been to blame. And if these Indians take to the war path now—which they are sure to do—then I want to say to you, sir, the bloodshed that results will not be the fault of the Indians. The responsibility must rest entirely on the white man. Those are my sentiments as a man, sir. As an Army officer I have always obeyed orders. I am not guilty of the charges for which I have been convicted."

Not only is it possibly the longest speech ever delivered in a western film, it is also the most personal and impassioned. And the actor who spoke the lines knew exactly what he was talking about.

Wade Boteler, Chief White Eagle and Tim McCoy.

THE THUNDERING HERD

PARAMOUNT, 1933

Directed by Henry Hathaway. Written by Jack Cunningham and Mary Flannery, based on the novel by Zane Grey. Photographed by Ben Reynolds. 62 minutes.

CAST:

(Tom Doane) Randolph Scott; *(Millie Fayre)* Judith Allen; *(Randall Jett)* Noah Beery; *(Clark Sprague)* Harry Carey; *(Bill Hatch)* Buster Crabbe; *(Jane Jett)* Blanche Frederici; *(Jude Pilchuck)* Raymond Hatton; *(Prewitt)* Barton MacLane.

Zane Grey and Randolph Scott had much in common. Neither was a westerner but it was their identification with the West that made both of them millionaires. Neither the writer nor the actor merited a great deal of praise from the critics but each won devoted followings.

Grey, born in Zanesville, Ohio, in 1875, began his career as a dentist in New York City, but a dentist with a hankering to write. Aside from a magazine article or two, success eluded him until he made a trip to the West in 1908. That did it; he found his niche. Two years later, his first novel, *Heritage of the Desert,* appeared on the market, followed by *The Riders of the Purple Sage,* which sold one million copies in its first year, and which would be filmed four times—by William Farnum (1918), Tom Mix (1925), George O'Brien (1931) and George Montgomery (1941), with the concensus leaning toward the Montgomery version as being the closest to the spirit of the novel. After that first sale to Hollywood in 1918, Grey had no trouble peddling the film rights to dozens of his novels. A man with canny foresight, Grey leased his work to the producers for a period of seven years, after which the rights reverted to him, enabling him to sell the novels again for remakes. However, he did not, as people expected, use the money to buy himself a ranch in the West. Grey indulged himself in his favorite sport, deep sea fishing, and traveled the world. He settled in Altadena, not far from Los Angeles, and there he died in 1939 from a sudden heart attack—but the income and the constant filming of his stories went on and on.

Randolph Scott became a quintessential movie westerner, a veritable icon of western lore whose features

Harry Carey and Randolph
Scott

gradually seemed as natural a part of the wide open spaces as the buttes and the mesas. He was, however, very much a southern gentleman, a Virginian from the upper crust, who had little interest in the cowboy life away from the cameras. Scott was born of a wealthy family and ended up one of the richest men in Beverly Hills, due to a talent for business that was even more acute than his considerable skill in maintaining a film career over a period of more than 30 years. Unlike most actors, who read *Variety* and *The Hollywood Reporter* during breaks in filming, Scott read *The Financial Times* and *The Wall Street Journal*. Courtly of manner, he was well respected by those with whom he worked; the veteran director Michael Curtiz, who directed him in *Virginia City* (1940) said, "Randy Scott is a complete anachronism. He's a gentleman, and so far, he's the only one I've met in this business full of self-promoting sons-of-bitches."

When David O. Selznick was casting *Gone With the Wind,* fans of various stars deluged the producer with suggestions for the main roles. The actor whom the public, including author Margaret Mitchell, seemed to want for Ashley Wilkes was Scott, whose accent and bearing were perfect for the character as written. Selznick chose the more esteemed Leslie Howard, who later made no secret of the fact that he thought the role vapid. Scott had actually played a Wilkes-like role in *So Red the Rose* (1936), as a southern gentleman who loves plantation owner Margaret Sullavan, fights for the Confederacy and returns to rebuild the South. Sadly, the film was a flop and its failure probably lessened Scott's chances at getting the Ashley Wilkes role.

Born in Roanoke, Virginia, in January of 1899, Scott was a descendant of early settlers in the state. His mother was from an old-guard North Carolina family; she married textile manufacturer George G. Scott and their son was educated at a number of private schools before attending Georgia Tech. There a back injury prevented him from attaining his goal of becoming an all-American football player. After college, he began an apprenticeship in textile manufacturing but shocked his family with his interest in the theatre. His father's advice was to get it out of his system by trying it and then return to the sensible business of textiles. He gave his son a letter of introduction to the only man Scott senior knew with any connections in the entertainment industry—Howard Hughes.

Scott managed to meet the elusive Hughes, who arranged for him to get work as an extra in a George O'Brien western, *Sharp Shooters,* in 1928. The experience was enough to convince Scott that the movies and not the theatre was the line he should pursue. To learn about acting, of which he practically knew nothing, he attended the Pasadena Community Playhouse for two years, with odd jobs on the side—one of them coaching Gary Cooper's accent for *The Virginian.* Scott's performance in the play *Under a Virginia Moon* at the Vine Street Theatre in Hollywood in early 1932 brought him several studio offers, and he decided to accept the one from Paramount. The handsome, charming young Scott was clearly star material but the studio was not sure in which direction to steer him. After he had done a variety of small roles, it occurred to Paramount to give him the lead in a planned series of Zane Grey pictures.

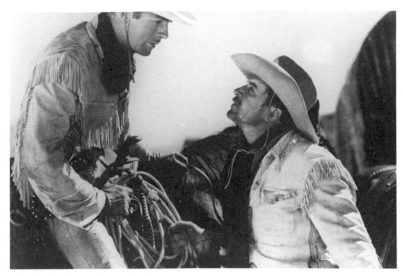

Randolph Scott and Monte Blue.

Harry Carey, Randolph Schott and Raymond Hatton.

Randolph Scott, Monte Blue
and Harry Carey.

Scott, who had ridden horses most of his life, including fox hunts in Virginia, now began an apprenticeship in westerns that would eventually lead to superstardom in the Hollywood West.

The Grey films to which Paramount assigned Scott were actually remakes. All of them had been made in the '20s, mostly with Jack Holt playing the hero, and the studio not only used a great deal of footage from the previous films but also dressed Scott and the other actors in similar costumes to match the shots. First came *Heritage of the Desert*, released in September of 1932, followed by *Wild Horse Mesa, Man of the Forest, To the Last Man* and *Sunset Pass*. All the Scott-Grey films were slickly made and the choice of a favorite can only be personal.

The Thundering Herd was first made by Paramount

in 1925 with Jack Holt in the lead as buffalo hunter Tom Doane. A large amount of footage from that version was used in the Scott version, particularly the shots of Indian encampments and the wagon train attack, all filmed in Wyoming during the winter. The footage is somewhat antique but it is clearly authentic. The Scott film begins with a panel: "In the fall of 1874, there occurred one of those wild rushes for sudden wealth that have characterized the American West. This time, it was the lure of buffalo hides, for which a rich commercial market had been developed. The White Man again invaded Indian territory and ruthlessly slaughtered the buffalo herds of the Red Man. Outfitting and shipping depots sprang up at strategic points. Of these, the most remote, deep in the buffalo country, was Sprague's trading post." Under these words appears the signature of Zane Grey.

Sprague (Harry Carey) is a tough but fair dealer, whose chief hunter, Jude Pilchuck (Raymond Hatton), warns him there is trouble brewing because some of the other hunters are stealing hides and blaming the Indians. One of them is Randall Jett (Noah Beery), whose hard and bitter wife, Jane (Blanche Frederici), resents the lecherous attention he pays to their adopted daughter, Millie (Judith Allen). Millie is about to marry Tom Doane, but to thwart this, Jett pulls his wagon, his family and his crew out of the camp and heads into the country, there to steal more hides. Tom follows but is beaten and shot by Jett while attempting to escape with Millie. Jett then ties the unconscious Tom onto his horse, which wanders around until found by Sprague and Pilchuck.

After recuperating, Tom sets out on a hunting expedition and soon finds the Indians on the warpath. The Indians cause a buffalo stampede which Tom manages to divert to save his party. Hearing that Jett has raided other hunters, Tom rides off to locate him, and hopefully find Millie. This turns out to be less of a problem than he had imagined. The jealous Jane Jett promises her husband that he shall never have Millie; they fight and the nasty couple both die as a result. Millie rides off and is soon found by Tom, whose next problem is

helping the wagon train fight off the Indians. This done, all looks well for a bright future.

The Thundering Herd gives a good account of the buffalo wars but the film's producers are not quite as sympathetic toward the plight of the Indians as Grey iin his novel. The footage clearly shows why the Indians declared war—the slaughter of the buffalo deprived them of their source of food and clothing—but they still appear to be vicious savages standing in the way of progress. However, *The Thundering Herd* was made to entertain, not to educate.

Paramount thereafter put Scott in *The Last Round-Up, Wagon Wheels, Rocky Mountain Mystery* and *Home on the Range.* Appearing in these ten Grey pictures over a two year period was an exposure that would shape the course of Scott's career. In the ensuing years, he would appear in a variety of movies, musicals, drawingroom comedies, dramas and war stories, but every now and then he would be called to the saddle for such roles as the US Marshal tracking *Jesse James*

(1939), as Wyatt Earp in *Frontier Marshal* (1939), and as the husband of *Belle Starr* (1941). In 1948, he decided to go West and stay there.

Heritage of the Desert was not only Randolph Scott's first western, but also was the first film directed by Henry Hathaway. He would become a past master with action/adventure movies over a career that lasted for 40 years. Hathaway directed seven of the Scott-Grey films, including *The Thundering Herd,* and much credit is due him for the success of the films. The pacing and the characterizations are much superior to anything being done in the B western arena of those years. Hathaway had worked on the 1925 version of *The Thundering Herd* as an assistant director, as he had on the six other original versions of the Grey films he later made with Scott. He was therefore the perfect choice to remake them and to know how to integrate previous footage. Hathaway was always grateful that he was able to begin his career as a director in this manner, "It was the finest training a man could possibly have."

Raymond Hatton, Randolph Scott, Judith Allen and Harry Carey.

SCARLET RIVER

R K O ,   1 9 3 3

Produced by David Lewis. Directed by Otto Browser. Written by Harold Shumate. Photographed by Nicholas Musuraca. 57 minutes.

CAST:

(Tom Baxter) Tom Keene; *(Judy Blake)* Dorothy Wilson; *(Jeff Todd)* Creighton Chaney; *(Babe Jewell)* Betty Furness; *(Ulysses Mope)* Roscoe Ates; *(Sam Gilroy)* Edgar Kennedy; *(Buck Blake)* Billy Butts; *(Clink McPherson)* Hooper Atcheley; *(Benny)* Jack Raymond; *(Dummy)* James Mason; *(Yak)* Yakima Canutt.

In almost all the films Hollywood has made about itself, whether searing dramas like *Sunset Boulevard* (1950) and *The Bad and the Beautiful* (1953) or comedies like *Sullivan's Travels* (1941) and *Singin' in the Rain* (1952), the portrait is seldom flattering. What we mostly see is an industry populated by ambition, conceit, ego and egocentricity. This is true, although to a less severe extent, in the dozen or so westerns that deal with the making of westerns. The first was *The Moving Picture Cowboy,* which Tom Mix made for the Selig Polyscope Company in 1914. Mix concocted the picture himself and in it spoofed the mock heroics of movie cowboys. The hero brags about all the stunts he does on film, but the truth is that he is not capable of any of them. Spurred by the success of the film, Mix did two more of similar content in 1916. In *A Mix-Up in Movies,* he plays a cowboy who robs a bank when he sees a film company staging a robbery, but changes his mind when he falls in love with the leading lady; in *Shooting Up the Movies,* he is an outlaw who rescues a girl from what he believes to be danger, not knowing that it is part of a movie set-up. Again he falls in love and again it is love that leads him to the right side of the law.

The pleasing nonsense of the Mix movies about the movies more or less set the style for all the others that involved Hollywood's cowboy stars in the heyday of the B western. In 1936, Charles Starrett was *The Cowboy Star,* who proves he can be brave in real life, and the same year, Gene Autry scored a hit with *The Big Show,*

30

Cowboy star Tom Keene as cowboy star Tom Baxter.

in which he played a dual role, a mean and surly cowboy star and the genial, brave stuntman-double for the star. In 1937, George O'Brien made *Hollywood Cowboy* and, like Starrett, showed he was as brave off screen as on. The following year, Buck Jones appeared in *Hollywood Round-Up,* as a stunt man who wins the love of the leading lady when she realizes he is a much better man than the temperamental star for whom he doubles. Over the years, Richard Dix, George Montgomery and Roy Rogers appeared in similar fare, but it was not until 1951 that Hollywood made a major feature about movie westerners—*Callaway Went Thataway,* with Howard Keel as a drunken, washed-up hero whose old film on television bring him back to public interest. The accent was on comedy, as was also the case in *Hearts of the West* (1975), in which Jeff Bridges plays a naive would-be novelist who winds up as an extra in westerns and Andy Griffith as a wily old stuntman who befriends him, and in Blake Edwards' *Sunset* (1988), in which Bruce Willis (as Tom Mix) and James Garner (as Wyatt Earp) join forces in Hollywood of the '20s to solve a murder.

Of the B westerns dealing with picture making, the best is *Scarlet River* (1933), starring Tom Keene, who was signed for a series by RKO in 1931. Keene was a

Roscoe Ates, Tom Keene, Edgar Kennedy, Betty Furness and Dorothy Wilson

stage actor with no experience of western life, and his western movies never rivaled those of Buck Jones and George O'Brien. After making *Scarlet River,* he appeared in only one other RKO western before the studio cut him loose, after which he was chosen by King Vidor as the lead in what would become a classic film about the Depression, *Our Daily Bread* (1934). However, his performance did not bring him any major offers and he thereafter signed up for series westerns with minor companies. He eventually changed his name to Richard Powers and worked as a supporting player in a variety of films, dying in 1963 at 59.

In *Scarlet River,* Tom Keene is cowboy star Tom Baxter, who goes on location to make a picture with his leading lady, Babe Jewell (Betty Furness), and his high-strung director, Sam Gilroy (Edgar Kennedy), only to become frustrated with the noises and intrusions. As he and Babe play a scene by a covered wagon, a busload of land developers pull up and ruin the shot; as he pans for gold in a creek, a stream of marathon runners pass before the camera, and as he goes to film a scene in a cabin, he finds it being turned into a cafe. Tom and his director give up and return to the studio.

On his way into the commissary for lunch, Tom passes Joel McCrea, who kids him about his problems. Inside, Tom says hello to Myrna Loy and then sits at a table with a group of people, one of whom is Bruce Cabot. Overhearing Tom complaining about shooting on location, an executive tells of receiving a script from someone on a ranch, with a photo and a note telling that it is available as a location. Tom decides that Scarlet River Ranch is the place to make his picture.

But that too is beset with problems. Its owner, Judy Blake (Dorothy Wilson), is losing money on the operation but cannot understand why, or why her foreman Jeff Todd (Creighton Chaney—soon to change his name to Lon Chaney, Jr.), is encouraging her to sell, while at the same time proposing marriage. Todd is in cahoots with Clink McPherson (Hooper Atcheley), who knows he can control the area's water rights once he acquires the ranch. When Baxter starts filming at the ranch, he quickly suspects Todd as the man responsible for cattle poisoning and haystack fires, and Todd becomes uneasy as he sees Judy and Baxter becoming fond of each other. To get the movie people to quit the location, McPherson kidnaps Judy, leaving a note promising to

Billy Butts, Tom Keene and Yakima Canutt.

Yakima Canutt, Billy Butts, James Mason, Tom Keene, Edgar Kennedy and Betty Furness.

return her once they have left. They appear to go and Todd scoffs, "There's your movie heroes for you—first sign of trouble and they head back to Hollywood."

Tom Baxter, of course, is not about to leave Judy in the lurch. Disguised as a cowhand, he infiltrates McPherson's hideout and attempts to free the girl. Seeing that Judy is in danger, the duplicitous Todd moves in her defense and gets shot down by McPherson for his efforts. Tom is about to be thrown over a cliff when the movie company arrives by truck, firing with pistols loaded with blanks, although the villains assume the shots to be real. Baxter then goes after McPherson and overpowers him. The movie hero is a real hero, winning the love of Judy in the process.

Scarlet River uses one of the oldest of western plot devices—the one about the lady ranch owner being cheated out of her property, until the hero arrives to save her—but in this instance the situation is given flavor by imposing the movie-in-the-making structure. In his literate script, Harold Shumate worked in some

of the digs common in other films dealing with Hollywood. The director, played by Edgar Kennedy, who specialized in comic frustration, is forever calling for his assistant at the first sign of trouble, "Oh, Benny!" But the best line in the film is spoken by Babe Jewell when the admiring Judy asks if hero Tom actually does all his own stunts: "Sure he does. Tom wouldn't let anybody else do a stunt he wouldn't do himself. He's not just a movie actor, he's a real guy." That Betty Furness delivered the line without a guffaw is a credit to her acting ability.

Tom Keene's stunts in *Scarlet River* were performed by Yakima Canutt, who also played a small role in the film. Canutt, who started his career as a champion rodeo rider, played heroes in silent westerns but switched to bit-parts, mostly villains, in the '30s, while at the same time building what would become Hollywood's top reputation as a stunt man. He doubled for most of the celebrated movie heroes and in time became a second-unit (action sequences) director, the chariot race in *Ben-Hur* (1959) being his greatest achievement. In *Scarlet River,* he performed for the first time a stunt that became a specialty—that of riding after a runaway wagon, leaping from his horse onto the lead wagon horse and then falling between the team, with the wagon passing over him. In this film, he performs the stunt when the villainous foreman, Todd, claims he can do any stunt a movie actor can do. He tries it and fails; then Keene does it properly, but in both cases, it is Canutt who actually does the danger-ous leaping and dragging. Canutt's best performance of this stunt appears in *Stagecoach* (1939), as the Apache who tries to stop the coach, only to be shot from the lead horse by John Wayne. In the Hollywood West of the '30s and '40s, few men were more employed than Yakima Canutt.

In telling a good yarn as well as giving some glimpses into the business of making westerns, *Scarlet River* is a little gem of a picture.

Filming Betty Furness and Tom Keene.

Buck Jones

THE SUNDOWN RIDER

COLUMBIA, 1933

Directed by Lambert Hillyer. Written by Lambert Hillyer, based on a story by John Neville. Photographed by John Boyle. 65 minutes.

CAST

(*Camp O'Neill*) Buck Jones; (*Mollie McCall*) Barbara Weeks; (*Lafe Armstrong*) Pat O'Malley; (*Laughing Maxie*) Wheeler Oakman; (*Houseman*) Niles Welch; (*Jim Hunter*) Bradley Page; (*Sheriff Rand*) Frank La Rue; (*Gabe Powers*) Ward Bond.

No man in films personified the virtues of the American cowboy better than Buck Jones. He had about him an air of authority and decency, and a sense that he believed in what he was doing. He certainly enjoyed making westerns and that enjoyment was conveyed to the millions of youngsters who became his loyal fans. Even people who did not particularly like westerns allowed that there was something different about Jones. There was never any hint of scandal in his life, he carefully maintained an image he felt appropriate to his work and, unlike some other cowboy stars, he was

grateful for the lifestyle he had been lucky enough to attain. He was once with William (Hopalong Cassidy) Boyd when the two were spotted and surrounded by young boys eager for their autographs. Boyd was annoyed and told "the little bastards" to go away. Said Jones, "Careful, Bill. Without these little bastards, you don't have anything."

He was born Charles Gebhardt in Indiana in December of 1891 and picked up the nickname Buckaroo as a youngster because he loved to ride horses. It was not until he went into the picture business after World War I that his employers came up with the solid Anglo-Saxon name of Jones to replace his own Germanic sounding one. He was a baby at the time his family moved to Oklahoma, where he grew up on a small ranch owned by his father. A lively lad with a hankering to wander, he joined the Army in January of 1907 by lying about his age, claiming to be three years older than 15. He became a part of G Troop in the Sixth Cavalry and first saw action along the Mexican border in skirmishes with banditos. In September of that year, Jones encountered a great deal more action when his regiment was sent to the Philippines to contain the warfare being waged against the government by the Moro rebels. In late 1909, he received a severe bullet wound in his left leg, causing him to be shipped home and discharged from the service. It took him nine months to recuperate from the wound but he then reenlisted and served another three years.

Jones was in Texas City, Texas, when he left the Army in October of 1913, coinciding with an appearance in that city by the Miller Brothers 101 Ranch Wild West Show. He applied for a job as a horse handler but within months he had become one of the show's top performers. In 1914, while playing in New York's Madison Square Garden he met a 15-year-old equestrienne named Odelle Osborne. A year later, he married her and she was his wife until his untimely death 27 years later. They performed together but with America's entry into the war, they took a job in Chicago preparing horses for Army service. Thus engaged, he was relieved from further military duty. The couple returned to circus life after the war but by late 1918, with his wife pregnant with what would be their only child, daughter Maxine, Jones headed for Los Angeles to try, as had hundreds of ranch and circus cowboys before him, to get work in western movies. With his ability as a rider and his pleasing looks and manner, it turned out to be not too difficult.

Like all the others, Jones lined up for work outside the studio gates early in the morning. He was often picked and soon came to the attention of an actor, William Farnum, who suggested to the management of Fox Pictures that here was someone they might consider grooming. The Fox folks did, mostly because star Tom Mix was so difficult with his constant demands for more money and production delays that the studio had to threaten him with replacement. Jones was given his first starring role in 1920, *The Last Straw,* and appeared in 60 Fox films over the next eight years. Most were westerns but occasionally he was put into modern action pictures like *Skid Proof* (1923), as a racing driver. By 1928, his luck seemed to run out. Fox, like all the studios, was concerned about making westerns with the coming of sound, and they let Jones go. He then produced a picture, *The Big Hop,* with his own money and lost most of his investment. Things became even worse. He organized The Buck Jones Wild West Show, which ground to a halt after two months, with a loss to him of a quarter-million dollars.

After two years off the screen, he had his manager, Scott Dunlap, negotiate a contract with producer Sol Lesser for a western series that would pay Jones $300 a week, much less than he had been receiving at Fox but an offer he accepted without hesitation. The early

sound westerns were awkward due to the cumbersome equipment, but they quickly improved, and it was now that Buck Jones came into his own. He realized that much better stories could be told with sound and he was careful about picking his material. He made 60 westerns during the '30s, including four serials, and his work was solid, reliable and consistently popular. Indeed, by 1936, Buck Jones was No. 1 at the western box office.

The Sundown Rider, released on the last day of 1933, is a good example of his work. It is a rather gritty, darkly-hued western, scripted by the man who also directed it, Lambert Hillyer, who had done 25 of William S. Hart's westerns and had written 16 of them. He had also worked with Tom Mix. In describing Jones, Hillyer said that he was a perfect compromise between the austere Hart and the flamboyant Mix. In *The Sundown Rider,* Jones is Camp O'Neill, a cowboy on his way to accept an offer from his friend, Lafe Armstrong (Pat O'Malley), to work on the latter's ranch. As he nears it, he stops at an encampment, where a group of cowhands are branding cattle. He is greeted in a friendly manner, unaware that the leader of these men, Laughing Maxie (Wheeler Oakman), is a crook switching brands. As other riders approach, Maxie and his men take off, leaving Camp, who is now accused of being a rustler. Despite his protestations, he is punished by being branded on the chest. In agony, he climbs on his horse and proceeds with his journey.

In town, he meets Lafe and tells him the story, and that he intends to find the man who branded him. Lafe warns him this is both easy and dangerous—Maxie owns a gambling saloon in town and has many gunmen on his payroll. Hearing that Camp is after him, Maxie posts one of his men inside the saloon, but Camp spots the gunman's reflection in a mirror and shoots him. Facing Maxie, telling him he is a man who always pays his debts, Camp beats him, deliberately cutting his face to leave a mark. But a shot is fired and Maxie drops to the floor dead. It is assumed that Camp is the killer but the shot was actually fired by the saloon card dealer, Houseman (Niles Welch), who has been badly treated by Maxie. Now pursued by the law as a killer, Camp takes off with Lafe to the latter's ranch. Mortally wounded by a bullet, Lafe advises Camp to proceed to the ranch of Mollie McCall (Barbara Weeks), who needs help. Urging Camp to assume his identity, Lafe dies holding off the sheriff's posse until his friend can get away.

Mollie welcomes the man who seems to be Lafe Armstrong and gladly accepts his offer to be her new foreman. She has been losing cattle and suspects foreman Gabe Powers (Ward Bond) of stirring up her troubles. Camp thrashes him and throws him off the

Buck Jones and Niles Welch

ranch, whereupon Powers reports to the man by whom he is really employed, Jim Hunter (Bradley Page), the owner of the bank in Sundown. Hunter is aware that Mollie's ranch is sitting on a rich oil deposit. He refuses to extend her more credit and points out that her loan is shortly due. He always, however, gives his creditors until the very last ray of sundown on the day the debt is due. Camp suggests to Mollie that she sell her cattle, which requires a difficult drive she has up to now been unwilling to tackle, and Hunter instructs Powers to stop the drive.

On his way to Sundown for another job as a dealer, Houseman is shot by Powers, who knows how Maxie died, but he lives long enough to clear Camp. Powers fails to stop the cattle drive, and after making the sale, Camp gallops back with the money in order to arrive before the sun sets on the debt dateline. On the way back, he is bushwacked by Powers, who loses his life when Camp's men come to the rescue. At the bank, Mollie waits with Hunter, who tells her time has run out. But Camp gets there just as the last ray of sun flickers on the wall—in the company of the sheriff and with evidence that Hunter is a crook.

The Sundown Rider ends with Camp and Mollie looking into the fading sunset. Slowly, his hand comes up her back and rests on her shoulder—and a fine

Buck Jones and the four jail birds he recruits to help him. The one in the check shirt is Glenn Strange, one of the most employed character actors in the history of the B Western.

Buck and the boys go to work.

example of a 1933 B western draws to a close. Among other things, it defies the general belief that in these western programmers the cowboy hero kissed only his horse. In the Buck Jones westerns, there was always strong intimation of romance, although the shy-around-women hero was never blatantly amorous. That would not have sat well with the young fans, who preferred Jones to ride his white horse Silver at top speed and to either outdraw the villain or beat him to a pulp. With Buck Jones, there was never any doubt that he could do all of this, or, from a more business point of view,

that he could come up with good yarns. He was a man who loved western literature and read avidly. That had much to do with his success. He was serious about making westerns and, of all the cowboy stars, there is the least uniformity in his pictures. Each of them is a little different, set in various periods and places and using various styles. Sometimes he overdid the eagerness to be different and the stories lines became diffused, but by and large, his westerns maintained a high and interesting standard.

Buck Jones and Barbara Weeks.

IN OLD SANTA FE

MASCOT, 1934

Produced by Nat Levine. Directed by David Howard. Written by Colbert Clark and James Gruen, based on a story by Wallace MacDonald and John Rathmell. Photographed by Ernie Miller and William Nobles. 62 minutes.

CAST:

(*Kentucky*) Ken Maynard; (*Lila Miller*) Evalyn Knapp; (*Charlie Miller*) H. B. Warner; (*Chandler*) Kenneth Thomson; (*Tracy*) Wheeler Oakman; (*Cactus*) George Hayes; (*Himself*) Gene Autry; (*Himself*) Smiley Burnett; (*Red*) George Burton; (*Nick*) George Cheseboro.

Riding a horse is a skill, but with some people, it is an ability that comes as naturally as breathing. It was with Ken Maynard who rode a horse as if he were a part of it. As a circus trick rider, he could flip back and forth over the sides of the horse in full gallop, ride two horses at once, standing with one foot in each saddle, and mount the horse from running jumps. It was his horsemanship that made him a movie star. Part of that

success came from having a horse that was far more intelligent than the norm and one that also seemed to have a sense of theater. In 1926, Maynard bought a light palomino for 50 dollars, the best 50 dollars he ever spent. The horse, a half-Arabian, half-American saddle horse, which he named Tarzan, was already ten years old. It would be his co-star through his best years in westerns. Tarzan was easy to train; he nodded when spoken to, responded when called, and rolled over and played dead on cue. Maynard was so attached to the horse that when Tarzan died in 1940, he buried him in secret and refused for years to admit that the horse had gone. He seemed to have a kinder regard for Tarzan than for any human, including his three wives, and he was never mean or abusive to the horse, as he was to most of the other creatures in his life. Ken Maynard was probably the most difficult man who ever appeared in westerns.

In his years of stardom, it was always claimed that Maynard was born in Texas, which in the minds of most western buffs seemed like a natural place for a cowboy to be born. Maynard was never a cowboy. He was born in Indiana in July of 1895, the son of a man who ran a small construction business. The father found he had sired a boy with a rebellious nature and a tendency to run away from home. When Maynard was 16, his parents gave up trying to control him and he joined a traveling carnival show, from which he graduated to various Wild West shows as a rider. He joined the Army in 1917, serving in the Corps of Engineers but never going overseas. Afterwards, he was hired by the Ringling Brothers Circus, with which he became the top cowboy attraction. They encouraged him to also be a rodeo contestant, knowing that he could easily win titles. Between the circus and the rodeos, Maynard made big money. However, there was bigger money to be made in Hollywood, and he signed with Fox Pictures in late 1922.

Maynard found himself with little to do at Fox because the studio was placing all its emphasis on its Tom Mix and Buck Jones productions. He left after two years and joined Davis Distribution, a small company willing to give him star billing in a serial. This gave Maynard enough success to be offered a contract with First National, soon to be absorbed by Warner Bros., and it was the 18 features he made for them that made him a cowboy star. When he moved over to Universal in 1929, he was in the peak of condition, his horsemanship spectacular. By 1933, he was making $10,000 a week, one of the highest salaries ever earned by a movie westerner. But there were problems, all of them stemming from his stubborn, perverse nature. He was temperamental and demanding, he wanted things done his way and flew into tantrums when they were not, and he was one of those unfortunate men who become frightening when drunk—and Maynard drank heavily.

Maynard severed a contract with Universal in 1934 because they would not give him his way and he was picked up by Nat Levine, the owner of tiny Mascot Pictures, a company trying to build its image. Levine planned to use Maynard in a string of features, but after *In Old Santa Fe* and the serial *Mystery Mountain,* he changed his mind. *In Old Santa Fe* received a bigger than usual budget, a good script and plenty of experienced players, including the gentlemanly H. B. Warner, the man who played Christ in *King of Kings* (1927), as the father of the heroine. And for an extended musical sequence in the middle of the film, Levine introduced a young singer named Gene Autry.

The film is set in the present day, with most of the action taking place on a dude ranch, owned by Charlie Miller (Warner), who daughter Lila (Evalyn Knapp) takes a shine to Kentucky (Maynard) after nearly running him over in the desert while speeding in her convertable. Also at the ranch is a slick easterner, Chandler (Kenneth Thomson), whose father was once a crooked associate of Miller's and who now intends to blackmail Miller into handing over half the property, as well as the hand of his daughter in marriage. Realizing that Kentucky is a threat, Chandler moves to get rid of him. When Kentucky enters the ranch's horse race in the desert, Chandler has his henchman, Tracy (Wheeler Oakman), cut Tarzan's saddle strap, causing it to break lose during the race. But Kentucky simply discards the saddle in full gallop and continues bareback (a splendid example of Maynard horsemanship). When that ploy fails, Tracy next trips the horse with a wire, causing horse and rider to fall, with Kentucky losing the race. To add to his woes, Kentucky finds Chandler claiming ownership of the horse, having goaded Ken-

Ken Maynard.

Ken Maynard, Kenneth Thomson and Evalyn Knapp.

tucky's crusty old sidekick, Cactus (George Hayes), a half owner, into betting on Tarzan to win—betting being a weakness of Cactus.

Chandler also knows that Miller is a part owner of a local gold mine, and when he hears that a heavy vein has been struck, he makes plans for robbery. He frames Kentucky by letting him stop a stagecoach being chased by bandits; the wounded driver explains he is carrying the gold, whereupon Kentucky takes it with the purpose of returning it to the ranch. On the way back, he is arrested by the sheriff because the driver has been killed and Kentucky is the suspect. Cactus helps Kentucky break out of jail and they go back to the ranch, where Chandler is having problems with Tracy, who tries to snatch the gold. Chandler kills him and tries to frame Kentucky, who now pulls a ruse. In front of the sheriff and all the guests, Kentucky reads a letter from Tracy which pins the blame for everything on Chandler. Kentucky actually reads from a blank piece of paper but Chandler's furious response incriminates him. All is well, except in the mind of Cactus, a man who has never had any patience with "wimmen." He snorts in disgust at the sight of Lila in Kentucky's arms.

In Old Santa Fe, an exceptionally well-made and amusing picture of its kind, marked the high water mark in Ken Maynard's career. After Maynard completed the Mascot serial *Mystery Mountain,* Nat Levine

let him go. He had become far too difficult to deal with, abusive when drunk and argumentative on the set if something did not meet with his approval. Levine had planned to star Maynard in another serial, *The Phantom Empire* but decided instead to give it to Gene Autry, whose work in *In Old Santa Fe* had generated a lot of comment. It was this serial that triggered Autry's phenomenal success in films. Within a year or so, he eclipsed the popularity not only of Maynard but also of all the other cowboy stars, none of whom could understand why the rather passive and far from virile Autry could do so well with his musical westerns. And so *In Old Santa Fe,* not a foot of which takes place in *Santa Fe*—the meaning of B western titles was rarely anything to ponder—marked a turning point in Hollywood, the rise of Autry and the decline of Maynard.

Maynard was in his 40th year at the time of working for Levine and already his appearance was, because of the drinking, beginning to change for the worse. He became increasingly pudgy and no longer the agile acrobat. But he was still a name with which to reckon and Columbia signed him for a series of eight westerns. In 1936, he was No. 5 at the western box office, the following year No. 9, and then his popularity quickly faded away. He made four cheap westerns for Grand National in 1937, followed by four even cheaper ones for Colony. By 1940, nobody wanted him. Then three years later, he was hired by Monogram and co-starred with another old timer long out of favor, Hoot Gibson, for a series called *The Trail Blazers*. The pictures were dreadful and after six of them, Monogram dumped Maynard, who had become obnoxious and whose demands for more money made no sense in view of the poorly received product. In late 1944, a company called Mattox hired him to star in *Harmony Trail*, an ironic title. There was no harmony on this trail, and the film career of Ken Maynard wheezed to a halt.

Maynard lived for almost another 30 years, but they were mostly sad years. He appeared with circuses and western shows, but by the late '50s, he and his wife Bertha, a former circus rider, were living in near poverty in a trailer in San Fernando. After she died in 1968, his disposition and his drinking grew steadily worse and he was kept alive by a few benefactors, one of whom was Gene Autry, who had idolized Maynard before he himself became a star and who never allowed his support of Maynard to be known. In January of 1973, Maynard, a physical wreck, was taken to the Motion Picture Country Home in Woodland Hills and

there he died two months later. Despite all the misery and travail, he was honored at his funeral as one of the greatest of the cowboy stars. He was certainly the most mercurial of them; a very handsome young man with a flashing smile, he could be charming on the one hand and so truculent on the other that his career was bound to suffer. But in his heyday, Maynard was a master horseman and a fine entertainer.

In Old Santa Fe marked not only the birth of Gene Autry's career but also was a turning point for George Hayes, the greatest of all the western sidekicks. Hayes, born in Wellsville, New York in 1885, made a good living as a stage actor until he began appearing in films iin 1929. After a few roles in westerns, he decided that the guise of a crochety old character was his best shot. In 1933, he appeared as a supporting player with John Wayne in *Riders of Destiny* and pleased audiences so much that Monogram, to whom Wayne was then contracted, used him in the following ten Wayne westerns, with Hayes more and more becoming a lovable old grump. The guise jelled so well in *In Old Santa Fe* that he would do nothing else for the rest of his career.

Ken Maynard, Evalyn Knapp and George Hayes.

43

Producer Harry Sherman was so impressed with Hayes' role as Cactus that he decided to use him in his planned series of Hopalong Cassidy pictures, as Windy Halliday, Hoppy's loyal but ever complaining pal. Hayes left Sherman in 1938 and accepted a better offer from Republic, where he gained even stronger identity as a Roy Rogers sidekick known as Gabby. After appearing in *The Cariboo Trail* with Randolph Scott in 1950, Hayes decided to retire. He had reached 65 and he had had enough. By then, he had appeared in 169 movies, most of them westerns, and he had enjoyed a remarkable success. The truth about George Hayes is that he made a more consistent living and earned better money than most of the cowboy stars he supported. In the '30s, he averaged almost one film per month, a track record possibly not equaled by any other player in Hollywood. He enjoyed 19 years of retirement, dying in a Burbank hospital in 1969, and never gave in to any request to come back to the picture business.

A footnote to the story of Ken Maynard: while Gene Autry was undoubtedly the first successful singing cowboy, it was Maynard who was the first movie cowboy to sing, albeit none too well. One of his best films, *Strawberry Roan* (1933), was actually built around the song of that title. However, he never sang again in films once Autry was launched. To Maynard's credit, he did not stop the writers of *In Old Santa Fe* from poking fun at his singing. The film opens as he and Hayes ride along, with Maynard singing and Hayes grimacing and finally commenting, "I've heard coyotes I liked better."

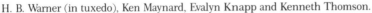

H. B. Warner (in tuxedo), Ken Maynard, Evalyn Knapp and Kenneth Thomson.

Harry Carey

THE LAST OUTLAW

R K O   1 9 3 6

Produced by Robert Sisk. Directed by Christy Cabanne. Written by John Twist and Jack Townley, based on a story by John Ford and E. Murray Campbell. Photographed by Jack Mackenzie. Music by Alberto Colombo. 72 minutes.

CAST:

(*Dean Payton*) Harry Carey; (*Chuck Wilson*) Hoot Gibson; (*Calvin Yates*) Henry B. Walthall; (*Sally Mason*) Margaret Callahan; (*Dr. Mason*) Frank M. Thomas, Sr.; (*Billings*) Russell Hopton; (*Al Goss*) Tom Tyler; (*Joe*) Harry Jans; (*Jess*) Ray Meyer; (*Tom*) Frank Jenks.

John Ford began his directing career in 1915, making two-reel westerns at Universal. His first feature, a five-reeler, running close to an hour, was *Straight Shooting,* starring Harry Carey, with whom he would be a close friend for the remainder of Carey's life. One of the two-reelers Ford made in 1919 was *The Last Outlaw,* the story of a man who comes out of jail after a long period to face a different kind of world. Ford was the co-author of the script, a fact acknowledged by RKO when they

remade the story in 1936 as a vehicle for Harry Carey, although this version was considerably elaborated upon by the two assigned scenarists. To give the film even more of a nostalgic twist, RKO gave Hoot Gibson co-billing with Carey, in whose Universal pictures Gibson had made his mark, one of them being *Straight Shooting.* Gibson, a genuine Nebraska cowboy, was 20 in 1912 when he was named World Champion All-Around Cowboy at the Pendleton, Oregon, rodeo. This was his springboard to work as a stuntman in western movies, followed by bit parts that evolved into leads. His first feature film, following many two-reelers, was *Action* in 1921, directed by John Ford. Enormously popular all through the '20s, Gibson saw his career run out of steam by the early '30s and his hiring for *The Last Outlaw* probably had much to do with the influence of Ford and Carey.

Harry Carey's place in the history of western film is a special one. Except for those aware of his work in silent film—what little of it remains—he is remembered as a craggy, gruff character actor, seemingly always an

Player, Harry Carey and Tom Tyler.

old codger, the stern looks masking a warm heart. He was born in the Bronx in 1878, the son of a judge, and he studied law at New York University. In order to convalesce from a severe bout of pneumonia at 21, he was sent to the ranch of a friend in Montana. While there, he wrote a play and called it *Montana,* afterwards deciding to stage it and act in it. A new career emerged. Carey toured with the play for three years, then picked up work as an actor in other people's plays, which by 1910 led to work in the movies. He became a member of D. W. Griffith's company and worked consistently from then on. Signing with Universal in 1915, Carey found his identity becoming more and more western, particularly after doing a series as Cheyenne Harry, many of which he wrote himself.

Carey married Olive Fuller Gordon, the actress who co-starred with him at Universal, and they bought a working ranch in the San Fernando Valley. Their son, Harry, Jr., was born in 1921 and as soon as he became of age he, too, appeared in westerns, especially those made by John Ford, as did Olive Carey. The Careys were very much a part of the Ford family. Harry senior never had to worry about work. In 1931, by then 53, he played the lead in MGM's *Trader Horn,* which in-

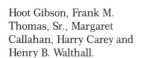

Hoot Gibson, Frank M. Thomas, Sr., Margaret Callahan, Harry Carey and Henry B. Walthall.

46

volved him in African locations for a year, and after that came a stream of either leading parts in B westerns or character roles in a variety of A pictures. He made three western serials for Mascot and a series of his own for Ajax. As a crusty westerner dressed in plain garb, he appealed more to the older rather than the younger audience.

Carey could hardly be better in this film. As Dean Payton, a once-feared bandit who is paroled after 25 years in jail, he seems exactly the man he is playing. A man with his own code of ethics, the first thing he notices after being turned loose in the modern world is the lack of courtesy and the ill temper of people in what is now called Center City, which he once knew as Broken Knee. He is several times almost knocked down in traffic and nearly arrested for jaywalking by a short tempered policeman. Payton goes to see the man who captured and jailed him, a respected adversary, Calvin Yates (Henry B. Walthall), and finds him long demoted from sheriff to under sheriff. The sheriff is a slick politician named Billings (Russell Hopton), who is concerned about his press publicity for the upcoming election. Payton meets his daughter, Sally (Margaret Callahan), adopted by his old friend, Dr. Mason (Frank M.

Thomas, Sr.), and decides it is better not to let her know he is her father. He next goes to play poker in a saloon and gets cheated, but a spectator, rancher Chuck Wilson (Gibson), comes to his defense, resulting in a new friendship. When Chuck meets Sally, he starts to make a play for her.

Payton, Chuck and Sally go to the movies and watch a western, *Heart of the Plains,* starring singing cowboy Larry Dixon (Fred Scott). When Dixon sings "My Heart's on the Trail," Payton cringes. So does Chuck, who asks Sally, "You actually like that feller?" She does. Later, Chuck dresses up in fancy western duds to impress Sally and Payton is appalled, "Just when I was beginning to like you, you go and turn moving picture cowboy on me." But Chuck soon wins back Payton's respect when he joins the old man in foiling the attempt of gangster Al Goss (Tom Tyler) and his two partners to escape justice after a bank robbery.

Sally is in the bank when it is robbed and Goss takes her as a hostage. Payton jumps on the running board of the getaway car and falls off. He is arrested and jailed as a suspect but Yates and Chuck get him out. Learning that Goss is heading up into the hills where Yates long ago tracked Payton, the three men saddle up and take

Margaret Callahan and Harry Carey.

Hoot Gibson, Henry B. Walthall and Harry Carey.

Hoot Gibson, Harry Carey and Henry B. Walthall.

48

chase, while the sheriff and all his modern forces of cars, radio and airplanes prove futile. Goss is tracked to the very cabin in which Payton was holed up. The old outlaw now asks advice from Yates about the tactics by which he was captured, and he uses them to overpower Goss and his men. "Where were you shooting from when you had me in there?" Payton fires at the water supply, resulting in barrels bursting on the roof; ruins the chimney, causing smoke to billow inside, and shoots the tires of the car—while Chuck blasts away the radio from which is emerging the voice of Larry Dixon singing "My Heart's on the Trail." The frustrated Sheriff Billings arrives too late and Sally is delighted to learn that the brave old fellow is her father, which she already begun to suspect.

Much of *The Last Outlaw* takes place in the city but the last shot shows Payton, Chuck and Yates from the rear riding off into the familiar landscape, a doff of the stetson to western movie tradition. Seen today, the film has even more punch and poignancy than when first shown. The 1936 world into which the Carey character emerges is light years from 1911, when he was put away. Progress has been made but some of it is dubious, especially in regard to human behavior. Years later, there would be many films lamenting the passing of the Old West but in this minor 1936 picture RKO produced what is possibly the first to make the point about the changes that civilization brought to the West. There are many moments of satire in *The Last Outlaw,* as it pokes affectionate fun at the New West, commenting on old virtues and new values, and even ridicules what was then a new source of Hollywood wealth—the singing cowboy.

Carey, 58 at the time of making it, was the ideal choice for *The Last Outlaw,* and it is possibly his finest performance. As a B picture, it quickly passed into the vaults, mostly forgotten except by those who recalled it as a Carey triumph. John Ford intended one day to remake it and persuaded Carey to purchase the rights to the film. He did so, causing RKO to surrender the negative, which seems to have disappeared. By the time Ford was ready, Carey was ill, dying on September 21, 1947, in his 70th year, a beloved and valued character actor in an industry not noted for its sentimentality. More than a thousand people attended his funeral.

When John Wayne made *Angel and the Badman* (1947), his first film as a producer, it was a foregone conclusion that he would employ Carey. Carey not only was his idol but the actor upon whom Wayne had modeled his own western image, including the stance and the manner of speaking. The last western in which Carey appeared was Wayne's *Red River,* but he never lived to see it. Harry, Jr., was also in it, as he was in the Ford-Wayne *Three Godfathers* (1948), which bears the dedication, "To the memory of Harry Carey—bright star of the early western sky." In 1956, when Ford and Wayne made the classic *The Searchers,* there was an even more personal tribute. Olive Carey and Harry, Jr. were, as expected, among the players, and both were reduced to tears by Wayne's last piece of action in the picture. As *The Searchers* ends, Wayne, standing in a cabin doorway almost in silhouette, folds his arms, grasping his left elbow with his right hand—as Harry Carey had done so many, many times in his western movies.

Harry Carey with his greatest admirer, John Wayne, in *Angel and the Badman* (1947).

49

TROUBLE IN TEXAS

GRAND NATIONAL, 1937

Produced by Edward F. Finney. Directed by R. N. Bradbury. Written by Robert Emmett. Photographed by Gus Peterson. 63 minutes.

CAST:

(Tex Masters) Tex Ritter; *(Carmen)* Rita Cansino; *(Barker)* Earl Dwire; *(Squint)* Yakima Canutt; *(Duke)* Dick Palmer; *(G-Man)* Hal Price; *(Sheriff)* Fred Parker; *(Lucky)* Horace Murphy; *(Pinto)* Charles King; *(Announcer)* Tom Cooper; *(Sheriff)* Glenn Strange; *(Bix)* Jack Smith.

Gene Autry and Roy Rogers were far and away the most successful of Hollywood's singing cowboys, but the man held in higher regard by lovers of western folk songs is Tex Ritter. He starred in 60 minor westerns between 1936 and 1945 and managed to gain popularity despite the mediocre material. Autry and Rogers were well guided and funded by Republic; Ritter began in westerns made on threadbare budgets and, when he was later signed by studios like Columbia and Universal, he was given second billing to William Elliott and Johnny

Mack Brown. However, Ritter would eventually fare better than most of his B western competitors because, after quitting the movies, he achieved much greater fame as a balladeer and recording artist.

Woodward Maurice Ritter was born on a farm near Murvaul in eastern Texas in January of 1905. He attended the University of Texas in Austin with the object of becoming a lawyer, but his singing in the glee club brought him to the attention of Professor J. Frank Dobie, who was then and for many years thereafter regarded as America's foremost authority on folk music of the southern and western states. He encouraged Ritter not only to develop as a singer but to study and collect folk songs, and this would have a profound affect upon the course of his career. Ritter often said, "Dobie played a large part in making me what I am today."

Ritter had to leave the university for lack of money and he took a series of odd jobs before being hired by radio station KPRC in Houston to sing western ballads, with Dobie supplying material. Ritter became the first major singer of western songs on radio, and by the time

Tex Ritter and Rita Cansino (Hayworth)

Finney declared himself a producer and shrewdly placed Ritter under contract to himself and not the studio. He persuaded Grand National to let him produce a western series with a budget of $10,000 per picture, of which Ritter received a 25 percent. They made 12 westerns for Grand National and then, when that company floundered, switched to Monogram. Of the dozen, the best is *Trouble in Texas,* which is of above interest to film buffs because the leading lady is a 19-year-old named Rita Cansino, who immediately after this engagement changed her last name to Hayworth. This was not her only B western; the previous year, she began her movie career playing a bit in *Under the Pampas Moon,* then the lead in a pair of Tom Keene westerns, *Rebellion* and *Old Louisiana,* and The Three Mesquiteers picture *Hit the Saddle.* Her best early western would come after the Ritter film when she co-starred with George O'Brien in *The Renegade Ranger,* by which time she was beginning to show the presence that would soon result in stardom.

In *Trouble in Texas,* Rita is a federal agent named Carmen, whose boss sends her out West on an assignment and tells her to gain employment as a dancer in a

of his death, he had acquired one of the largest collections of such material in the country. His success on radio led to his being hired by a touring band, which he left in 1930 when he went to New York to try his luck. It was with him at that time of great economic depression and he was hired by the Theatre Guild to play a cowboy in *Green Grow the Lilacs,* which Richard Rodgers and Oscar Hammerstein would turn into a musical a dozen years later. Early in 1932, he was hired to play Sage Brush Charlie in the play *The Roundup,* a success which resulted in invitations to appear at colleges to sing and talk about western music, and in his being signed as the star of a radio series titled *Lone Star Rangers.* Appearances on that and many other radio shows built his reputation, and once Gene Autry established the new era of the movie singing cowboy, it was only a matter of time before Hollywood would find Ritter.

The man who got Ritter to put his name on a movie contract was Edward Finney, then the advertising manager for a new company, Grand National Pictures.

Tex Ritter and Rita Cansino

Fred Parker, Horace Murphy and Tex Ritter.

saloon owned by a man named Barker (Earl Dwire), suspected of heading up a gang of rodeo racketeers. "It's up to you to find out how they operate. Everytime they've had anything to do with a rodeo, the top contenders have all died very mysteriously." Also trying to unravel this mystery is Tex Masters (Ritter), who arrives in the town of Middleton with his sidekick, Lucky (Horace Murphy), to enter the annual rodeo. Tex's brother had died in a rodeo five years earlier and he has been trying ever since to find out how and why.

On the way into Middleton, Tex thwarts a stagecoach holdup by a pair of thugs, Squint (Yakima Canutt) and Pinto (Charles King), both of whom tackle Tex on separate occasions in town, each getting soundly thrashed. Tex and Carmen become interested in each other and she tries to warn him of the dangers of becoming involved in the rodeo. Shrugging off her admonition, he puzzles why she should be working for

a man like Barker. Neither can tell the other the truth about their motives. On the final day of the rodeo, Pinto is instructed to get rid of Tex, in the manner used to kill the previous victims—to stick a poisoned pin in the rope halter by which the rider clings to his bucking horse. Lucky catches Pinto in the act of placing the needle, but becomes so distracted by watching the events that Pinto easily escapes and warns his boss that the jig is up, "Let's clean out the bank and head for the border." Carmen alerts Tex to what is going on and he rides into town, where he nabs some of the gang, with Barker managing to get away in a wagon. Tex pursues and after a dangerous fight, during which he falls between the traces of the galloping team, he brings the dastardly villain to justice. Now able to tell Tex she is a government agent, Carmen lets it be known she wants to quit her job and settle down on a cattle ranch. Says Tex, "I know just the spot."

Trouble in Texas is routine B western fodder, but made lively by the pleasing style of Ritter, here interspersing the action with four songs—plus a graceful dance by Rita—and a large amount of stock footage of rodeos, obviously drawn from a number of events, none of which match the meager rodeo being staged for the film. Much of the footage, of parades, Indian dances, bull dogging, bronco busting and races, is obviously vintage but of interest because of its authenticity. But the amount of stock footage and the number of musical numbers makes it easier to see how Finney was able to produce pictures like this in five days and on tiny budgets.

Yakima Canutt, playing a bigger role than usual as a thug, is also the double for Ritter in the dangerous wagon chase at the end, pulling the stunt at which he was a master—falling between runaway horses and allowing the wagon to pass over him. Also deserving mention is Charles King, who appeared in most of Ritter's Grand National and Monogram westerns and was invariably beaten senseless by Tex. Constantly employed during the heyday of the B western, King played ugly brutes in as many as 200 pictures. Years later, looking back on his early westerns, Ritter smiled, "I guess I was pretty tough. Roy and Gene sang more but I killed more. And old Charlie King, well, I must have killed him at least 20 times, and usually behind that same rock."

The energy and the charm that marked Ritter's early westerns gradually diminished. Had he the backing and the budgets given Autry and Rogers, it might have been different. By 1945, he had had enough of making minor westerns. More interesting work was available as a singer on radio and at personal appearances. He had made many recordings during the years as a cowboy movie star but when he joined Capitol Records in 1942, he emerged as a major recording artist, with songs like "Rye Whiskey" and "Jealous Heart" placing him at the top of the country and western charts. His greatest success in the movies was one in which he was not seen; producer Stanley Kramer chose him to sing the narrative ballad in the Gary Cooper classic, *High Noon* (1952), which brought composer Dimitri Tiomkin and lyricist Ned Washington an Oscar, and which was performed by Ritter on the Oscar broadcast. His esteem as a balladeer grew, with more and more offers from television shows and wide record sales.

In 1965, Ritter was asked to join *The Grand Ole Opry* in Nashville, and it was in that city that he spent much of the remaining nine years of his life. On January 2, 1974, while visiting a friend who was in jail in Nashville, he was struck by a heart attack and died instantly—just ten days short of his 69th birthday. Surviving him were his widow Dorothy Fay, whom he had met when she played Buck Jones' leading lady in *The Stranger from Arizona* (1938), and his sons Tom, who was born with a birth defect, and John, who was to become a major star in television and films. Ritter's passing was a great loss to all who knew and admired him. He was a genial, dignified, knowledgable man, and his mark in the history of western film, like his genuine Texas accent, is distinct.

Yakima Canutt, Rita Cansino (Hayworth) and Tex Ritter

THE CHEROKEE STRIP

WARNER BROS., 1937

Produced by Bryan Foy. Directed by Noel Smith. Written by Joseph K. Watson and Luci Ward, based on a story by Ed Earl Repp. Photographed by Lu O'Connell. Music by Howard Jackson. Songs by M. K. Jerome and Jack Scholl. 58 minutes.

CAST:

(Dick Hudson) Dick Foran; *(Janie Walton)* Jane Bryan; *(Tom Valley)* David Carlyle; *(Molly Valley)* Helen Valkis; *(Link Carter)* Ed Cobb; *(Army Officer)* Joseph Crehan; *(Judge Ben Parkinson)* Gordon Hart; *(Joe Brady)* Frank Faylen; *(Blade Simpson)* Milton Kibbee; *(Bill Tidewell)* Jack Mower; *(George Walton)* Tom Brower; *(Mink Abbott)* Walter Sondering; *(Barty Walton)* Tommy Bupp.

Dick Foran was a man who enjoyed a comfortable career in Hollywood from the age of 23 until he died in 1979 at 68. He appeared in a variety of films—a lead player in B pictures and a supporting one in the A league—but it is his work in westerns by which he is best remembered. It was a line imposed upon him, certainly not one to which he was born. Foran started

life in New Jersey, the son of a United States Senator, and after education in private schools, he was sent to Princeton. Gifted with a fine, light baritone voice, he was more interested in singing and acting than studying and left the university before graduating. In Los Angeles in 1934, he was hired to sing in *Stand Up and Cheer,* the musical that edged six-year-old Shirley Temple to stardom, and did well enough to be signed by Warner Bros. as a contract player. An impressive performance in Bogart's *The Petrified Forest* proved that Foran had a good presence on film and for the next four years, Warners kept him constantly at work, as the studio did all its contract players.

After making five quickie westerns with John Wayne in 1932 and '33, Warners abandoned the field as being insufficiently profitable. However, with the success of Gene Autry in 1936 and the opening up of a much wider market for musical westerns, Warners now decided to get back into the celluloid sagebrush business. It was a studio run like a factory, with ample resources, facilities and a vast number of artisans and players on the payroll, one of whom was a handsome young actor with a pleasing personality and a nice singing voice. Warners also happened to have one of the finest music departments in the industry. It would not be hard to cash in on the bonanza Republic was enjoying with Autry—or so Jack Warner thought.

The first of what would be 12 Foran musical westerns was *Moonlight on the Prairie*, released in November of 1935, followed by *Song of the Saddle, Treachery Rides the Range, Trailin' West* and *The California Mail* the same year, then in 1937: *Guns of the Pecos, Land Beyond the Law, Cherokee Strip, Blazing Sixes, Empty Holsters, Devil's Saddle Legion* and *Prairie Thunder*. All were well-produced little packages, several notches above the usual run of B westerns, with most using a goodly amount of stock footage from the Warner library, especially the material shot for the Ken Maynard pictures made in the late '20s. In regard to music, the Foran westerns were head and shoulders above the competition. Most B westerns of the '30s contained barely any scoring, and whenever music did well up, it was usually done with recorded tracks, often of abys-

Jane Bryran and Dick Foran.

At right Dick Foran shakes hands with David Carlyle, who would shortly change his name to Robert Paige.

Dick Foran and Glenn Strange.

mal quality. Not so at Warners, where each of the Foran westerns was separately scored, mostly by Howard Jackson, and generally contained a pair of songs written by staff tunesmiths, composer M. K. Jerome and lyricist Jack Scholl. If anything, the songs were a little too good for the pictures, most of them being ballads more in keeping with the Broadway stage than the open range, especially when voiced in bravura style by Foran. This was not the way Autry was rounding up his posse of fans.

The only one of the Jerome-Scholl songs to find any lasting popularity was "My Little Buckaroo," which Foran sang in *The Cherokee Strip*. In this outing, Foran appears as Dick Hudson, a young lawyer bound on hanging out his shingle in the Oklahoma of 1889. It was the time when the government opened up the territory for settlers, who, on April 22nd of that year, where allowed to stake out land for themselves at no cost. When first seen, Dick is happily riding along singing "Traveling Home," when he is fired upon. The shooter is a boy, Barty Walton (Tommy Bupp), who claims he is just target practicing. As Dick berates the lad, Barty's sister Janie (Jane Bryan) arrives to side with him and call Dick a bully. A few moments later, Link Carter (Ed

Ed Cobb, Helen Valkis and Dick Foran.

56

Cobb) comes on the scene and Dick senses trouble, recalling Carter's past crimes, and the two fight. Dick knows that with Carter on hand the settlers about to take part in the land rush will be cheated.

In the new territory, Carter becomes the primary business force, starting up the town of Big Rock and appointing the mayor and the sheriff. Everything is run by Carter and Dick finds little business for his law office. The sheriff is Janie's father, George Walton (Tom Browser), who has allowed himself to become compromised by Carter. Dick, while riding through the nearby countryside, finds cattle being rustled. He pursues one of the cattle nappers, who turns out to be Janie. She explains she is simply trying to get back cattle stolen by Carter and that her father has had to go along with Carter because of threats to the family. Walton finally decides he cannot condone Carter's increasing control and gives Dick incriminating evidence, which causes the old man to be shot and wounded. After Dick's friend, rancher Tom Valley (David Carlyle—soon to change his name to Robert Paige), storms into Carter's office to accuse him of a list of crimes, he is gunned down in the street. Carter denies the murder but the crowd has had enough of him and moves to lynch him. Dick suggests that there is a better way—a court trial, at which he establishes not only guilt of murder and extortion but the fact that Carter had entered the territory illegally a day before the government decree.

As *The Cherokee Strip* draws to its inevitable happy ending, Dick drives Janie in a buggy over the ground on which they will settle and sings, "The Prairie Is My Home," which Jerome and Scholl had written for *Guns of the Pecos*, two movies ahead of this one, and which turned up in several of the others in this series. Aside from a melodic line verging on the operatic, the song came closer than any of the others to being a theme for the Foran westerns. The film also benefitted from the expert editing of Thomas Pratt, who skillfully interwove stock footage of previous films dealing with the Oklahoma land rush with new material. That epic event has been touched upon in several films, most notably in William S. Hart's silent classic *Tumbleweeds* (1926) and *Cimarron* (1931). Another asset of this Foran movie was the casting of Jane Bryan as the heroine. B westerns were regarded as apprenticeships for contract players and few went on to major careers. Bryan was a talented young actress, giving fine performances in films like *The Old Maid* (1939) with Bette Davis, *Each Dawn I Die* with James Cagney, and *We Are Not Alone* with Paul Muni. But in 1940, aged 22, she opted for family life and left the picture business.

After making the last of the dozen musical westerns, Dick Foran found himself a success and a failure. His efforts placed him No. 6 in the Top 10 western stars of

Dick Foran and Ed Cobb.

1936 and No. 4 the following year, no mean achievement. However, his studio was more interested in profit than popularity. Warners found the Foran westerns unsaleable in the major cities and although the small town movie houses were eager for more, Warners could not compete on rental terms with the smaller studios that specialized in B westerns. Modest as the Foran budgets might have been, they still had to take into account the huge Warner Bros. overhead, which made the product cost out of kilter with the limited income.

When Universal offered Foran a contract in 1940, Warners told him he was free to take it. He started off with Universal making two of the better western serials, *Winners of the West* and *Riders of Death Valley*, co-starring in the latter with Buck Jones. After that, the studio used him in a slew of modestly budgeted action pictures, horror items and musicals, films that provided a living but no distinction. But it was with Universal that Dick Foran would find his finest cinematic moment. As the romantic lead in the Abbott and Costello comedy *Ride 'Em Cowboy* (1942), he not only did well playing Bronco Bob, a writer of western stories who pretends he can do all the cowboy things he writes about, but also introduced a beautiful ballad that would become a standard, Don Ray and Gene dePaul's "I'll Remember April." And he sang it very well.

THE PAINTED STALLION

REPUBLIC, 1937

Produced by J. Laurence Wickland. Directed by William Whitney, Alan James and Ray Taylor. Written by Barry Shipman and Winston Miller, based on a story by Morgan Cox and Ronald Davidson and an idea by Hal G. Evarts. Photographed by William Nobles and Edgar Lyons. Musical direction by Raoul Kraushaar. 12 episodes.

CAST:

(*Clark Stuart*) Ray Corrigan; (*Walter Jamison*) Hoot Gibson; (*Alfred Dupray*) LeRoy Mason; (*Zamorro*) Duncan Renaldo; (*Kit Carson*) Sammy McKim; (*Jim Bowie*) Hal Taliaferro; (*Davy Crockett*) Jack Perrin; (*Oscar*) Ed Platt; (*Elmer*) Lou Fulton; (*The Rider*) Julia Thayer.

No form of western was more preposterous than the serial. If Hollywood cowboys lived in a West that never was, those in the serials populated a virtual western never-never land. In serials, the villains were more dastardly and the heroes more bold, to say nothing of being incredibly lucky. A hero in a western serial could survive virtually any form of catastrophe. He could live through horse and cattle stampedes—miraculously there was always a rock to climb behind or a tree to leap into—he could escape landslides, massive Indian attacks or any outrageous plot device designed to end his life. When the coach or wagon in which he was trapped was propelled over a cliff, he always managed to jump out before it went over, although that piece of filming was never shown until the start of the next chapter.

Serials go back to the early days of silent film but they became a major attraction after sound came to the aid of the movie producers, who quickly realized that sound itself was a vital part of whipping up excitement with hordes of Saturday matinee youngsters. The first sound serial was Universal's *The Indians Are Coming,* starring Tim McCoy in 1930, and that studio would make another 68 serials before the last one in 1946. Republic made 66 of them and Columbia churned out 57, in addition to batches made by smaller companies. Since they all contained 12 to 15 chapters each, the total amount of film devoted to serials is indeed large—and somewhat overlooked by film historians.

About a third of the serials were westerns, which is not difficult to understand in view of the audience for whom they were made or the fact that it was a relatively inexpensive form of picture making. The most successful western serial was Republic's *The Lone Ranger* in 1938, which inevitably led to *The Long Ranger Rides Again* a year later. However, a good case can be made for *The Painted Stallion* as the most fondly-remembered western serial. Made by Republic in 1936, it seemed to have a little magic about it, partly because it was filmed on location in southwest Utah, near St.

George—a region often used by Hollywood thereafter—but mostly because the title horse was ridden by a beautiful Indian girl, who looked about as Indian as Marilyn Monroe. That such a creature would be found in this setting made no sense whatsoever, but serials had nothing to do with sense. There were fairy tales.

Hal G. Evarts (1887–1934), a Kansan noted for his knowledge of western lore, published his three-part story *The Painted Stallion* in *The Saturday Evening Post* in 1925. When his widow sold the rights to Republic, she found, as have so many others, that selling a story

Ray Corrigan, Hoot Gibson and Hal Taliaferro.

to a film company does not ensure that it will be filmed as written. By the time a flock of scenarists had settled on the final script, it bore no relation to Evarts' original and all the late writer received in the credit titles was, "Based on a story by . . ." What emerged was a conventional tale of a wagon train making its way along the Santa Fe Trail, challenged by a would-be territorial dictator named Alfredo Dupray (LeRoy Mason) and protected by a guardian angel in the form of an Indian maiden on a painted stallion, a girl who shoots whistling arrows to warn the trekkers and fend off the villains. Republic chose blond, blue-eyed, 23-year-old Julia Thayer to play this fanciful part and it turned out to be the only role by which she would be remembered. At one point in the film, the improbable heroine is referred to as a spirit, "All the peons and Indians think the stallion is a ghost horse and the rider an Indian spirit." Not until the very end of the serial is there any explanation. The leader of the wagon train, Walter Jamison (Hoot Gibson), asks the Governor of New Mexico (Gordon DeMain) about the girl and is told, "There's a story among the Comanches of a baby girl, the sole survivor of a massacred settlement, brought up by the Comanches and because of her golden hair they worship her as a goddess, a goddess of peace." Be that as

Ray Corrigan and Charles King.

Ray Corrigan, Maston Williams and LeRoy Mason.

60

Hal Taliaferro, Hoot Gibson and Jack Perrin.

it may, the hero, Clark Stuart (Ray Corrigan), finds the rider of the painted stallion to be a flesh-and-blood beauty, and when last seen, they are riding off into the sunset together.

The plotline of *The Painted Stallion* has the hero empowered by Washington to proceed to Santa Fe in 1823 to negotiate a treaty with the Mexican governor, following Mexico's recent break with Spain. He joins a wagon train setting out from Independence, Missouri. To beef up the historical aspect of the serial, Republic decided to place a pair of legendary real life frontier figures as members of the trek—Jim Bowie and Davy Crockett, although neither could have been involved in such an adventure in 1823. They also placed another name westerner, Kit Carson, making him a 12-year-old boy (Sammy McKim), getting his apprenticeship as a frontiersman from the likes of Bowie and Crockett. As a stretching of historical fact, this was not too far off the mark. Carson would have been 14 in the year of this story and probably saw something of wagon train life, not that Republic was interested in educating the audience. It was simply that having an eager young lad

with a famous name was a dependable piece of casting in a western serial, one in which he could be rescued several times by the hero.

The first few chapters deal with the perils of the trek across the harsh landscapes and the opposition of the Indians. Things become really rough for the trekkers as they near the end of the trail and approach Santa Fe, where Dupray wishes to set up a private empire. Formerly the governor, he has been deposed by the severing of ties with Spain but he knows the riches of the area and seeks to make them his own, which necessitates sabotaging any treaty with the United States. Hence the constant attacks on the wagon train and the perpetual dangers in which Stuart finds himself, dangers which would be more evident if not for the intervention of the Indian girl who watches over him and shoots her arrows of warning. She also at one point rescues him from the bottom of a gully after he has been chased over the edge by the galloping villains at the end of Chapter Ten, which is fair play since he had saved her from the same thugs in Chapter Three, at the end of which they jumped off a high cliff into a lake.

61

Stuart naturally survives the leap, just as he does the assorted explosions, fires, wagon collisions and an avalanche.

Eventually, Dupray concedes to the failure of his plans to establish his own province and decides to depart with the wealth he has acquired. This is stashed in a cave in the rugged mountains, where Stuart and the Rider attempt to stop him, only to be captured themselves. But Jamison and his men arrive in time and attack. In the ensuing battle, Dupray and his principle lieutenants meet their justly violent end and the newly-arrived governor promises that all will be well in New Mexico from now on.

The Painted Stallion can perhaps be best described as pleasantly absurd. Like all serials, its devices of peril for the hero are ridiculous and defy critical comment. Such films were not made for critics and barely received any mention in the press. They were made for the enthusiastic youngsters who attended the matinees and they were invariably successful. What gave this one a little more quality was the fact that its producer, J. Laurence Wickland, was a man with a genuine love of the outdoors, and wherever possible, he shot on scenic locations. He took his cast and crew to Utah for two weeks and while there, he elevated his 21-year-old script supervisor, William Whitney, to the post of principle director because he liked the young man's enthusiasm for the project. The enthusiasm showed in the final product; the appointed directors, Alan James and Ray Taylor, were seconded to action sequences, and the three hours of material were edited into 12 chapters by Murray Seldeen.

Wickland wisely chose old-time western star Hoot Gibson for his name value, although the role of the wagonmaster is at best secondary. The choice of the unknown Julia Thayer as the rider turned out to be inspired, but it is Ray Corrigan as the hero who carries the serial. Large and beefy, Corrigan started in films as a stuntman and bit player, and he was contracted by Republic in 1935. Within a year, the studio decided to feature him as Tucson Smith in its series titled *The Three Mesquiteers,* the most successful of the westerns built around the trio format. Corrigan did 24 of these films, mostly with Robert Livingstone as the romantic Stoney Brook and the comedic Max Terhune playing Lullaby Joslin. Taking time out to appear as the star of *The Painted Stallion* helped Corrigan build his popularity with the fans, as his employers clearly knew it would. Republic, no less than the bigger studios, was a well-run business enterprise.

William Boyd.

TEXAS TRAIL

PARAMOUNT, 1937

Produced by Harry Sherman. Directed by David Selman. Written by Jack O'Donnell, based on the story *Tex* by Clarence E. Mulford. Photographed by Russell Harlan. 58 minutes.

CAST:

(Hopalong Cassidy) William Boyd; *(Windy Halliday)* George Hayes; *(Lucky Jenkins)* Russell Hayden; *(Barbara Allen)* Judith Allen; *(Black Jack Carson)* Alexander Cross; *(Hawks)* Robert Kortman; *(Boots)* Billy King; *(Brad)* Rafael Bennett; *(Major McCready)* Karl Hackett; *(Shorty)* Jack Rockwell; *(Jordan)* Philo McCullough; *(Smokey)* John Beach.

The best known character in all of western fiction is Hopalong Cassidy, and the fact that he is the best known is due more to the actor who played him on screen than to the author who created him. As personified by William Boyd, who was 40 when he took over the role, Cassidy is a rock-firm moralist, genial except when angered, almost avuncular and with a well tailored, dark and sober hat, shirt and pants, made the

more striking by his always riding a white horse. He is as close to being a Knight of the range as has ever been seen.

As formed in the mind of Clarence E. Mulford (1883–1956), in a long series of interconnected novels which began with *Bar-20* in 1907 and ended with *Hopalong Cassidy Serves a Writ* in 1941, Cassidy is at first a young roughneck, cussing and tobacco-spitting, constantly in trouble because of a foul disposition, who ages through the novels but never changes his basically hard-bitten nature. He is also a bitter, unlucky man, a cowhand who turns gunman after losing a wife and son to illness—and he is merely one of the numerous characters who populate the novels. In some, he does not appear at all.

Both Mulford and Boyd were unlikely men to end their lives identifiable almost entirely because of Hopalong Cassidy. Mulford was a quiet, mild-mannered man who grew up in New York and became a civil servant. Fascinated with the West as a youngster, he researched its history with a passion, gradually building up hundreds of files of material. After successfully placing some short stories, he turned out *Bar-20,* and he was a successful western novelist thereafter. Unlike Zane Grey, whose success with western fiction was triggered by a visit to the West, Mulford never ventured westward until 1924. In 1935, he was contacted by Harry Sherman, a producer of more than 20 years' experience in films, who suggested making a series based on the Cassidy character. Sherman explained that he had little money at this point but that he was willing to give five percent of the income to Mulford. The author sensed a good thing and accepted.

William Boyd, born in Ohio in June of 1895, grew up in near poverty in Oklahoma. When his laborer father was killed in a work accident, Boyd, then 12, left school in order to earn money to support a large family. By his late teens, he had drifted westward, where he worked in lumber camps in Arizona and fruit farms in California. He became a truck driver, a car salesman and a chauffeur. In 1918, an actor suggested, because of Boyd's good looks and his striking white hair, that he try getting work as a movie extra. It proved to be fairly easy and Boyd started at Famous Players-Lasky, which merged with, and became known as, Paramount at about the time he arrived. Within a couple of years, he

Russell Hayden, William Boyd and George Hayes.

was playing bits for Cecil B. DeMille who, in 1926, elevated him to stardom in *The Volga Boatman.* Boyd did well at the box office and started to lead a high life of financial plenty and giddy glamor, which included an over indulgence in drinking. He easily made the transition to sound film, but by 1935 his popularity had waned. When Sherman offered him the role of Cassidy and explained he could pay only $5000, Boyd wasted no time in accepting.

Boyd was not Sherman's first choice for Cassidy. Thinking to keep the character somewhat close to the Mulford invention, Sherman offered the part to character actor James Gleason, who specialized in playing crusty and slightly cantankerous men. But Gleason was not interested in the small money offered and Sherman then turned to Boyd. After reading the script, Boyd suggested a more heroic interpretation of Cassidy, and Sherman, eager to get into production now that he had a distribution deal set up with Paramount, agreed. He would later argue with Boyd about the interpretation but the shrewd actor knew what he was doing. *Hop-a-long Cassidy,* later retitled *Hopalong Cassidy Enters,* was released in July of 1935 and the public response was immediate. In the first year of the Cassidy pictures, Boyd played parts in three other films, but after the fifth Cassidy outing, *Three on the Trail,* he never again played any other character. No film actor ever assumed so completely another identity as did William Boyd.

Billy King, William Boyd and Karl Hackett.

William Boyd and Billy King.

The Cassidy pictures—there would be a total of 66—are the finest series of B westerns ever turned out. Right from the start, with Paramount backing, the production values, the scripts and the acting were miles ahead of the competition. Sherman shot all of his exteriors on location, around Lone Pine in the Owens Valley, an area of ideal western scenery, some 200 miles north of Los Angeles. To the west of Lone Pine lies Sequoia National Park, which includes Mount Whitney, the highest point in California. Just to the south is Owens Lake and 30 miles to the west lies Death Valley. The critics often commented on the beauty of the photography.

The first 20 or so of the Cassidy pictures were claimed to have been based on the Mulford novels, but in truth there is barely the slightest resemblence. The credit titles of *Texas Trail*, the 14th Cassidy film, gives the source as Mulford's *Tex* (1922), yet there are no similarities between the film and the book, in which Cassidy does not even appear. By this time Boyd's Hoppy was so popular that no one other than Mulford raised any protest. Mulford sneered at the series but not the income.

While the Cassidy films place the action only generally in the late 19th century, *Texas Trail* clearly takes place in 1898, with the outbreak of the Spanish-American War. Cassidy is called to Fort Bowie by Major McCready (Karl Hackett), who asks for help in supplying the cavalry with badly needed horses. Cassidy

Alexander Cross, Russell Hayden, William Boyd and George Hayes.

65

agrees not only to take the assignment but also to encourage his cowboys to prepare for enlistment and take training. Previous attempts by the Army to collect horses have failed because of rustlers. The main culprit, unknown to anyone, is rancher Black Jack Carson (Alexander Cross), who plans to track Cassidy once he has rounded up 500 horses and then steal them. Cassidy gradually assembles the horses and corrals them in Ghost Creek Canyon. Carson has ten of his own Triple X horses run in with the herd and thus has a good reason to arrest Cassidy and his men as rustlers. They are tied up as the Carson gang plan to spirit the horses over the Mexican border. To Cassidy's aid come two allies. The first is Carson's house guest, Barbara Allen (Judith Allen), the new schoolmarm, who overhears Carson and his men plotting and rides to inform McCready; the other is McCready's young son, Boots (Billy King), who takes it upon himself to seek out Hoppy, the man he idealizes. Boots finds the tied-up men at night, and Cassidy the next morning sets about changing the situation. He starts a large fire, which panics the stolen herd and causes the Carson gang to

William Boyd, captured by Alexander Cross.

lose control. The cavalry soon arrives and Cassidy hands Carson over to the Army, along with the horses they need. Then, in the final scene, a commissioned lieutenant, he rides off with his now uniformed men to fight with Teddy Roosevelt's Rough Riders in Cuba.

Texas Trail, like all the early Cassidy pictures, is a highly skillful piece of western film fare, distinguished by the fine photography of vast numbers of horses galloping amid the stark scenery of the northern part of Death Valley. The script also plays up the characters of Cassidy's two sidekicks, the handsome young Lucky Jenkins (Russell Hayden) and the crochety old Windy Halliday (George Hayes). Hayden played the part in 27 of the films and Hayes in 21. It was always expected, and never failed, that the impetuous Lucky would get into trouble, most often because of paying too much attention to the leading lady, and that Windy would complain about everything under the sun and tell dubious stories about past adventures. In time, the two actors would leave the series but they were replaced by others in virtually the same characterizations.

In 1941, after making 41 Cassidy films, Harry Sherman severed his connection with Paramount, feeling he could do better elsewhere, and the remaining 25 were

released by United Artists. Sherman and Boyd had never been in complete accord over the interpretation of Cassidy, Sherman feeling that it might have been closer to what Mulford had in mind, and Boyd was forever hounding him for better scripts. In 1944, Sherman decided he had had enough of Cassidy and called a halt, which displeased Boyd very much because by now his screen identity was so completely Cassidy that he could get no other work. Two years later, having raised the capital, Boyd purchased the rights to the character and made 12 more films under his own banner, although because of rapidly rising costs, they were of an ever diminishing quality. By the summer of 1948, it was all over, or so it seemed to Hollywood, which was now beginning to fear the coming of television. Boyd made another bold move, this time selling almost all his property and assets in order to acquire ownership of the Cassidy films. It was a move which would turn him into a millionaire.

By releasing the films to television, at a time when the new industry was desperate for product, Boyd not only made money but recaptured the glory and the popularity of the early years of the pictures. Additionally he produced a television series of 30-minute Cas-

sidy stories, as well as playing the role on radio and organizing merchandizing tie-ins. And for his old boss, Cecil B. DeMille, he did a cameo appearance as Hoppy in *The Greatest Show on Earth* (1952), the only time Hopalong Cassidy was ever seen on the screen in color. In 1958, Boyd sold his interests and enterprises for $8-million and retired to a quiet life with his fourth wife. He had no children and it was often rumored that he did not care much for them. As he passed the age of 70, his health began to decline and he became more and more reclusive. Boyd was 77 when he died in 1972, a victim of cancer and Parkinson's disease, a sad ending for a man who left such a glowingly heroic image as Hopalong Cassidy, an image that was entirely of his making.

Boyd's track record in western film compares to no other. No other film actor ever created a character and played him for 17 years with such lasting identity. And no other ever so radically changed his own lifestyle, from that of a rather aimless Hollywood playboy to the guise of western paragon, one who gave up hard liquor and took to drinking white wine once he became the beloved Hoppy, which was something Clarence E. Mulford could never understand.

67

John Wayne and Johnny Mack Brown.

BORN TO THE WEST

PARAMOUNT, 1937

Directed by Charles Barton. Written by Stuary Anthony and Robert Yost, based on the novel by Zane Grey. Photographed by J. Devereaux Jennings. 52 minutes.

CAST:

(Dare Rudd) John Wayne; *(Judith Worstall)* Marsha Hunt; *(Tom Fillmore)* Johnny Mack Brown; *(Hardy)* John Patterson; *(Hammond)* Monte Blue; *(Hooley)* Sid Saylor; *(Buyer)* Lucien Littlefield; *(Fallon)* Nick Lucats; *(Brady)* James Craig; *(Sam)* Johnny Boyle; *(Sheriff)* Jack Kennedy.

The notion that John Wayne became an overnight star when he appeared in *Stagecoach* in 1939 makes little sense to anyone with knowledge of westerns. He certainly moved into a wider range of stardom but by that time he had already been in films for 11 years and he had made 38 westerns. In 1936, he was No. 7 in popularity at the B western box office, which is as high as he got. At the time John Ford picked him to play the Ringo Kid, Wayne had slipped to No. 9. In that limited league, his days were numbered. As a B westerner, he approached neither the popularity of Gene Autry nor the prestige of Buck Jones. It was not until he became a major player that Wayne blossomed into a charismatic actor, and one who would enjoy an astonishing longevity and popularity as an international star. Since his death in 1979, he has passed into almost legendary status.

Born in Iowa in May of 1908, Wayne grew up in Glendale, California, and attended the University of Southern California on a football scholarship. Being a star tackle on the popular USC Trojan team proved his entry in the film business. The team was several times filmed, and in the summers, Wayne found employment as a prop boy for Fox Pictures. While working on *Mother Machree* in late 1927, director John Ford took a liking to him and gave him a bit part in the film. Slightly bigger bits in six other Fox productions brought him to the attention of director Raoul Walsh, who decided to take a big chance and give Wayne the lead in *The Big Trail*, which was indeed big. It was a super western running two hours and filmed in 70mm and requiring the installation of special equipment in theatres. Now the start of the Great Depression, *The Big Trail* played in limited engagements and its young star found himself tainted, and partly blamed, with a big failure. After small parts in two other films, Fox let him go. Columbia hired him as a supporting player in one Buck Jones and two Tim McCoy westerns, plus other bits, and then they dumped him, something Wayne never forgot. He vowed not to set foot inside Columbia ever again, despite later offers. Work at a low salary playing leads in a pair of Mascot Serials, *Shadow of the Eagle* and *Hurricane Express* in 1932, brought him some popularity, resulting in Warner Bros. starring him in a series of programmers, five of which were westerns. The profits were not big enough for Warners to continue with him but strong enough for Monogram to sign him for 16 westerns, each made on a miniscule budget. If nothing else, they registered John Wayne as a Hollywood westerner.

In 1935, Republic signed him for a series of eight, after which, desperate to get away from cheap westerns, he tried playing heroes in a variety of action pictures at Universal. The results were not encouraging, and when Paramount offered him the lead in *Born to the West* in early 1938, he accepted with alacrity. It was a Zane Grey story, made by a major studio, and it had the added advantage of teaming him up with another young actor who had managed to make a name for himself in westerns, Johnny Mack Brown.

As with Wayne, it was Brown's ability as a football player that opened the door to the movie business, except that in Brown's case he was a major player. An Alabaman, born in 1904, he never lost the southern accent or the courtly manner that marked him as being a little different from the other cowboy stars. As a halfback on the University of Alabama's football team, he became a sports hero, particularly on New Year's Day, 1926, when he caught a 75-yard pass in almost motion picture fashion, leading a 'Bama win over the University of Washington 20-19. Exactly one year later, playing at the Rose Bowl in Pasadena, an actor friend arranged a screen test at MGM. It was a breeze and Brown straightaway was given a role in a baseball picture, *Slide, Kelly, Slide*. For MGM, Brown became a leading man in comedies and dramas, and it was not until 1930, when King Vidor chose him to play *Billy the Kid*, that he began his identification with the West. Although a major presentation, it was not a major success and Brown went back to a variety of films.

Brown was not an accomplished actor, and after MGM let him go in 1931, he accepted whatever came his way. A Mascot serial in 1933, *Fighting With Kit Carson*, seemed to suggest that his best bet was with six-guns, spurs and saddles, and over the next four years, he did western series for Supreme and Republic,

and two serials for Universal. However, by the time Paramount offered him second billing in *Born to the West* in late 1937, his career, like that of Wayne, was not on very solid ground. But this film would make a difference for both of them.

Born to the West was just about the only Zane Grey story that Paramount had not previously made into a movie. With its expertise and facilities, the studio was able to give a B western such as this a better look and feel than the minors. Paramount had a well laid-out western town on the backlot, plenty of contract players and lots of stock footage of cattle drives and stampedes, of which the first few minutes of this film is somewhat confusedly composed. And because of the Hopalong Cassidy pictures, it also had location facilities set up around the spectacular scenery of Lone Pine, and it sent the cast and crew there for several days of exteriors. Thanks to a good script by Stuart Anthony and Robert Yost, the parts given Wayne and Brown were more interesting than the norm in this kind of fare. Wayne plays a rather charming scalawag named Dare Rudd and Brown is his cousin Tom Fillmore, a solid rancher, banker and head of the Cattleman's Association.

When first seen, Dare and his sidekick Hooley (Sid Saylor) are drifters in need of work. They come across

Sid Saylor, Johnny Mack Brown, John Wayne and Marsha Hunt.

a battle between cowboys and rustlers, and join in, hoping that by ending up on the winning side, they will be hired. They pick badly and flee, chased by Fillmore, who corners them and discovers that he has been chasing his cousin. Dare easily talks his way out of the situation and Fillmore invites him to come into town the next day and visit him. Dare does so, but not until he and Hooley have been tossed out of a saloon for cheating at poker and brawling. Dare boasts that he is "the best poker player this side of the Mississippi." Fillmore offers him a job, but Dare dislikes the idea of honest labor and says he would rather drift on—until Fillmore's girlfriend Judy (Marsha Hunt) walks into the Fillmore Bank. After one look at her, Dare decides to accept the offer to stay, even though the job is just that of a chuckwagon cook. He works hard to impress Judy, and with her nudging of Fillmore, he gets promoted to head the drive of Fillmore's cattle to market.

Trouble is in the air, due to Hammond (Monte Blue), the man who not only owns the saloon but also runs a well-organized rustling operation. Lyn Hardy (John Patterson), who has been working as Fillmore's foreman, is actually in the employ of Hammond. Dare gradually suspects Hardy and foils his attempt to take over the cattle drive. After he sells the cattle and is now in possession of a large amount of cash, Dare's vanity is played upon by Hammond, who tricks him into a poker game, and using marked cards, Hammond, who has hired an ace player, Brady (James Craig), divests Dare of all the funds. But Hooley rides for Fillmore, himself a reformed poker ace, and upon arrival, Fillmore starts to win back the money. In desperation, Hammond tries to cheat and Fillmore reaches for his gun. He is wounded in the melee but he and Dare shoot their way out of the saloon and take off, pursued by Hammond and his men. Hooley rides to get Fillmore's cowpunchers, who arrive in time to save Dare and his cousin. Fillmore gives Dare a chance to get away with the money, thinking that is all that interests his rascal relative but he is pleasantly surprised to find signs of reformation. Dare admits that he is not the best poker player this side of the Mississippi.

Dare decides to leave, thinking that Judy's heart is really with Fillmore, who by this time knows it is not. He tells Judy that Dare has left by the north trail. She rides after him and tells him that Fillmore wants him for a partner. He asks her, "Do you?" She nods, and with that they head back to the ranch—along with Hooley. In B westerns, sidekicks could always count on fidelity.

Born to the West is among the very best pictures of its class and it did much for Wayne and Brown. The style that Wayne had been honing for the past seven years here seemed to finally jell. Playing a rogue, he gives the part more charm than he had previously been able to bring to bear. Following this, he was hired by Republic to play the role of Stony Brooke in that studio's popular *Three Mesquiteers* series. It was while doing a series of eight of these items that Wayne was called by Ford for *Stagecoach*—and the eventual ascension into western superstardom.

Johnny Mack Brown was afterwards contracted by Universal as their No. 1 westerner. Following a pair of serials, *Flaming Frontiers* (1938) and *The Oregon Trail* (1939), he did 30 westerns for them over the next four years, which made him consistently popular. When Universal dickered about renewing his contract, he switched to Monogram and starred in 67 of the studio's cowboy pictures. By the time he ended with Monogram in 1952, Brown had chalked up one of the longest track records of any movie westerner. He was now 48 and long in the tooth for this game. He was also, due to heavy drinking, getting hefty, and the spark was gone. Brown was still a southern gentleman but a rather tired one. He retired from the screen, but in 1965, he strapped on his six-shooters once again for cameos in *Requiem for a Gunfighter* and *The Bounty Killers*, both films produced by western authority Alex Gordon, who in each case attempted to populate his sagebrush saga

70

Sid Saylor, Johnny Mack Brown, Marsha Hunt and John Wayne.

John Wayne, Johnny Mack Brown and Sid Saylor.

with every old western star he could corral. The following year, Brown did another bit in *Apache Uprising,* but for his fans it was rather disturbing seeing him as a portly, slow-moving oldtimer. He seemed older than his years and somewhat sad. That he was. Johnny Mack Brown died of a kidney ailment at the age of 70 in 1974.

Johnny Mack Brown and John Wayne.

71

Smith Ballew.

RAWHIDE

20TH CENTURY-FOX, 1938

Produced by Sol Lesser. Directed by Ray Taylor. Written by Dan Jarrett and Jack Natteford, based on a story by Jarrett. Photographed by Allen Q. Thompson. Musical direction by Michael Breen. 59 minutes.

CAST:

(*Larry Kimball*) Smith Ballew; (*Himself*) Lou Gehrig; (*Peggy Gehrig*) Evalyn Knapp; (*Ed Saunders*) Arthur Loft; (*Bascomb*) Carl Stockdale; (*Pop Mason*) Si Jenks; (*Sheriff Kale*) Cy Kendall; (*McDonnell*) Lafe McKee; (*Butch*) Dick Curtis; (*Gilliam*) Cecil Kellogg; (*Biff*) Slim Whitaker.

The success of Gene Autry was astonishing. By 1936, having been seen in only a handful of musical westerns the previous year, he was No. 1 among the cowboy stars and he maintained that position until 1942, when he went into the Army. Then Roy Rogers assumed the top spot and stayed No. 1 until 1954, by which time the era of the B western had come to the end of the trail. Autry resumed his career in 1946 and immediately regained his popularity—as No. 2. He and

Rogers were virtually neck and neck for the next eight years. Many were the attempts to cash in on their success as singing cowboys but few even came close. One of them was Smith Ballew.

Ballew was born in Texas in 1902, but he was never a cowboy. At the University of Texas, he conducted the college dance band and sang, and did so well that this set the course of his career. He went to New York in 1925, and over the next ten years, Ballew sang with various bands—he even had one of his own for a while—appeared on the radio and made a large number of recordings. His baritone crooning pleased a lot of people. Hollywood beckoned, and in 1936, he appeared opposite Frances Langford, as a singing cowboy, in *Palm Springs*. Sol Lesser then signed Ballew to make a series of eight westerns for his Principal Pictures, only five of which were filmed because, when Lesser stopped releasing his product through 20th Century-Fox and switched to RKO, that studio decided it could do without Ballew. RKO's own western programming was, in its opinion, ample.

Lou Gehrig leaves Grand Central Station, heading west.

Ballew's first two pictures, *Western Gold* and *Roll Along Cowboy,* made little impression at the box office and Lesser then made efforts to jack up the product. He brought in Ray Taylor, long an expert director of B westerns, and the next film, *Hawaiian Buckeroo,* was a distinct improvement, mostly because it revealed to moviegoers something not generally known—that there was considerable ranching activity on the main island of Hawaii. Then came *Rawhide,* which turned into a gem of its kind, followed by the genial *Panamint's Bad Man.* With any luck, Ballew might have gone on in this fashion, but luck was not with him. His career as a Hollywood singing cowboy was over almost as fast as it had begun. The lanky Ballew, all six-foot-five of him, thereafter played bits in other people's westerns and quit the business in 1950, when he became an executive with Hughes Aircraft. Two years later, he accepted a position with Convair in Fort Worth, Texas, where he lived for the rest of his life, dying in 1978.

Rawhide is one of those blessed little pictures where the sum total is somehow more than the parts. Sol Lesser hired veteran script writer Dan Jarrett, who used an original story, which he whipped into a more-than-usually involved western screenplay, and one which would sadly turn out to be his last. But the real joy of *Rawhide* is Lou Gehrig. Lesser had the happy

Cecil Kellogg and Smith Ballew.

73

Smith Ballew, held up by Dick Curtis.

inspiration, of asking the legendary baseball player to co-star with Ballew. This would be the only film for Gehrig, which is a pity because, had it not been for his enormous success in baseball and for the illness that claimed his life at the age of 37, he could easily have had a career as a movie character actor. Gehrig was a cheerful, outgoing New Yorker and, although he had never acted before, he appears in *Rawhide* to be completely at ease in front of the cameras.

Rawhide begins in New York's Grand Central Station as Gehrig tells a bunch of reporters that he is quitting baseball—he plays himself in the film—and going out West to live with his sister, Peggy (Evalyn Knapp), with whom he owns a ranch. He is looking for peace and quiet, which he is not about to find. There are crooked people in the nearby town of Rawhide, he learns, who have taken over the Ranchers Protective Association and turned it into a racket, forcing ranchers to join as a means of controling the sale of hay and sundry supplies. The association's aged, bedridden founder C. G. Mc-Donnell (Lafe McKee), is unaware that his manager, Ed Saunders (Arthur Loft), is running the racket and using violence to bring the ranchers into line. Lawyer Larry Kimball (Ballew) is having little luck persuading the ranchers to stand up to Saunders but he finds a feisty ally in Gehrig, who does not take to Saunders' suggestions about joining the association. Larry also

meets Peggy, with the inevitable mutual interest. Rather than pay the exhorbitant prices imposed by Saunders, Larry and Gehrig haul in hay from a distant point, only to be attacked by bandits and have their wagons run off the road.

Gehrig is disgusted and, with Larry's help, fights back. Puzzled by the apparent consent of the ailing McDonnell, Larry breaks into the latter's house and finds him a prisoner, unaware of what is going on. Larry shoots one of Saunders' henchmen who is about to do in the old man with poisoned milk. In the meantime, Peggy has decided that the pressure being applied by Saunders is too hard to fight; she is about to sign with him when Larry and Gehrig arrive to prove that they have enough evidence of his crookedness to end the scam. Saunders, sensing the end, takes off, to be pursued by Larry, who easily catches up with him.

The plotlines of *Rawhide* were, even by 1938, time honored but they are carried off with style. Four songs sung by Ballew space out the action, and the film is populated by plenty of extras in the streets, the saloon and out-on-the-range galloping around. But it is the presence of Lou Gehrig that lights up the picture, somewhat overshadowing the mild-mannered Ballew. He looks like a man having a whale of a time. The New York Yankees first baseman took to the cinematic range like the Yankee Stadium infield. The highlight of the

74

Lou Gehrig and Smith Ballew, after the barroom brawl with billiard balls.

Si Jenks, Smith Ballew and Lou Gehrig.

film is the barroom brawl in which he and Ballew take on the villain's hired guns, with Gehrig knocking a number of them out by pitching billiard balls at their heads with stunning accuracy. Later, to stop the sister signing the contract with the villain, Gehrig, the south-paw, borrows a bat and ball from an admiring team of kids playing baseball and pitches a ball right through the office window. And at the end, having put up a pretence of wanting to settle in the quiet West, Gehrig shows his true colors when a telegram arrives advising him to report for spring training—and he is off back East like a shot.

Rawhide is a happy souvenir of a remarkable man. Gehrig joined the Yankees in 1923, played in 2,130 consecutive games and participated in seven World Series before falling victim to a rare disease. He was tricken with amytropic lateral sclerosis, a neurological disfunction which would subsequently be known as Lou Gehrig's Disease. He announced his withdrawal from baseball to a crowd of 62,000 fans at the Yankee Stadium on July 4, 1939, and he died on June 2, 1941. A year later, Gary Cooper played Gehrig in *The Pride of the Yankees,* an Oscar-winning highlight in Cooper's career and a splendid tribute to the great ball player. Somewhat ironically, the man to whom Smith Ballew has always been compared because of his appearance and manner was Gary Cooper.

George O'Brien.

LAWLESS VALLEY

RKO, 1938

Produced by Bert Gilroy. Directed by David Howard. Written by Oliver Drake, based on a story by W. C. Tuttle. Photographed by Harry Wald. Music by Roy Webb. 59 minutes.

CAST:

(Larry) George O'Brien; *(Norma)* Kay Sutton; *(Bob North)* Walter Miller; *(Tom Marsh)* Fred Kohler, Sr.; *(Jeff Marsh)* Fred Kohler, Jr.; *(Fresno)* Lew Kelly; *(Tim Wade)* George McQuarrie; *(Sheriff)* Earl Hodgins; *(Speedy)* Chill Wills; *(Anna)* Dot Farley.

Of all the movie cowboys, the one who most looked as if he could take care of himself in a saloon brawl was George O'Brien. Those who had to "fight" him in such brawls knew they were up against a man who knew how to use his fists. In the Navy in 1918, he had become the light heavyweight boxing champion of the Pacific Fleet, and he was one film westerner who never used a double in his fight scenes. O'Brien seldom required a double for anything. He had been a stuntman before being an actor and he kept himself in superb physical

condition. He was a cheerful, gregarious, loquacious kind of man, with a cheeky charm that marked him as being very different from the average film westerner. O'Brien was the only one of them who is also remembered as the star of one of the great silent films, F. W. Murnau's *Sunrise* (1927), in which he co-starred with Janet Gaynor.

O'Brien was born in San Francisco in April of 1900, the son of a policeman who rose to become a commissioner and a director of penology. He learned to ride at any early age when his father got him an after-school job currying the horses of the city's mounted police, as well as working on the weekend at the Los Gatos ranch of a family friend. In high school, a dynamo of energy, he excelled in swimming, football and basketball. With America's entry into World War I, which coincided with his 17th birthday, O'Brien eagerly joined the Navy and became a pharmacist's mate. Discharged in late 1919, he began to study for a possible career in medicine but a meeting with Tom Mix changed everything. Mix was in San Francisco, performing in a rodeo, and through a mutual friend, O'Brien was presented to the famed movie cowboy, who, impressed by the young man's strapping build, offered him a job at 15 dollars a week as a camera assistant. Lugging equipment around for a year led to chances to perform as an extra and a stunt double, and then to bit parts. He came to the attention of John Ford in 1924 when the director was looking for someone to play the lead in what would become an epic western, *The Iron Horse,* running, in its first release, the better part of three hours. Ford tested dozens and decided that the beefy, bright-eyed and bushy-tailed O'Brien was what he wanted. The two were friends until Ford died in 1973.

The Iron Horse, which employed O'Brien for half a year, was the great hit of 1924. Now under contract to Fox, O'Brien was given star treatment and used in an average of four films per year. With the exception of *Three Bad Men* (1926), again with Ford, none was a western. However, by the end of the '20s, Fox had lost both Tom Mix and Buck Jones, and now, in the new era of sound film, the studio needed someone to star in a western series. O'Brien was the logical choice, and for the remainder of his movie career, virtually all his films were westerns. Among the best of the Fox sagebrush sagas were the Zane Grey classic *Riders of the Purple*

Fred Kohler, Sr., Fred Kohler, Jr., Kay Sutton and George O'Brien.

Kay Sutton and George O'Brien

George O'Brien and Walter Miller at work.

77

Sage (1931), and *Frontier Marshal* (1934), in which he played Wyatt Earp. In 1936, O'Brien accepted an RKO contract, and it was a westerner for that studio that O'Brien is best remembered.

All of the 20 films O'Brien made for RKO over the next four years were well constructed programmers. RKO, the smallest of the major studios, seemed to have a fondness for westerns and its product was above average. O'Brien was No. 2 at the western box office in 1936 (Buck Jones was first) and he stayed in the Top 10 all through his RKO sojourn. The care that was put into his westerns paid off, and in O'Brien the studio had a man of unusual appeal, one who was an athlete, a charmer and a believable actor. And among the best of the RKO series is *Lawless Valley* (1938).

Lawless Valley has O'Brien as Larry Rhodes, out on parole after serving only a year and a half of a prison sentence for stagecoach robbery. He is, of course, innocent, and in returning to Valley Junction, his intention is to find the man who framed him and caused the apparent suicide of his father. On the way home, he strikes up a friendship with an amiable drifter, Bob North (Walter Miller), and takes him back to the ranch

of his former employer, Tim Wade (George Mc-Quarrie). The hiring of both quickly comes to the attention of the town's most powerful citizen, rancher Tom Marsh (Fred Kohler, Sr.), whose son, Jeff (Fred Kohler, Jr.), is engaged to marry Norma (Kay Sutton), Larry's former sweetheart. Norma still carries a torch for Larry but Marsh is her legal guardian and the custodian of her ranch. The Marshes do everything they can to get Larry to violate his parole but fail at every turn.

Tim gives Larry the pistol with which Larry's father is said to have shot himself—an unusual gun, a Colt 41. Larry finds that there is something wrong with the spring and sends it to a gunsmith. Marsh hears about this and tries in vain to retrieve the gun. Larry attempts unsuccessfully to rescue Norma, whom Marsh tells that he will not harm Larry if she agrees to go through with the wedding. After getting a sworn statement from the gunsmith that he mended the spring of the Colt 41 following the stagecoach holdup and the alleged suicide, Larry faces the crooked sheriff (Earl Hodgins), long a lacky of Marsh, who breaks down and admits that it was Marsh who robbed the coach of $50,000 and

Walter Miller, George O'Brien, Lew Kelly, Chill Wills and Earl Hodgins.

killed Larry's father. Larry and Bob race to the Marsh Ranch, stop the wedding and nab Marsh, father and son. And Bob turns out to be a federal marshal, assigned to string along with Larry because of the doubts held about the charge on which Larry was jailed.

Lawless Valley is a slick western, with a few novel twists but held together mostly because of O'Brien's breezy performance. As in all his RKO westerns, he appeared to be bubbling over with energy, including a good deal of swift riding, none of which required a double, and the stylish fisticuffs for which he was well known. But all things must come to an end and O'Brien and RKO parted company in 1940. He was a little tired of this kind of product and the studio felt a younger man might do better for them in the long run. In choosing Tim Holt to fill the O'Brien boots, RKO picked a winner. Holt would make 47 westerns for the studio.

O'Brien had joined the Navy Reserve after leaving active service in 1919 and he was keenly interested in the military. He resumed active service in 1941 as an officer and was involved in combat in the Pacific, serving as a beachmaster in more than a dozen landings. He was wounded and decorated, and discharged in late 1946 with the rank of commander. Hollywood at the time seemed little interested in him and all O'Brien could get on his return was a supporting role in the Dennis Morgan musical *My Wild Irish Rose* (1947). John Ford came to the rescue and gave him a major role in the cavalry epic *Fort Apache* (1948), with a similar recall to duty the following year in *She Wore a Yellow Ribbon*. He would have been used again by Ford in the third of the cavalry trilogy, *Rio Grande*, filmed in the summer of 1950, but by then the Korean War had broken out and O'Brien rejoined the Navy. Back in Hollywood two years later, he played the lead in a cheap western, *Gold Raiders*, which co-starred him with The Three Stooges, after which he called it quits.

No longer interested in Hollywood, O'Brien devoted himself to more service with the Navy Reserve, producing a stage pageant, *The Spirit of the Navy*, making documentary films for military personnel and for civilians about to be involved in the military, and performing special assignments with NATO and SHAPE. John Ford, also a wartime naval officer and active in the Reserve, worked with O'Brien on some of the documentaries, and when Ford made his last western, *Cheyenne Autumn* in 1964, O'Brien was once more a cavalry officer on screen. He never again appeared in a film.

When asked which were his favorites, George O'Brien did not hesitate to say that they were those he made with his friend John Ford, starting with *The Iron Horse*, the film that made him a star and ending with the cavalry pictures in which he was one of an old family of Fordian players. He was an unusual western star, an ebullient man far removed from the classic silent cowboy, and a man as devoted to the Navy as to films. His wife, actress Marguerite Churchill, his co-star in *Riders of the Purple Sage*, divorced him in 1948 after 15 years of marriage, when he went off to the Korean War. Neither of his children had any interest in Hollywood; his son Darcy became a professor of English Literature and his daughter Orin a string player with the New York Philharmonic.

O'Brien's was a rich, full life until a stroke in 1979 left him partially paralyzed, a cruel fate for such an active man. Six years later, he died in a nursing home in Broken Arrow, Oklahoma, well into his 86th year.

HEART OF THE NORTH

WARNER BROS., 1938

Produced by Bryan Foy. Directed by Lewis Seiler. Written by Lee Katz and Vincent Sherman, based on the novel by William Byron Mowery. Photographed in Technicolor by L. William O'Connell. Music by Adolph Deutsch. 80 minutes.

CAST:

(*Sergeant Alan Baxter*) Dick Foran; (*Joyce MacMillan*) Gloria Dickson; (*Elizabeth Spaulding*) Gale Page; (*Corporal Bill Hardsock*) Allen Jenkins; (*Corporal Jim Montgomery*) Patric Knowles; (*Judy Montgomery*) Janet Chapman; (*Inspector Stephen Gore*) James Stephenson; (*Whipple*) Anthony Averill; (*Red Crocker*) Joseph Sawyer; (*Mac Drummond*) Joseph King; (*Dave MacMillan*) Russell Simpson; (*Larry Young*) Arthur Gardner; (*Father Claverly*) Pedro de Cordoba; (*Lunnnon Dick*) Alec Hartford; (*Captain Ashmun*) Robert Homans; (*Burgoon*) Anderson Lawler; (*Pedeault*) Bruce Carruthers; (*Tom Ryan*) Garry Owen.

No country has had as many films made about its national police force as Canada—by another country. The Canadians themselves have made very few movies about the Mounties, the Royal Canadian Mounted Police, but in the Golden Age of Hollywood, cinematic tales of their exploits were numerous and probably did more for Canadian identity than anything produced by the Canadian tourist industry. Not that the films actually had much to do with Canada. Hollywood's Mountie pictures were mostly westerns in which the heroes and the villains wore different kinds of hats—boy scout stetsons and fur caps. They were filmed for the most part in the mountains to the east of Los Angeles, up around Lake Arrowhead and Big Bear Lake, where the scenery is not greatly different from that of the Canadian Rockies. And since that area was within a two-hour drive of the studios, it was much easier than going to Canada.

Hollywood began spotlighting the Mounties early in the game of movie make-believe. Tom Mix played a redcoat in *The Cyclone* in 1920, the very year the Royal Canadian Mounted Police was so designated and made the national police body—prior to that they had been the Royal Northwest Mounted Police, and it was in that regional capacity that most of the fiction has been written about them. No police force has ever been so romanticized and nothing ever written about them brought them more attention than Rudolph Friml's operetta *Rose Marie,* particularly in the 1936 MGM version, which sported Nelson Eddy and the stirring "Song of the Mounties."

Most of the top cowboy stars made at least one film wearing the scarlet tunic and the dark blue riding britches with the broad yellow stripe. Buck Jones was *McKenna of the Mounted* (1932), Tom Tyler was *Clancy of the Mounted* (1933), George O'Brien was *O'Malley of the Mounted* and James Newill was *Renfrew of the Royal Mounted* (1938). Newill made eight pictures as Sergeant Renfrew, who, like Nelson Eddy had a fine baritone voice—youngsters growing up with these films could easily be forgiven for believing that being a baritone was a requisite for joining the RCMP—but the actor who made the most Mountie movies was Kermit Maynard. Two years younger than his brother Ken and an equally fine horseman, he appeared in ten, beginning with *The Fighting Trooper* in 1934. All were purportedly based on the novels of James Oliver Curwood, who specialized in writing about the great Northwest. Charles Starrett made five appearances as a Mountie and one of the films, *Secret Patrol* (1936), was actually filmed in Canada, not that it made any difference to the audience.

Zane Grey's contribution to RCMP lore, *King of the Royal Mounted,* became a B western in 1936, with

Gloria Dickson, Dick Foran and Gale Page.

Dick Foran, Anthony Averill, Allen Jenkins and Pedro de Cordoba.

Dick Foran, Russell Simpson and Gloria Dickson.

Robert Kent playing the title part, and then blossomed into a serial in 1940, with Allan Lane as King. Lane did so well with the Saturday matinee popcorn brigade that he had to make another serial in the same guise, *King of the Mounties,* two years later. Hollywood appeared to have touched a vein of gold. In the wake of Sergeant King came a surge of RCMP serials: *Perils of the Royal Mounted* (1942), *The Royal Mounted Rides Again* (1945), *Dangers of the Canadian Mounted* (1948), *Canadian Mounties versus Atomic Invaders* (1953) and *Perils of the Wilderness* (1956), which has the distinction of being the last serial made in Hollywood.

The most ambitious film about the Mounties was Cecil B. DeMille's *Northwest Mounted Police* (1940). It was a respectful treatment of the Riel Rebellion of 1885 but for Canadians it appeared an odd tribute, since the hero was a Texas Ranger played by Gary Cooper. But it was better than having the Canadian West won by a couple of dogs—"Chinook" and "Rin Tin Tin," the wonder hounds in two series of Mountie pictures starring Kirby Grant and Dick Simmons. Canadians were also somewhat peeved to find Gene Autry and Roy Rogers coming up to help the redcoats, as they did in *Gene Autry and the Mounties* (1951) and *North of the Great Divide* (1950).

Errol Flynn was a Mountie in Raoul Walsh's *Northern Pursuit* (1943), as was Tyrone Power in *Pony Soldier* (1952) and Alan Ladd in Walsh's *Saskatchewan* (1954), which Universal spent a lot of money making entirely in Alberta. For British release, the title were changed to the more readily understandable *MacDonald of the Mounties* and *O'Rourke of the Royal Mounted*. One of the more authentic depictions of RCMP life was given by Dick Powell in *Mrs. Mike* (1950), but it lacked the action fans expected of movies about Mounties. Robert Ryan gave a respectful performance as an RCMP inspector in Burt Kennedy's *The Canadians* (1961), dealing with the migration of American Indians into Canada following the defeat of Custer in 1876, but the film was dull and soon faded away.

Of all the many films Hollywood has made about the RCMP, the best in terms of both entertainment and some concept of the job of the police force in the Northwest is *Heart of the North,* filmed in Technicolor by Warners in 1938 in the beautiful scenery around Big Bear Lake. The story is set in the Mackenzie River district of the Northwest Territories, with aerial shots of that area incorporated into the film. It is centered in the fur trapping and gold mining community of Fort

Dick Foran and James Stephenson. The corporal is Allen Jenkins.

Endurance, where their goods are shipped down river to Edmonton, Alberta. Trouble is in the air due to theft, and drunken old Dave MacMillan (Russell Simpson) accuses Mac Drummond (Joseph King), the shipping agent and manager of the trading post, of crookedness, which nobody takes seriously. His daughter Joyce (Gloria Stuart) is smitten with Sergeant Alan Baxter (Dick Foran), but he is engaged to snooty city girl Elizabeth Spaulding (Gale Page), who wants him to resign from his severe duties. When the boat carrying a large supply of furs and gold is boarded by Red Crocker (Joseph Sawyer) and robbed, it is Baxter who is sent in pursuit of Crocker and his gang, taking with him Corporal Hardsock (Allen Jenkins) and fledgling Constable Young (Arthur Gardner). Crocker pitches sticks of dynamite at the pursuing Mounties in their canoes and Young is badly injured. After taking him back to the post, Baxter is held responsible for bungling the job and relieved of duty by martinet Inspector Gore (James Stephenson).

Determined to bring Crocker to justice and find out who is behind all the trouble, Baxter appropriates a Forestry Service aircraft and, with Hardsock, takes off. When they finally find Crocker and his men, they dive down and fire upon them, but Crocker shoots back and cripples the plane. After crash landing in a lake, Baxter and Hardsock pursue on foot, and following a great deal of gunfire and fisticuffs, Crocker is overpowered. In the meantime, Gore sends out an RCMP aircraft to find Baxter and return the group to Fort Endurance. They arrive just in time to stop the angry trappers and miners from lynching MacMillan, whom they have decided is the cause of all their trouble. Baxter forces Crocker to confess to the crowd, and Drummond slinks away. Spotting him, Tommy Ryan (Garry Owen), a Mountie who has suffered a nervous breakdown, follows him and guns him down, because Drummond once trampled on a sapling Ryan was planting. Baxter is promoted to inspector by Gore, who is happy to get away to another post. Baxter realizes it is Joyce he loves and Elizabeth concedes the loss.

Heart of the North is by no means a great film. It just happens to be the best produced of all the Hollywood programmers about the Royal Mounted. It contains many of the story cliches germain to this kind of picture but they are carried off with pacing and vigor, in addition to the having the advantage of Technicolor. This was the first Mountie film made in color and audiences could finally see that the tunics were indeed scarlet, while also learning that Mounties at work wear a dark khaki, cutaway-collar jacket. The scarlet is for dress and ceremony, as is the use of horses. Not a single horse appears in *Heart of the North*, which is as it should be because the job in the present day requires every kind of motorized vehicle, including boats and aircraft. Like so many of the more respectful movies about the Mounties, this one begins with an opening panel of tribute, and includes a statement by Colonel John French, the original commissioner of the Royal Northwest Mounted Police, "You are agents of justice. Where the law is unknown—make it known. Where the law is broken, get your man." It is, of course, that rallying cry of "get your man," plus the handsome uniform and the spectacular setting, that has made the RCMP a ripe subject for novels and movies.

ARIZONA BOUND

MONOGRAM, 1941

Produced by Scott J. Dunlap. Directed by Spencer G. Bennet. Written by Jess Bowers. Photographed by Harry Neumann. 57 minutes.

CAST:

(Buck Roberts) Buck Jones; *(Tim McCall)* Tim McCoy; *(Sandy Hopkins)* Raymond Hatton; *(Ruth)* Luana Walter; *(Joe)* Dennis Moore; *(Steve Taggart)* Tris Coffin; *(Miranda)* Kathryn Sheldon; *(Mack)* Gene Alsace; Horace Murphy; Slim Whittaker; I. Stanford Jolley; Artie Ortego; Ben Corbett.

In 1941, both Buck Jones and Tim McCoy reached the age of 50. Each had attained a peak of popularity in the '30s, but by the end of the decade competition was increasingly tight. Cowboy stars, like athletes, had to give way to younger men. Jones and McCoy were starting to think of dismounting.

McCoy's best westerns were those he made for Columbia between 1931 and 1935. After that, the trail began to wind downhill. He signed with Puritan Pictures to do a series of ten at a salary of $4000 per western,

and then agreed to a contract with Imperial for eight at the same wage scale. Imperial reneged and McCoy took the studio to court. He won the case and received the full amount specified by the contract but the court fight kept him off the screen for the second half of 1936 and all of the following year—not a good career move for a cowboy star of this period. He was next seen in four Monogram westerns in 1938, followed by eight for Victory Pictures, all with small budgets. Still he was drawing his $4000 per movie. McCoy was now doing it strictly for the money. He long had maintained a ranch in Wyoming, where he spent his time between films, and now he was thinking of making the residence permanent. In late 1939, he accepted an offer to do another series for producer Sigmund Neufeld of PRC, this time thinking that it would really be the end. Even the good money was hardly enough to justify appearing in these cheap pictures. But now came an offer with some appeal, and one that would involve Buck Jones.

Tim McCoy may not have cared very much about what was happening to his career in westerns. Not only did he have his ranch but as an officer in the Army Reserve he was already thinking about resuming active service in 1941. Buck Jones cared very much, it was his life. In late 1938, he concluded a series for Columbia but even though he placed third among the western Top 10 that year, no studio came forth with another offer. Jones appeared in only one film in 1939, a non-western, unappealingly titled *Unmarried*. In 1940, Republic hired him to portray a villain in *Wagons Westward*, the only unsympathetic role he ever played and one which brought howls of protest from his fans. However, the uproar resulted in Columbia giving him the lead in its serial *White Eagle*, followed by the second lead, supporting Dick Foran, in the Universal serial *Riders of Death Valley*. Hollywood apparently had been premature in shunting Buck Jones to the sidelines.

It was Scott Dunlap, Jones' closest friend and manager, who came up with the idea of doing a series that would co-star Jones and McCoy. Once McCoy agreed to the proposal, for his usual $4000 per picture, Scott took the idea to Monogram, a studio eager for product. A deal was struck immediately and the *Rough Riders* series was launched. A budget of around half a million dollars was set up for the first eight pictures—B westerns almost always were contracted in lots of eight—and *Arizona Bound* went into production. That and the following two, *Forbidden Trails* and *The Gunman From*

Tim McCoy, Buck Jones and player.

Bodie, are generally regarded as the best of the group, with a gradual diminishing of production quality with *Ghost Town Law, Down Texas Way, Below the Border, Riders of the West* and *West of the Law*, the final one being released in October of 1942. As with all series, the tendency of the producers was to spend most of the money at the start and then have to economize as the series progressed. Monogram had no cause to regret the investment. The films were widely popular. More than merely the youngsters enjoyed seeing these elder citizens of the Hollywood West in tandem. All eight scripts were written by a woman, Adele Buffington, a veteran writer of western stories, who used the pen name Jess Bowers.

Another tried and true western player, Raymond Hatton, was brought in to make the Rough Riders a trio, a format that had become popular by this time largely due to the success of Republic's *The Three Mesquiteers* series. In all eight pictures, the three men play the same roles, as United States Marshals working undercover. Jones is Buck Roberts, McCoy is Tim McCall and Hatton is Sandy Hopkins, a role set up for mostly comedic purposes. Each film has the men being called out of retirement, Roberts and McCall from their ranches and Hopkins from his hotel business in Texas. At the start of *Arizona Bound,* Roberts receives a telegram asking him to proceed to Mesa City, which is being plagued by the robberies of stagecoaches bearing

Tim McCoy and Buck Jones.

Buck Jones.

the gold being shipped out of the town. The villain is Steve Taggart (Tris Coffin), who owns the saloon. There Roberts and Taggart recognize each other as former antagonists, Roberts having once sent him to jail. Taggart claims he is now a respected businessman and Roberts pretends he no longer has anything to do with law enforcement, he is simply a cattleman. McCall walks in and is assumed by his dress and manner to be a parson, although one who not only totes a gun but also beats Taggart at poker, insisting that the winnings will go toward building a church. Hopkins enters and appears to be nothing but an old drifter.

Roberts offers to drive the next stagecoach out of town, using a different route, but he is overheard by one of Taggart's men. Taggart sees this is a way of framing Roberts. When the coach is held up, one of the men rides away after saying "Thanks, Buck." The co-driver, Joe (Dennis Moore), has Roberts arrested and

taken back to town, where he is jailed. McCall and Hopkins help him to break out, after which Roberts explains to Ruth (Luana Walter), the lady who runs the gold shipment office, that he switched boxes, expecting a hold-up, and that the gold is safely hidden in her office. Taggart and his men now make getaway plans but in the ensuing battle among them, the townspeople and the three marshals, the gang members are either killed or captured. Roberts, McCall and Hopkins say goodbye and head back to their own businesses—until their next adventure.

Like all the other pictures in the series *Arizona Bound* is a solid little western, conventional in its scope and story but carried off with the skill of old hands at this game. Jones and McCoy obviously enjoyed being back in the spotlight—especially Jones—and the public welcomed the pairing of two men who had become almost legendary western figures by this time. Monogram was delighted with the results and offered a new contract—but there would be no more of these Rough Riders.

Despite the series' success, it was clear to McCoy that he was very much a supporting player for Jones. His interest in being a star of B westerns had gone. He was wondering how to soften the disappointment for Jones in telling him that he had no intention of renewing the contract when a perfect excuse came his way. In the spring of 1942, he was recalled by the Army for active service, which resulted in him serving in England, France and Germany as a liaison officer between ground and air tactical units. Among his decorations were the Bronze Star and the French Air Medal. He made no effort to resume his film career after the war but accepted cameo roles in *Around the World in 80 Days* (1956), Samuel Fuller's *Run of the Arrow* (1957), in which he played a general who negotiates a peace treaty with the Sioux, and old serial hand Spencer Bennet's *Requiem for a Gunfighter* (1965). McCoy wrote an autobiography, "Tim McCoy Remembers the West," in 1976 and he died two years later at the United States Army hospital at Fort Huachuca, Arizona, in his 87th year.

Monogram planned another series for Buck Jones but only one film, *Dawn on the Great Divide*, was made. It was released on December 18, 1942, by which time Jones had been dead for three weeks. He and Scott Dunlap went on a combination publicity and bond-selling tour, ending up in Boston on November 28. That evening, they were entertained by film distributors at the Cocoanut Grove night club. A bus-boy accidentally set fire to the papier-maché decorations while trying to fix a light bulb and the old building became an immediate inferno. Jones was rushed out by his friends but he went back in to get Dunlap, not knowing that Dunlap had made his own escape. Jones was pulled out again but by then his face and body were badly burned and his lungs seared. He died two days later, one of the almost 500 people who lost their lives in that fire.

The very last shot of Buck Jones, at the end of *Dawn on the Great Divide*, sees him turning and waving goodbye. When the film was screened at Monogram for the cast and crew, everyone was reduced to tears, as were many admirers when the film was released. A special kind of presence had left the western picture business, a man of genuine substance was gone. Among his admirers was John Wayne, who appeared with Jones in *Range War* (1931). Many years later, musing that there should be a memorial somewhere in Hollywood for Jones, he said, "They certainly forgot old Buck." Hopefully not.

Dennis Moore, Luana Walter, Buck Jones, Tim McCoy and Raymond Hatton.

INTERMISSION

The B western did not die with Buck Jones. If this book gives that impression, it is because at the time of his death I was 15 and my interest in that kind of film had passed. With the fallacious kind of maturity that comes with puberty, I had decided that B westerns were no longer worthy of my patronage. These were now the years of the Second World War, my interests had widened, including a burgeoning curiosity about sex that found most of its outlet in gazing at the images of beautiful women on film. It would not be until years later, as someone studying and writing about the history of film, that I would go back and examine both my own wonder at these pictures and their significance as American culture. In the main I would find, as do all who try to retrace the enthusiasms of childhood, that the material was slight, if not a little absurd. But I had no trouble understanding what it was about these films that had entranced me as a child, as they had millions of others. They were simple stories of obvious heroes and villains, set in a world far removed from anything I knew. Now I can no longer look at them with the uncritical eyes of a child but I take pleasure in believing that my admiration all those years ago for men like Buck Jones and Tim McCoy was not misspent. They really were Good Guys.

If the B western did not die in 1942, it was at least heading down trail, and one from which it would never return. There are two reasons for this. One is that the making of the program western had by this time become a slicker form of industry, turning out a smoother product due to better production facilities. But there was less joy in the work, the spirit was beginning to dry up. The West itself had modernized and it was no longer supplying Hollywood with genuine cowpokes looking to make an easier dollar riding for the cameras rather than laboring on the range. Besides, many of them were now in the Army riding around in tanks. Making westerns by 1942 was much more an actor's business than a cowboy's avocation. The innocence had gone. Sophistication did not sit well in a B western saddle.

The other reason is that the major studios discovered

the West in 1939 and began turning out westerns that made the little pictures look somewhat feeble in comparison. Of the thousand or so westerns made in the '30s, barely a handful were major productions. The West at that time seemed to belong at the Saturday matinee, a near oblivion from which it was rescued by John Ford with his *Stagecoach*. Ford had started his career making westerns but with the coming of sound he appeared to have deserted it. Now he found it again and became its champion. After Ford, the deluge. Warner Bros. struck gold placing Errol Flynn in *Dodge City* and Cecil B. DeMille gave *Union Pacific* epic treatment. James Cagney had fun being *The Oklahoma Kid*, Tyrone Power was an improbably handsome *Jesse James* and eastern tenderfoot James Stewart began a profitable western identity with *Destry Rides Again.*

By the end of 1942, not only Buck Jones was gone. Tom Mix was long gone, and the likes of Ken Maynard and Hoot Gibson were over the hill. Colonel Timothy J. McCoy was back in the Army, George O'Brien was back in the Navy and John Wayne had graduated from Class B to Class A. Gene Autry, after time out for military service, would keep the musical western a viable investment, as would Roy Rogers, and William Boyd kept Hopalong Cassidy in the saddle until 1948. Charles Starrett rode all the way to 1952, chalking up a record that no other screen cowboy could match—130 westerns over a 15 year period and all with the same studio, Columbia. The genial Johnny Mack Brown, get-

ting heftier all the time, also managed to make it to 1952, along with William Elliott, Rex Allen, Allan 'Rocky' Lane and Tim Holt. But with television looming over the land, the writing on the canyon walls was all too clear. Wayne Morris, in 1954, had the dubious distinction of starring in the last set of B westerns ever made. They had had a good run for the money—all of 50 years, much longer than the historical period in which they were set.

I rediscovered the West in 1946 with *My Darling Clementine*, thanks to John Ford, who had apparently rediscovered it himself. Now I could again enjoy all that splendid scenery, galloping horses and gunplay but with the addition of interesting stories, well acted and directed, well photographed and musically scored. To put it in musical terms, my romance with the West had gone from B Minor to A Major. Now it seemed that virtually any kind of story could be told in a western setting, they could deal with love and hate, lust and greed, honor and regret, from the freudian *Pursued* to the philosophical *Ride the High Country* to the resignation of *The Shootist*. The western became more truthful and realistic—but still a fantasy, as it must be. Everything, even a newsreel, takes on fantasy once it is photographed, edited, narrated, musically scored and projected on a screen. It is unwise and unreasonable to expect anything more than that. The real West is easy to find, as is its history.

PART TWO:
THE WEST IN A MAJOR

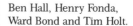
Ben Hall, Henry Fonda,
Ward Bond and Tim Holt.

MY DARLING CLEMENTINE

20TH CENTURY-FOX, 1946

Produced by Samuel G. Engel. Directed by John Ford. Written by Samuel G. Engel and Winston Miller, based on the novel *Wyatt Earp, Frontier Marshal* by Stuart Lake. Photographed by Joseph P. MacDonald. Music by Cyril J. Mockridge. 97 minutes.

CAST:

(*Wyatt Earp*) Henry Fonda; (*Chihuahua*) Linda Darnell; (*Doc Holliday*) Victor Mature; (*Old Man Clanton*) Walter Brennan; (*Virgil Earp*) Tim Holt; (*Morgan Earp*) Ward Bond; (*Clementine Carter*) Cathy Downs; (*Granville Thorndyke*) Alan Mowbray; (*Billy Clanton*) John Ireland; (*Ike Clanton*) Grant Withers; (*Mayor*) Roy Roberts; (*Kate Nelson*) Jane Darwell; (*John Simpson*) Russell Simpson; (*Dad*) Francis Ford; (*Bartender*) J. Farrell MacDonald; (*James Earp*) Don Garner; (*Barber*) Ben Hall; (*Hotel Clerk*) Arthur Walsh; (*Coach Driver*) Jack Pennick; (*Sam Clanton*) Mickey Simpson; (*Phin Clanton*) Fred Libby.

The Ox-Bow Incident (1943) was probably the first Hollywood western to take a cold, hard look at the less heroic aspects of life in the West. It came into being only because Henry Fonda and director William Wellman

badgered Darryl F. Zanuck into making it, promising to do assignments neither of them really wanted to do if Zanuck would let them film Lamar Trotti's treatment of the Walter Van Tilburg Clark novel about a lynching. The result was an uncompromising look at the darker, meaner side of the Old West, dealing with mob violence and lawlessness. It was the nearest to Greek tragedy that Hollywood had yet come in its depiction of western history and Zanuck delayed its release for a year, feeling that there would be little market for such a bleak picture. He was right. The film did poorly at the box office and it is only with time that it attained a reputation as a classic western, but stylistically it was an immediate turning point.

It was the last film in which Henry Fonda was seen before joining the Navy for wartime service. When he returned to Zanuck and 20th Century-Fox three years later, he, like other actors whose experiences in combat had broadened their views on humanity, was looking for better and more realistic material. Fonda was fortunate. John Ford had also just returned from naval serv-

Henry Fonda.

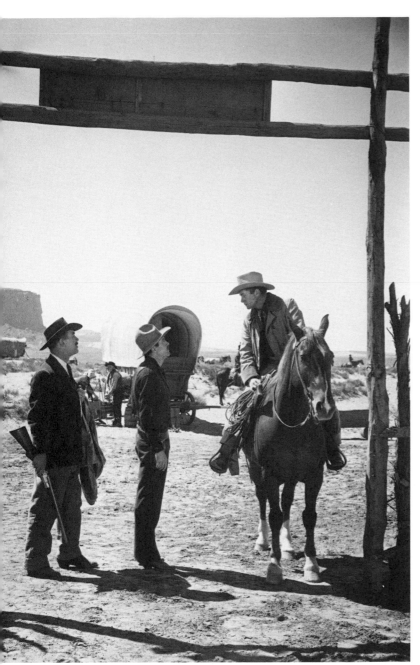

Ward Bond, Henry Fonda and Tim Holt.

different. He was true to his word, producing a western that stands as a classic, a darkly hued, realistic one but touched with a feeling of poetry. Like so many of the Ford films, it is a tale of family life, in this case the conflict between an evil family and a good one.

Clementine begins with Earp and his brothers Morgan (Ward Bond), Virgil (Tim Holt) and Jim (Don Garner) driving their herd of cattle across southern Arizona. A pair of men ride up. Old Man Clanton (Walter Brennan) and his son Ike (Grant Withers) offer to buy the cattle but Wyatt turns them down. That evening, the three older Earps leave Jim to tend the cattle and ride into Tombstone to have a look at the town known for its wild lifestyle. Wyatt subdues a drunken gunman and as a result he is offered the job of town marshal, which he declines. He changes his mind after going back to his campsite and finding Jim murdered. As marshal, he now comes into conflict with Doc Holliday (Victor Mature), who seems to be the dominant figure in Tombstone. Doc is a cultured man but ill with tuberculosis and seemingly bent on self destruction. However, he respects Wyatt's integrity and the two men become friendly, in a guarded sort of way.

Doc's dancehall girlfriend Chihuahua (Linda Darnell) dotes on him and becomes jealous when his eastern fianceé, Clementine Carter (Cathy Downs), arrives in Tombstone, having gone to much trouble to find him. Doc tries to send her away, saying that neither he nor his present ways can offer her anything, and then becomes jealous himself when Clementine meets Wyatt, who is smitten with her in his shy, bumbling manner. Under Wyatt's firm hand, Tombstone begins to take on the appearances of order and calm, and the members of the church committee hold a dance to celebrate the laying of a foundation. Wyatt invites Clementine to go with him and she accepts. But the calm is disturbed when Wyatt notices Chihuahua wearing a medallion that belonged to Jim. He has suspected the Clantons as being responsible for the rustling of his cattle and the killing of Jim, and once he learns from Chihuahua that she was given the medallion by Billy Clanton (John Ireland), he knows he has a case.

The confession causes Chihuahua to be shot by Billy, who is wounded by Virgil as he runs away. Virgil chases Billy to the Clanton home and moves to arrest him, but the Old Man kills Virgil. In the meantime, Doc, summoning up his past skill as a surgeon, operates on Chihuahua in an attempt to save her life. The operation at first seems successful but Chihuahua soons dies. With that, Doc throws in with the Earps, who have challenged the Clantons to an open fight. The forces meet at the OK Corral and after an extended battle all the Clantons lose their lives as does Doc Holliday. Clementine decides to stay in Tombstone and become

ice and he felt the same way. He wanted Fonda to play Wyatt Earp in *My Darling Clementine,* which Samuel G. Engel and Winston Miller had adapted from Stuart Lake's novel, *Wyatt Earp, Frontier Marshal.* Fox had dealt with the material twice before; George O'Brien did *Frontier Marshal* in 1934 and the title was used again five years later, with Randolph Scott in the lead. However, the obstinate Ford claimed he had known Earp and that he had talked with the legendary westerner about life in wild Tombstone and about the gunfight in the OK Corral, and that his version would be

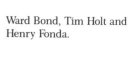

Ward Bond, Tim Holt and
Henry Fonda.

a schoolmarm and Wyatt, who has to leave town with
brother Morgan on family business, tells her he will
return.

Despite its air of authenticity, *My Darling Clementine*
is not a factual treatment of Tombstone and the Earps,
as Ford well knew. This is obvious from his decision to
film it in Monument Valley—his first trip back after
shooting *Stagecoach* there seven years previously—
which lies on the northern boundary of Arizona and not
in the south, where Tombstone is actually situated. Doc
Holliday did not die at the OK Corral and that legendary
gunfight took place in a small area and was over in
minutes, not as depicted by Ford in a wide setting and
a drawn out battle. But none of this really matters. The
Ford Doctrine was clearly stated in 1962 with *The Man
Who Shot Liberty Valance,* in which besotted old newspaperman Dutton Peabody says, "This is the West.
When the legend becomes fact, print the legend." Ford
backed up his argument by pointing out that anyone
wanting historical facts can easily find them. What he
wanted to do with *Clementine* and his other westerns
was to tell a story about values, especially the loyalty
of the family unit and the range of good and evil in men.
Somewhat ironically, the moody, dark spirit of this film,
artistically photographed by the great Joseph MacDonald, makes the fable appear realistic. Such was the
genius of Ford.

Henry Fonda was a perfect choice for Wyatt Earp,
just as he had been for Tom Joad in Ford's *The Grapes*

Henry Fonda and Cathy Downs.

of Wrath in 1939. Quintessentially American, Fonda had a rather withdrawn air about him, which well suited Ford's concept of Earp as a quiet, laconic, homespun man. Four years of wartime service seemed to further accentuate Fonda's proud, removed, common-man persona, one that would make him ideal for western films, especially as the embittered colonel in Ford's next western, *Fort Apache.* (In between, Ford and Fonda made the non-western, *The Fugitive.*) An honest, unbending and sometimes difficult man in person, those qualities served him well in playing simple, proud men making their way in the west.

Clementine also marked a return to the screen after wartime service for Tim Holt. His performance as Virgil Earp is excellent, as had been his work in Orson Welles' *The Magnificent Ambersons* (1942) and as it would be in John Huston's *The Treasure of Sierra Madre* (1948). Yet despite critical acceptance, Holt chose to return to the security of B westerns at RKO rather than tackle a variety of roles. He had done well with a string of westerns before going into the Air Force and he did even better with them afterwards. He was a handsome but slightly glum looking actor and it is interesting to imagine how he might have fared away from the cinematic West. As an actor, he did not fare well after he stopped making westerns in 1952. Claiming never to have liked Hollywood, he moved to Oklahoma and he was engaged in various businesses before dying of cancer at the age of 54.

My Darling Clementine also contains performances of note by two actors whose careers were highlighted by their work in westerns—Walter Brennan and Ward Bond. For Brennan, the part of Old Man Clanton was a deviation from his usual guise as a grumpy but good hearted sidekick. Here he is a bitter, callous criminal, who treats his sons as if they were dogs on leashes and considers them as if they were property, and yet he is as loyal to them as Wyatt Earp to his brothers. Brennan won three Oscars as a Best Supporting Actor, one of them for playing Judge Roy Bean in *The Westerner* (1940), and he was 75 when he retired, after playing in *Support Your Local Sheriff* (1969). Ward Bond never won any Oscars but his employment record was one any actor would envy. Starting in 1929 with a bit part in *Salute,* which also featured his friend John Wayne, Ward went from film to film—200 of them—until his death from a heart attack at the age of 55 in 1960, at which time he was playing the lead in the television series *Wagon Train.* A western thug for most of the '30s, he became a member of John Ford's stock group in 1938 with *Submarine Patrol* and the only Ford films he missed thereafter were those he was too busy elsewhere to work in. He made a dozen films with Wayne, of which his flamboyant performance as the minister-lawman Sam Clayton in *The Searchers* (1956) is probably the most memorable.

Walter Brennan and Henry Fonda.

Robert Mitchum.

PURSUED

WARNER BROS., 1947

Produced by Milton Sperling. Directed by Raoul Walsh. Written by Niven Busch. Photographed by James Wong Howe. Music by Max Steiner. 101 minutes.

CAST:

(*Thorley Callum*) Teresa Wright; (*Jeb Rand*) Robert Mitchum; (*Medora Callum*) Judith Anderson; (*Grant Callum*) Dean Jagger; (*Jake Dingle*) Alan Hale; (*Prentice McComber*) Harry Carey, Jr.; (*Adam Callum*) John Rodney; (*The Sergeant*) Clifton Young; (*Jeb (at 8)*) Ernest Severn; (*Adam (at 10)*) Charles Bates; (*Thorley (at 8)*) Peggy Miller; (*Army Captain*) Ray Teal; (*Coroner*) Ian Wolfe.

In the summer of 1942, 25-year-old Robert Mitchum, sick of being a sheet-metal worker in an aircraft factory in Burbank, California, took a notion to be an extra in the movies. He had no driving ambition to be an actor, he simply thought it would be easier than working in a noisy factory. Because of his height, his heft, his unusual face and a demeanor that suggested he could brawl his way out of a saloon if necessary, an agent

sent him to Harry Sherman, who was planning another set of Hopalong Cassidy pictures. Mitchum told Sherman of his checkered background as a drifter, a prize fighter, a longshoreman and a ditch digger, then added he had also been a cowpuncher in Texas. Everything was true except the last part. Sherman sent him out on location and assigned him to being a thug in *Border Patrol, Hoppy Serves a Writ* and *The Leather Burners.* Mitchum had found his niche; he was a natural for film work. He played bits in three other films, then Sherman called him back and used him in four more Cassidy stories, this time giving him small roles. Looking back on his Cassidy days Mitchum claims, "I got a hundred bucks a week and all the manure I could take home."

RKO took a chance on Mitchum in 1944 and starred him in *Nevada*, a Zane Grey story that had first been filmed in 1927 with Gary Cooper and again in 1935 with Buster Crabbe. With his brawn and his laconic manner, the Connecticut-born Mitchum seemed a natural for westerns. RKO immediately set him up with another Grey story, *West of the Pecos*, with which the studio had

Teresa Wright and Robert Mitchum.

done well in 1934 with Richard Dix. They did just as well with Mitchum, who might have been stuck with westerns had he not scored a big hit in 1945 with *The Story of G. I. Joe.* That one proved he was an actor of potentially greater scope than the limits of the celluloid range.

By the time he came to do *Pursued* at Warners at the end of 1946, Mitchum no longer needed to lie about his ability as a horseman. What he now needed to show was wider range as an actor because his role in *Pursued* was more complex than anything that had yet come his way. *Pursued* is regarded as the first psychological western, a kind of Greek tragedy amid the stark rocky landscapes of New Mexico, although actually filmed in the truly stark vistas of Monument Valley, the area opened up by John Ford. It is probably the first western to which the word *freudian* has ever been applied, dealing as it does with intense feelings of love and hate within family relationships, including murder provoked by adultery. Niven Busch, who had already set some kind of standard with passion out west in his *Duel in the Sun,* here provided an original screenplay, one which was bound to give his then wife, Teresa Wright, top billing, even though the crux of the story is very much the Mitchum role of Jeb Rand.

The film begins with Jeb's wife, Thorley (Wright), riding to meet him in the ruins of an old ranch, bringing him food and a map in order for him to plan a route of escape from the men in pursuit. Led by Grant Callum (Dean Jagger), a man possessed by hatred for Jeb and his family, the men are out to kill him, for reasons Jeb cannot yet understand. He tells Thorley that it has something to do with the ruins in which he has been waiting. All his life he has felt troubled and haunted by strange memories. He looks around, "I was here before—long ago." Flashback: Jeb as a small boy hides under a trap door as a gun fight rages above. It stops and a woman, Medora Callum (Judith Anderson), comes and takes the boy away. Lying dead on the floor are all the members of his family. Medora, a widow, brings Jeb up as one of her own, along with her son Adam and daughter Thorley.

As young grown-ups, Jeb and Thorley realize they love each other, which causes resentment from Adam (John Rodney), who was never fully accepted Jeb. With the outbreak of the Spanish American War in 1898, Jeb and Adam toss a coin to see which one will join the Army. Jeb goes, but after being wounded in action, he returns home to a hero's welcome and the presentation of the Medal of Honor. Adam's resentment is fostered by Callum, now a state prosecutor, who tells him the Rand family were thieves and killers, and that Jeb does not deserve the generosity he has received. Adam, who has run the family cattle business well while Jeb

Robert Mitchum and John Rodney.

was away, expresses increasing anger at having to share the income. Jeb suggests another toss of the same coin used before and again he loses. Adam furiously flings Jeb's clothes out of the house, provoking a savage brawl with him. Jeb leaves and Thorley promises to wait. That promise turns to hatred when Jeb kills Adam in self defense. At the hearing, Grant does his best to bring a charge of murder to bear but the verdict exonerates Jeb. Be that as it may, Medora now turns against Jeb and becomes angry when she hears that Thorley is seeing him again. Thorley explains that she intends to marry Jeb in order to ruin him. But this she cannot do and her love for him overwhelms the hatred. On their wedding night, Grant and all the Callums he has rounded up come to the ranch to kill Jeb. He escapes and heads for the old ruins, where Thorley comes the next morning. Gradually the pieces begin to fit in Jeb's mind.

The man who attacked and killed his family was Grant, whose brother was married to Medora, who had fallen in love with Jeb's father. With Old Testament wrath, Grant moved to avenge to his family's honor,

never resting until the last Rand has paid the price. Now Grant and the Callums arrive at the runs, and Jeb, in order to save Thorley from harm in a gun fight, surrenders. Summoned by Grant to witness the final act, Medora arrives and expresses her disgust. Grant fumes, "Now he gets his legacy—just like his father, who stole my brother's wife." While Jeb is led to a tree to be lynched, Thorley turns on her mother, "It's all because of your guilt. You never told him the truth so he could protect himself." As Grant is about to hang Jeb a shot rings out and Grant falls dead. Medora has put an end to the long quest for revenge. She turns and says, "I'm sorry, Jeb, for all the wrong I did you. Take your wife, go home."

Pursued is virtually a western *film noir,* underscored by Max Steiner with richly romantic-tragic music and filmed by the esteemed James Wong Howe, a cinematographer who made black-and-white film a high art. A great deal of the effectiveness of the film stems from Howe's dramatic use of lighting and deep focus settings. It has an intensity that might not have worked as well with color. The script is intelligent and the acting

Robert Mitchum, Teresa Wright and Judith Anderson.

Judith Anderson, Teresa Wright, John Rodney and Robert Mitchum.

precise. Mitchum conveys the confusion of a man haunted by fears he cannot understand and Judith Anderson is superb as the woman whose adultery is the basic cause of the tragedy, a woman of compassion, hurt by life and trying to make amends. The key to the film, however, is the performance of Dean Jagger as Grant Callum, a figure of hatred, possessed by festered pride and a single-minded bent for revenge. It is a warped Puritanism, made vivid by a setting so visually dramatic that it becomes almost biblical.

Calling the shots on this bizarre western was Raoul Walsh, a man himself vivid and dramatic. Known as a "man's man" all through the 40 years he worked in film, Walsh was an adventurous youngster who spent some time as a cowboy. He turned up in Hollywood in 1907 at the age of 20 and got work riding in westerns. Five years later, he wrote *The Life of General Villa* for film and played the part of the young Villa himself. Thereafter, he never lacked for employment and in 1915, he played John Wilkes Booth in *The Birth of a Nation*. He stopped acting after losing an eye in an accident and turned to directing. Among Walsh's silent classics are *The Thief of Bagdad* (1924) and *What Price Glory?* (1926). He directed the first sound western, *In Old Arizona*, in 1929 and a year later, he hired John Wayne to star in *The Big Trail*. Ten years went by before Walsh tackled another western, *The Dark Command*, which again starred Wayne. He began an association with Errol Flynn when he directed that quixotic actor's performance as the equally quixotic George Armstrong Custer in *They Died With Their Boots On* in 1941, but did not go West again until *Pursued*. He followed that with the slam-bang *Cheyenne*, starring Dennis Morgan, and Flynn's *Silver River*. There would be other epic Walsh westerns, most conspicuously *Colorado Territory*.

Robert Mitchum, Dean Jagger and Teresa Wright.

102

Henry Fonda, John Wayne, George O'Brien and Ward Bond.

FORT APACHE

RKO, 1948

Produced by John Ford and Merian C. Cooper. Directed by John Ford. Written by Frank S. Nugent, based on the story *Massacre* by James Warner Bellah. Photographed by Archie Stout. Music by Richard Hageman. 127 minutes.

CAST:

(*Capt. Kirby York*) John Wayne; (*Lt. Col. Owen Thursday*) Henry Fonda; (*Philadelphia Thursday*) Shirley Temple; (*Lt. Michael O'Rourke*) John Agar; (*Sgt. Major Michael O'Rourke*) Ward Bond; (*Capt. Sam Collingwood*) George O'Brien; (*Sergeant Mulcahy*) Victor McLaglen; (*Sergeant Beauford*) Pedro Armendariz; (*Mrs. Collingwood*) Anna Lee; (*Mrs. O'Rourke*) Irene Rich; (*Dr. Wilkens*) Guy Kibbee; (*Silas Meacham*) Grant Withers; (*Cochise*) Miguel Inclan; (*Sergeant Shattuck*) Jack Pennick; (*Mrs. Gates*) Mae Marsh; (*Sergeant Quincannon*) Dick Foran; (*Newspaperman*) Frank Ferguson; (*Bartender*) Francis Ford.

Not counting his early work in silent films and the Civil War sequence in *How the West Was Won* (1962), John Ford made 15 major westerns, starting with *The Iron Horse* in 1924 and ending with *Cheyenne Autumn*

40 years later. Most of them deal with aspects of military life in the West and three of them deal with it specifically: *Fort Apache* (1948), *She Wore a Yellow Ribbon* (1949) and *Rio Grande* (1950). They have become known as the Ford Cavalry Trilogy, a relationship made the stronger by John Wayne being the star of all three. The second appears to be the most popular—certainly a high point in the Wayne catalog—but a good argument can be made for claiming *Fort Apache* as a less sentimental and more accurate depiction of Army life and the campaigns against the Indians. The film has a gritty quality and perhaps because of being filmed in black-and-white, it seems closer to the textbooks of military history. And although Wayne receives top billing, the focal actor is Henry Fonda, playing a martinet, a meticulous by-the-book officer, who resents having been assigned to command a post in the West. Having held brevet rank as a general in the Union Army during the Civil War—now reduced to lieutenant colonel—and having recently returned from a tour of duty in Europe, he looks upon the new posting as a military slight.

A widower, Owen Thursday (Fonda) arrives at Fort Apache in company with his only child, daughter Philadelphia (Shirley Temple). As friendly and cheerful as her father is sullen and bitter, she soon becomes taken with Second Lieutenant Michael O'Rourke (John Agar), a recent graduate of West Point and the son of the post's veteran Sergeant Major (Ward Bond). Thursday is not in favor of romance between his daughter and the young officer but all the officers' wives do their best to promote it. There is nothing at the post that meets with Thursday's approval. He upbraids his officers for their casual dress and demands more acute discipline. The most respected officer on staff is Captain Kirby York (Wayne), whose long experience fighting Apaches has taught him respect for their skill and bravery in battle. He tries to impart this knowledge to Thursday, who dismisses it. To him the Indians are ignorant savages, to be tamed and confined to reservations.

Young O'Rourke takes Philadelphia out riding off the post and finds an Army wagon burned and its soldiers massacred. Reporting the finding to Thursday, the young trooper is warned not to take her out again. Thursday then orders York to lead him on an inspection of the scene of the killing and a tour of the area. They visit the post of Indian agent Silas Meacham (Grant Withers), where it becomes obvious that Meacham has been cheating the Indians in trade, supplying them with bad whiskey and selling them rifles. Thursday can now understand why the Apaches, led by Cochise (Miguel Inclan), have left the reservation and crossed the border into Mexico. However, it does not make him any more charitable toward the Indians. What he now sees is an opportunity to win a campaign that may bring him attention and a chance for promotion.

York advises Thursday against direct military action and, because of his previous personal contact with Cochise and the respect he has for him, volunteers to proceed as an emissary and try to persuade the Indian chief to return to American soil. York is successful and arrives back at Fort Apache just as Thursday is attending the dance held by the non-commissioned officers. Thursday orders the dance brought to a close and

Henry Fonda, George O'Brien, John Wayne and Grant Withers.

schedules an immediate briefing with his officers. He also decides on a direct military action against Cochise, aimed at forcing the chief and his people back to the reservation. York protests this as a violation of his understanding with Cochise but Thursday rejects any talk of conciliation. He leads his entire regiment out on campaign, and when York arranges a conference with Cochise, Thursday arrogantly demands complete submission and no terms of any kind. Cochise and his chiefs ride away in anger.

When York strongly advises against attacking the Indians, Thursday accuses him of cowardice and orders him to retire, and to take young O'Rourke with him. Thursday then leads his men against Cochise and is mortally wounded in battle. At one point, York comes to the rescue of the fallen Thursday, who rejects help and tells York, "When you command this regiment, and you probably will, command it." He then takes York's horse and saber, and joins the cluster of his surviving officers and men in a circular gully. After a few moments of silence, the sound of galloping horses grows louder. A mass of Indians surge over the soldiers and when the dust settles a minute or so later, all are dead.

Much later, perhaps two years, York is interviewed in his office at Fort Apache by a group of newspapermen, who want to know about Thursday and his now acclaimed Last Stand. With no allusion to military blunders or personal shortcomings, York supports the action as one of bravery, one which contributes to the army's tradition of service. "No man died more gallantly

Grant Withers, Victor McLaglen, John Wayne, Henry Fonda, George O'Brien and Pedro Armendariz.

106

John Wayne and Henry Fonda.

George O'Brien, Henry Fonda and Dick Foran to the left; Pedro Armendariz and Jack Pennick between flags, and Ward Bond and Victor McLaglen to the right.

108

John Wayne and the press conference in praise of the fallen leader.

or won more honor for his regiment." When a reporter speaks of the men who died, York replies, "They haven't died as long as the regiment lives."

Fort Apache was based upon James Warner Bellah's story *Massacre,* which was obviously inspired by what happened to Lt. Col. George Armstrong Custer at the Battle of the Little Big Horn in 1876. Bellah was an authority on the history of the military campaigns in the West and he respected both the courage of the Army and the Indians in their tragic conflict. So did Ford. The film is full of details of those times, more so than any other Hollywood account. It shows family life, the strong unity between men, the roles of the wives at the fort and their activities, and the rigors of Army duty in a severe land. Other than the bitter, frustrated Thursday and the venal Indian agent Meacham, there are no villains per se, only men caught up in history. Ford's respect for the Apaches is obvious, even though in his film they are played by the Navajos of Monument Valley, once again the setting for a Fordian evocation of the western past. His Indians are proud and honest warriors—and victims.

Critics have faulted Ford for his sentiment, and there is no denying his Irish soul occasionally tilted a little too much toward a sentimental view of family and Army life. It also tended to give the impression that the US Cavalry at the time was well populated with the Irish. It certainly had plenty of Irishmen in its ranks, along with men of many nationalities, indeed almost an American version of the French Foreign Legion in the years between the ending of the Civil War and the start of the 20th century. The criticism is a small one; more to the point is the success with which Ford captured the spirit of life in those times and the tribute he paid to the courage of both the soliders and the Indians, the tragedy of the conflict and the inevitability of it. This he continued to do in the two following films, *She Wore a Yellow Ribbon* and *Rio Grande,* both shot in Technicolor and both because of it tending toward a more heroic picturization. Both films are more John Wayne vehicles

110

than *Fort Apache*. In *Ribbon*, he plays a cavalry captain, Nathan Brittles, on the verge of retirement, but in *Rio Grande* he is again Kirby York, now a lieutenant colonel, in command of a regiment but having to deal with an estranged wife and a son who joins his regiment as a private. All three films give understanding of Army life but *Fort Apache* is the harder view, and probably truer. However, it was not until 1964 that Ford, in his last western, gave an uncompromisingly hard account of life for the Indians in the conflict with the white migration in the latter part of the last century. *Cheyenne Autumn* dealt so honestly with the grief imposed upon the Cheyenne nation that it seemed as if Ford was apologizing to the Indians for the manner in which he and so many other filmmakers had depicted them as dumb savages, devoid of rights, in so many movies of earlier years. Sadly the admirable *Cheyenne Autumn* would turn out to be the least successful of all his westerns.

The sentiment in *Fort Apache* is not confined to the characters in the story; it also has to do with Ford's choice of actors. In this regard, it is a sentiment that can be shared by western movie fans. In it appear three actors who were stars of series of B westerns in the '30s—Wayne, George O'Brien and Dick Foran. O'Brien was an excellent choice for the role of a veteran cavalry officer haunted by a past military blunder and quietly desperate to be transferred from Fort Apache, and Foran, in a much smaller role, plays a sergeant overly inclined to drinking. *Fort Apache* also required Foran to be very Irish and at one point to serenade the officers' wives with "Sweet Genevieve," which at least proved that he was still in good voice. It was the last time Foran ever sang in a film. After 1948, Hollywood offered few opportunities for middle-aged light baritones, certainly not in westerns.

STATION WEST

RKO, 1948

Produced by Robert Sparks. Directed by Sidney Lanfield. Written by Frank Fenton and Winston Miller, based on the novel by Luke Short. Photographed by Harry J. Wild. Music by Heinz Roemheld. Songs by Mort Greene and Leigh Harline. 91 minutes.

CAST:

(*Haven*) Dick Powell; (*Charlie*) Jane Greer; (*Mrs. Caslon*) Agnes Moorehead; (*Hotel Clerk*) Burl Ives; (*Captain Iles*) Tom Powers; (*Prince*) Gordon Oliver; (*Stallman*) Steve Brodie; (*Mick*) Guinn 'Big Boy' Williams; (*Mark Bristow*) Raymond Burr; (*Goddard*) Regis Toomey; (*Cook*) Olin Howard; (*Pianist*) John Berkes; (*Whitey*) Michael Steele; (*Pete*) Dan White; (*Ben*) John Kellogg; (*Bartender*) John Doucette; (*Sheriff*) Charles Middleton.

Luke Short was the pen name of Frederick Dilley Glidden, who at his death in 1975 at 67 had published some 60 western novels and fixed a solid reputation in the genre. Among his awards were those given by the Western Writers of America (1969) and the National

Cowboy Hall of Fame and Western Heritage (1974). His stories were skillfully plotted, lively, suspenseful, often violent and full of dramatic characters. The style tended toward the dark but the plots and settings ranged from the early days of ranching to modern detective tales. Short graduated from the University of Missouri with a degree in journalism but claimed he was fired from one newspaper after another as inept. He joked that whereas most newspapermen seemed to be failed novelists, with him it was the other way around. Unlike Zane Grey and Clarence E. Mulford, who never adventured in the West, Short spent two years as a trapper in northwestern Canada and lived for several years in New Mexico before settling in Colorado. His delving into western history provoked many of his stories.

Short did very well by Hollywood. His *Ramrod* became a superb Joel McCrea western in 1947 and MGM bought *Ambush* (1950) for Robert Taylor and *Vengeance Valley* (1951) for Burt Lancaster. His novel *High Vermillion* became Paramount's *Silver City* (1951), starring Edmond O'Brien, and Republic gave Brian Donlevy and

Rod Cameron the leads in its version of *Ride the Man Down* (1953). The following year Republic starred Cameron in *Hell's Outpost*, based on Short's *Silver Rock*. But 1948 was the year of triumph for Luke Short in the movies. Four of his novels became films that year. The first was Randolph Scott's *Albuquerque*, which was based on *Dead Freight for Piute*, followed by *Coroner Creek*, which also starred Scott and gave him one of his most critically acclaimed westerns to that point. Then came a pair of RKO productions, *Station West* and *Blood on the Moon*.

Station West is a good example of the Short western detective in action, with Dick Powell an excellent and obvious choice for the leading character. No actor ever made a more marked stylistic change in his screen persona than Powell. All through the '30s, he starred in lightweight musicals for Warner Bros., ever the boyish, smiling light baritone, frequently singing the songs that choreographer Busby Berkeley used as the basis for wonderful, often bizarre dance routines. By the end of the decade, Powell was desperately seeking to escape this limited image. After a variety of roles, he managed to persuade RKO to let him play Philip Marlowe in *Murder, My Sweet* (1945), a hard-edged treatment of

Raymond Chandler's *Farewell, My Lovely*. It was a dramatic turning point for Powell, which he followed with similarly tough characterizations in *Cornered* (1945), *Johnny O'Clock* (1947), *To the End of the Earth* (1948) and *Pitfall* (1948). Watching the Powell of these pictures, it is difficult to even associate him with the Powell of the Warner musicals.

In *Station West*, Powell is an Army Intelligence officer named Haven, who is sent to investigate the killing of two soldiers assigned to escort a gold shipment. He arrives in the small town that is the center of a mining area and checks into a hotel, where the guitar-strumming, singing clerk (Burl Ives) warns him that it is a tough, dangerous town. The surly, laconic Haven goes into the nearby saloon and quickly registers himself as argumentative. He makes a play for the beautiful singer, Charlie (Jane Greer), who also happens to be the owner of the place and a powerful citizen, which becomes apparent to Haven when her manager, Prince (Gordon Oliver), and her moose-like bodyguard, Mick (Guinn 'Big Boy' Williams), make him feel unwelcome. A young army lieutenant (Steve Brodie) suggests that if Haven is looking for a job, he can find one in the Army, which provokes sarcasm from Haven.

Dick Powell and Burl Ives.

Guinn 'Big Boy' Williams and Dick
Powell.

When the lieutenant leaves the saloon in anger,
Haven follows him to the home of Mrs. Caslon (Agnes
Moorehead), where Haven is presented to Captain Iles
(Tom Powers), the commander of the local garrison.
Iles has a low opinion of the Army Intelligence and their
methods but he has no choice except to comply with
Haven's orders. Haven points out to him the prob-
lems—the gold shipments are piling up at the Army
post, Wells Fargo will not convey it, the post is under-
manned and Iles' attempts to ship the gold have failed.
Haven must use his own ways of solving the situation.

Back in the saloon, Haven tries to engage Charlie in
bantering conversation, which causes Mick to spark a
fight with him. After a long and brutal brawl in the
street, Haven barely manages to win. In his hotel room,
Charlie comes to wash and bandage his cuts and
bruises. It seems she not only owns the saloon but has
shares in virtually every business in town, and she
offers him a job as her shipping and transportation

manager. Haven tells Mrs. Caslon that he would like to
try making a shipment from her gold mine to see what
might happen. The result is a hold-up, with Haven
knocked out and the driver, Goddard (Regis Toomey),
gunned down. Looking in the dead man's wallet, Haven
finds that Goddard was a Wells Fargo detective. He
then proceeds to Charlie's sawmill and, in poking
around, finds a large shipment of Army uniforms. Back
in town, he visits lawyer Mark Bristow (Raymond
Burr), a man hopelessly in debt to Charlie in gambling
losses, and has him notarize a statement to the effect
that he (Haven) was held up and robbed and had
witnessed the killing of Goddard.

Bristow shows the document to Charlie and Prince,
by way of getting himself in their favor, and they give
him a gun with instructions to kill Haven. The cowardly
Bristow is easily disarmed by Haven, who advised him
to get out of town. Bristow is shot by Prince as he tries
to leave but Haven manages to make his way back to

114

the sawmill, where he burns the uniforms, thwarting Prince's plans to remove the gold from the Army post. Returning to the saloon, he plans to arrest the woman who is behind all the crimes, although abetted beyond her wishes by Prince. Haven, who has fallen for Charlie, promises to do his best for her at the hearings. She offers him gold, "I believe every man has his price." He declines, "Some men don't believe that." She smiles, "But every woman knows it." He asks her where Prince is, and from the look in her eyes, he knows Prince is coming in the room—he turns and fires. Prince falls but a bullet from his gun hits Charlie, and she dies in Haven's arms, after he tells her he loves her.

As Haven gets on his horse and rides out of town, the hotel clerk strums his guitar and sings his fatalistic song, "The sun shining warm on the dust of the prairie . . . but it's heartless and cold . . . and a man can't grow old where there's women and gold." The tone of the song is appropriate for *Station West,* another almost *film noir* kind of western, and one marked by exceptionally sharp dialogue, although possibly of a kind more suited to the private eye films and radio programs Dick

Powell was doing in this period rather than to a western. Much of the impact of the film comes from the interplay between Powell and Jane Greer, fresh from her *femme fatale* triumph in *Out of the Past,* one of the classics of American *film noir.* Here the two are cynical observers of the human condition and emotionally drawn to each other even though they know there is little real hope for romance. The sultry, svelte Greer was an excellent choice for the villainess of *Station West,* although director Sidney Lanfield made her uncomfortable from the start by telling her the actress he wanted for the part was Marlene Dietrich. Ironically, Dietrich would play a very similar kind of role in 1952 in Fritz Lang's *Rancho Notorious.*

Except for two innocuous musicals with western settings, *Cowboy From Brooklyn* (1938) and *Riding High* (1943), *Station West* was Powell's only western film. However, he would gain an even wider identity with western lore in 1956, when, as part-owner and managing director of Four Star Television, he became the host of *Dick Powell's Zane Grey Theater,* an anthology series of half-hour productions which ran to 145

Dick Powell and Jane Greer.

115

Agnes Moorehead, Dick
Powell and Tom Powers.

Dick Powell and Raymond Burr.

116

episodes and in which he also appeared as an actor. Powell died in 1963 from cancer at the age of 58, having made a mark as a successful dramatic actor-director-producer that none would have predicted for the crooning star of '30s musicals.

Station West is also of interest to western buffs as the only film in which Guinn 'Big Boy' Williams appeared as a villain, indeed a glum thug. The fight between him and Powell is a savage one but in reality it is not one he would likely have lost. Six-foot-three and over 200 pounds, the Texas-born Williams was a football player and cowboy before arriving in Hollywood. He played the lead in a series of cheap westerns but his main success came from playing slightly dense but genial sidekicks to the likes of Errol Flynn, Randolph Scott and John Wayne, his final film being Wayne's *The Comancheros* in 1961. The hard drinking Williams died the following year from a heart attack at 62. He is well remembered as a cheerful screen lug, except in *Station West*, in which he is frighteningly sober and mean.

Jane Greer and Dick Powell.

Robert Mitchum and
Robert Preston.

BLOOD ON THE MOON

RKO, 1948

Produced by Sid Rogell and Theron Warth. Directed by Robert Wise. Written by Lillie Hayward, based on the novel *Gunman's Choice* by Luke Short, adapted by Harold Shumate. Photographed by Nicholas Musuraca. Music by Roy Webb. 88 minutes.

CAST:

(Jim Garry) Robert Mitchum; *(Amy Lufton)* Barbara Bel Geddes; *(Tate Riling)* Robert Preston; *(Kris Barden)* Walter Brennan; *(Carol Lufton)* Phyllis Thaxter; *(Jack Pindalest)* Frank Faylen; *(John Lufton)* Tom Tully; *(Milo Sweet)* Charles McGraw; *(Joe Shotton)* Clifton Young; *(Frank Reardon)* Tom Tyler; *(Fritz Barden)* George Cooper; *(Ted Elser)* Richard Powers; *(Cap Willis)* Bud Osbourne; *(Nels Titterton)* Zon Murray; *(Bart Daniels)* Robert Bray; *(Chev Avery)* Al Ferguson; *(Mitch Moden)* Ben Corbett.

Three weeks after the release of *Station West* in mid-October, 1948, RKO presented *Blood on the Moon*. There was nothing intentional about the timing. RKO had bought the rights to Luke Short's novel *Gunman's Choice* two years earlier but no one had come up with

a script that the studio considered good enough, or clear enough to make the complications of Short's plot suitable for telling within the framework of a film. Harold Shumate, long a specialist with western scenarios, had made an adaptation of the novel but declined to flesh it out and the project was shelved. It came to the attention of Robert Wise, who was looking for a major film after having been fairly successful with a string of modestly budgeted programmers. He gave it to a lady scenarist, Lillie Hayward, who came up with a script so good that the RKO brass thought of taking Wise off the project and handing it to a director with a bigger name. Wise put up a fight and, backed by production head Dore Schary, he went ahead with *Blood on the Moon*.

The fact that *Blood on the Moon* is a superbly hard-edged western, possibly the most *noir* of them all, has much to do with Wise. He joined RKO as an assistant editor at 20 in 1935 and gradually became a master film editor. When Orson Welles came to make *Citizen Kane*, he was given Wise as his editor, and when Welles made *The Magnificent Ambersons*, he chose Wise to again edit his work. Wise was editing the Val Lewton film

118

Curse of the Cat People in 1943 when Lewton fired the director and asked Wise to take over. It was the opportunity he had been waiting for. The photographer was the Czech-born Nicholas Musuraca and, when Wise was given the go-ahead on *Blood on the Moon*, this was the man he wanted to shoot his film, using the same kind of dark, shadowy effects.

Whatever knowledge and understanding of western life Robert Mitchum may have picked up from his previous work in the genre was well needed for this one. Here, he is a tough, simple cowpoke named Jim Garry and, when first seen, he is riding through a dark and rainy night. He makes himself a place to eat and sleep at the base of a tree and then has to jump into the tree to escape a herd of cattle that comes thundering by, ruining his saddle, bedroll and utensils. They are replaced by rancher John Lufton (Tom Tully), who wants to know why this lone cowboy is riding in the area. Trouble has erupted because the newly-appointed Indian agent, Jack Pindalest (Frank Faylen), is denying Lufton and the other local ranchers the right to graze on reservation land and is also rejecting their beef in favor of the cattle controlled by Tate Riling (Robert

Preston). Lufton tells Garry that Riling is trying to buy up ranches at rock bottom prices and bringing in gunmen as intimidation. Garry refrains from telling Lufton that he is actually on his way to join his old friend Riling.

Lufton has two daughters, the feisty Amy (Barbara

Charles McGraw, Robert Mitchum, Robert Preston and player.

Robert Mitchum, Barbara Bel Geddes and Tom Tully.

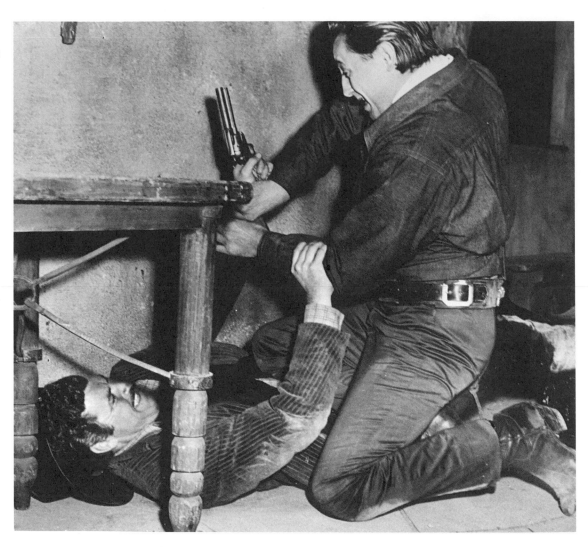

Robert Preston and Robert Mitchum.

Bel Geddes), who takes an immediate dislike to Garry when she meets him, and the more ladylike Carol (Phyllis Thaxter), who, unknown to her father, is being courted by Riling. Riling welcomes Garry and explains that his plan is to gain control of all the ranches and become the main seller of beef to both the Indians and the Army. Garry's doubts about the aims and methods of his friend quickly grow, particularly when a pair of Riling gunmen try to kill Lufton in the main street of Sundust. Garry stops them, winning admiration from Amy and puzzlement from Lufton. Among the small ranchers throwing in their lot with Riling are Kris Barden (Walter Brennan) and his son Fritz (George Cooper). Garry takes part in a raid on Lufton cattle, during which he sees one of Riling's men gun down Fritz. Figuring he is part of something rotten, Garry decides to move on. Riling catches up with him in a saloon of a nearby town to change his mind but Garry notices in a mirror the reflection of Riling's top gunman,

Reardon (Tom Tyler), positioned outside the door. Riling wants to know why Garry is leaving and he tells him: "It starts with your doublecross of a bunch of poor, jugheaded homesteaders and the hiring of gunmen—it goes on to your making love to a man's daughter to get her to turn against her own father—and you tried for Lufton today. It goes past that—to the death of Kris Barden's son, and it winds up right here with Reardon waiting outside to see if I go with you or if he shoots me in the back. I've seen dogs that wouldn't claim you for a son, Tate." The two men engage in a fist fight and Garry wins, although nearly exhausted by the effort. Then, as Reardon draws on him, another shot rings out and the gunman falls, cut down by Barden.

Garry goes to Lufton and tells him of Riling's plans and of Pindalest's involvement. Lufton has had to give in on the sale of his cattle to Riling but Garry proposes a scheme to delay it. He visits Pindalest at the Indian

120

Service post and explains that the ranchers are having trouble rounding up the cattle to meet the deadline because of the winter weather and that the sale should be put off for a week. As he makes an inspection tour with Garry, the agent agrees but then finds he is Garry's prisoner and set to be kept out of his post for a week. As Riling comes to his rescue, Garry is knifed by an Indian and left for dead. He makes his way to Barden's cabin and Barden goes for Amy, who comes to nurse him. A few nights later, Riling, Pindalest and a gunman arrive and demand that Garry be turned over to them. The siege goes on for hours and Garry creeps out in the dark, kills the gunman, knocks Pindalest unconscious and faces down Riling. Fatally wounded, Riling whispers, "Same old Jim. You and me together, we could have licked 'em—but you always had a conscience breathing down your neck."

Lufton and his men arrive and Garry turns Pindalest over to them. The agent protests his innocence but Lufton tells him that Garry has already outlined the scheme. Turning to Garry, the old rancher admits, "I guess I was wrong about a lot of things." Says Jim Garry, "I've been wrong about a few things myself." Nods Lufton, "We've been plenty stubborn." Amy looks at the two of them, "That's going to make two stubborn men in the family."

A good deal of the effectiveness of *Blood on the Moon* comes from the fine script Lillie Hayward fashioned from the Luke Short novel. The characterizations and the dialogue are perceptive, particularly in presenting the strengths and weaknesses of the two daughters. Especially effective is the scene in which the sensitive, vulnerable Carol finally faces Riling and accuses him of being a liar and a user. He claims "I did it for us—we need money before we can get married." She asks him if he loves her. He hesitates, and with that she walks out.

Blood on the Moon marked Robert Wise as a director

Tom Tyler, Robert Preston and Robert Mitchum.

121

to be reckoned with. In making a western, he strove for realism, choosing to shoot the film in the winter in Arizona's Oak Creek Canyon, in the vicinity of Sedona, achieving a dramatic bleakness well suited to the story. In order to have the clothing as authentic as possible, he hired an expert, Joe De Young, and in staging the knock-down, no-holds-barred brawl between Mitchum and Preston in the saloon, he told both them and their doubles that he wanted a fight that was realistic, one in which it would be obvious that the two men would be badly hurt. "I wanted to have them go at it as hard as possible, to fight like men of this kind would fight. I had seen too many of these silly western barroom brawls in which men pound each other like mad and then walk away barely winded. The winner in this fight had to be almost as exhausted as the loser, badly cut and bruised as would be the case."

Robert Mitchum's catalog of westerns is an interesting one. He immediately followed *Blood on the Moon* with the entirely different *The Red Pony*, Lewis Milestone's agreeable filming of the John Steinbeck novel about life on a California ranch. Mitchum played the amiable handyman Billy Buck. He did not go west again until 1952, this time with yet another vastly different kind of (contemporary) western, Nicholas Ray's *The Lusty Men*, an honest and sweaty look at the tough business of rodeo competition. Two years later, he traveled to the Canadian Rockies with Marilyn Monroe to make Otto Preminger's *River of No Return* and followed it with William Wellman's stark *Track of the Cat*, which Bosley Crowther described as being a Eugene O'Neill kind of western. *Man With a Gun* (1955) had Mitchum as a tough gunslinger, an unusual story of a man trying to find an estranged wife, and in the excellent *The Wonderful Country* (1959), he played a fugitive involved with Mexican bandits. Eight years drifted by before Mitchum took *The Way West,* as an embittered old trail scout, followed quickly with his performance as a drunken old lawman dragged back to respectability by John Wayne in Howard Hawks' *El Dorado*. Henry Hathaway's *Five Card Stud* (1968) presented Mitchum as a fire-and-brimstone minister and Buzz Kulik's *Villa Rides!,* his next film, had him as a Texas gunrunner working for Pancho Villa. Burt Kennedy's *Young Billy Young* and *The Good Guys and the Bad Guys* were both released in 1969, both being rather conventional, slam-bang westerns, one straight, the other tongue-in-cheek. If, as it seems, this pair ended his years as a movie cowboy, Mitchum can retire from the saddle with honor. He has ridden well.

Robert Mitchum and Walter Brennan.

COLORADO TERRITORY

WARNER BROS., 1949

Produced by Anthony Veiller. Directed by Raoul Walsh. Written by John Twist and Edmund H. North, based on the novel *High Sierra* by W. R. Burnett. Photographed by Sid Hickox. Music by David Buttolph. 94 minutes.

CAST:

(*Wes McQueen*) Joe McCrea; (*Colorado Carson*) Virginia Mayo; (*Julie Ann*) Dorothy Malone; (*Winslow*) Henry Hull; (*Reno Blake*) John Archer; (*Duke Harris*) James Mitchell; (*Marshall*) Morris Ankrum; (*Dave Rickard*) Basil Ruysdael; (*Brother Tomas*) Frank Puglia; (*Wallace*) Ian Wolfe; (*Pluthner*) Harry Woods; (*Prospector*) Housley Stevenson; (*Sheriff*) Victor Kilian; (*Station Agent*) Oliver Blake.

While making *They Shall Have Music* with Jascha Heifetz for Samuel Goldwyn in 1939, Joel McCrea complimented the renowned violinist on the authority of his playing. Heifetz returned the compliment, "Mr. McCrea, I don't have the least idea of how to ride a horse but when I see you do it I know that's how it should be done. You also have authority." With that

comment, Heifetz summed up McCrea's success as a film actor. No one, least of all McCrea, ever suggested he was gifted as an actor, but by wisely picking the right material, he was seldom less than persuasive—and in westerns far more than that. A modest, physically graceful man, McCrea was never driven by ambition; he appeared to amble through 30 years of movie stardom with ease, looking as comfortable in white tie and tails as in buckskins, and more than most actors he had an instinct for knowing what he could not do. He shocked Michael Curtiz when he turned down an offer to play Will Rogers, explaining that all he would be able to do would be a poor imitation. He convinced Curtiz that he was not qualified and suggested Will Rogers, Jr., who was later hired.

Of all the major actors who starred in westerns, McCrea was the only one to also be a full-time rancher, operating a large spread in Calabasas, some 30 miles west of Hollywood, and another in Nevada. Born in Pasadena, California, in November of 1905, McCrea was brought up with western lore. His maternal grand-

Dorothy Malone, Henry Hull and Joel McCrea.

father had crossed the country with a wagon train and his paternal grandfather had been an Army officer involved in the Indian Wars. McCrea lived in Hollywood as a child, where his father was an executive with the Los Angeles Gas and Electric Company, and he often watched movies being made. But at Pomona college, his announced ambition was to be a rancher. The head of the drama department, Benjamin David Scott, advised him that with his physique, height, good looks and easy manner, the best way to become a rancher would be to earn money in the movies and buy a ranch. McCrea took his advice and started to line up for work as an extra. It involved no great effort. Many of his school chums were the children of film executives and contacts were plentiful. Bit parts emerged and in 1929 McCrea was given a small role by Cecil B. DeMille in *Dynamite.* The next year, RKO hired him to star in the Alaskan adventure *The Silver Horde,* and Joel McCrea was a leading man from then on.

Despite his interest in ranching and his horsemanship, McCrea did not appear in a western until 1937 when Paramount starred him in its somewhat lumbering epic *Wells Fargo,* in which he played opposite Frances

Dee, whom he had married in 1933—and with whom in 1988 he celebrated a 55th wedding anniversary. By the time of making *Wells Fargo,* the McCreas were already living on their ranch in Calabasas, where he put to use all the skill he had picked up working on ranches during his summers as a teenager. The fact that he bought the property at Calabasas he attributes to Will Rogers, whom he met when he played a role in Rogers' *Lightin'* in 1930. "He was almost like a father to me. I loved that man and his philosophy. He knew I wanted a ranch and that I was saving up to get it. He told me to just go ahead and borrow some money because land in California couldn't go anywhere but up. When I was working with him a couple of years later on another picture, *Business and Pleasure,* I bought this ranch, and when I sold it 20 years later I made more money than I had in 35 years in motion pictures."

McCrea's second western was DeMille's *Union Pacific* (1939), with another five years passing before the next, *Buffalo Bill.* McCrea was, in these years, much better known as a reliable leading man in light dramas and comedies, scoring high points in Preston Sturges' *Sullivan's Travels* (1941) and *The Palm Beach Story*

124

(1942) and George Stevens' *The More the Merrier* (1943). In 1946, Paramount starred him in *The Virginian* and it was now, at the age of 40, that movie western life began for McCrea. For the remainder of his career he would appear in only one film that was not a western, *Shoot First* (1953), which he made in England. "As I grew older, I felt uncomfortable trying to be romantic with young actresses. I had started as a cowboy as a kid and now that I was a rancher I felt much more at home making westerns."

Buffalo Bill used McCrea in a highly romanticized account of William F. Cody and *The Virginian* was nice but conventional. But with *Ramrod* in 1947, McCrea hit his stride with a more adult and grittier kind of western. In it, he plays a ranch foreman used by a beautiful but unscrupulous lady employer (Veronica Lake) to further her ambitions, almost costing him his life. McCrea next co-starred with his wife in *Four Faces West*, which is remarkable as probably the only western ever made in

which not a single shot is fired. It is the story of a man who robs a bank to save his ranch and leaves the banker an I.O.U., impressing the pursuing sheriff with his humanity by stopping to attend a sick family. It was a perfect vehicle for the quiet, dignified McCrea style.

Warner Bros. wanted John Wayne for *Colorado Territory*, but he was tied up with other film commitments and director Raoul Walsh suggested McCrea. Possibly the most amiable and placid man ever to become a movie star, McCrea had long joked that he was the actor used whenever a producer was unable to land Gary Cooper, and when Walsh asked him if it bothered him to do something that had been slated for Wayne, he shook his head, "When the picture opens, I'll be the guy that's riding out there—people won't know how many were up for the part."

Colorado Territory is a re-working of *High Sierra*, which Walsh had directed with Humphrey Bogart in 1941. The idea of doing a western version intrigued

James Mitchell, John Archer, Joel McCrea and Virginia Mayo.

him. Instead of Bogart as gangster Roy Earle, McCrea is outlaw Wes McQueen, who breaks out of a Missouri jail and heads for Colorado to join his old gang, headed by crippled Dave Rickard (Basil Ruysdael). Sentenced to 20 years for bank and train robberies, McQueen is hounded by lawmen wanting to get him back behind bars. Riding on a stagecoach, he saves the lives of a man named Winslow (Henry Hull) and his daughter, Julie Ann (Dorothy Malone), when the coach is attacked by bandits, and the driver and guard killed. When McQueen arrives at the hideout in a deserted town, he comes across a pair of thugs in the gang, Reno Blake (John Archer) and Duke Harris (James Mitchell), whom he instinctively mistrusts. With them is a half-breed girl, Colorado Carson (Virginia Mayo), and for her he feels an immediate rapport. McQueen makes it known that he wants to retire from crime but Rickard talks him into one last job, one that will bring the gang a possible $100,000. Pulling off the job in spite of the treachery of Blake and Harris, who try to grab the money for themselves, he takes off with Colorado. They stop off at Winslow's house, where Julia Ann tries to betray McQueen for the reward money, but Colorado warns him and the two elude the pursuing posse. They head for the Mexican border but find themselves land locked in a canyon of old Indian dwellings. They defend themselves but the odds are too great, and McQueen and Colorado are shot to death.

Colorado Territory is a classic western, with a stunning use of landscape to accentuate the drama, contrasting the insignificant size of the characters with the immensity of the setting. The film has drive and impact, and benefits greatly from location shooting in New Mexico, where Walsh used a genuine, old fashioned narrow-gauge railroad, actual Indian cliff dwellings and the ruins of a deserted town. McCrea's portrayal of the doomed outlaw brought him more critical acclaim than he usually received, for which he credits Walsh. "I'd do stuff for him that I wouldn't have done for any other director. He was a gutty little bastard. And funny. In the scene where I was escaping from prison, I had to run across a swamp with dogs after me. There were logs and rocks in it and I fell down about four times and damn near broke my leg, but I got up and kept going

John Archer, Virginia Mayo, Joel McCrea and James Mitchell.

126

Henry Hull, Virginia Mayo and Joel McCrea.

because he was yelling, 'keep running, kid, keep running.' When I came out the other end, muddy, wet, cold and out of breath, I looked for Walsh, expecting him to tell me how great I had been and if it had been any other actor he'd have had to use a double, but he wasn't there. The assistant director said Walsh left halfway through the run, telling him it looked good and to use it. That's the way he'd do things. What a character!"

While making *Colorado Territory*, McCrea several times had lunch with his friend Gary Cooper, who was at Warners doing *Task Force*. One day, they were joined by Harry Warner, who at once point smiled at the two actors and said, "You guys are like Kellogg's Corn Flakes. When anybody reads your name, they know exactly what they're buying. Don't disappoint them. It's all right for Bogart to be a nice guy in this picture and a heel in the next but you guys can't do it." It was

advice neither Cooper nor McCrea needed but it was good to hear coming from one of the toughest business minds in Hollywood. Cooper, says McCrea, was the nearest to being a role model among other actors, "Not that I copied him. The only thing I did was to watch how sincere Coop was in his approach to acting, how honest he was, and then I tried to be honest in my own way and not go beyond my bounds." Of the old westerns stars, the one the young McCrea admired the most was William S. Hart. "I liked him better than Tom Mix because Mix was colorful but Hart was sincere. He thought everything he did on the screen was for real. He was great on authenticity and I admired that."

The venerable western producer Harry Sherman, who hired McCrea for *Ramrod* and *Four Faces West*, once said about him, "Joel is the greatest natural western actor since Mix and Hart, and he's the first natural horseman I've ever seen. No trick rider, just a guy who knows how to sit a horse with grace and authority." The authority on screen possibly had much to do with McCrea's other life as a rancher and landowner. At its peak, the McCrea ranch turned out a quarter of a million pounds of beef each year. In 1963, he sold off one thousand acres for $3-million, and gradually after that he sold off other parcels and reduced the property to the small area around his home in Camarillo. After *Colorado Territory,* he made another 20 westerns, playing Wyatt Earp in *Wichita* (1955), Sam Houston in *The First Texan* (1956) and Bat Masterson in *The Gunfight at Dodge City* (1959), which he intended to be his movie swan song—until three years later, when a script with the title *Ride the High Country* arrived in the mail.

Virginia Mayo and Joel McCrea.

128

Glenn Ford.

LUST FOR GOLD

COLUMBIA, 1949

Produced and directed by S. Sylvan Simon. Written by Ted Sherdeman and Richard English, based on the book *Thunder Gods Gold* by Barry Storm. Photographed by Archie Stout. Music by George Duning. 90 minutes.

CAST:

(Julia Thomas) Ida Lupino; *(Jacob Walz)* Glenn Ford; *(Pete Thomas)* Gig Young; *(Barry Storm)* William Prince; *(Wiser)* Edgar Buchanan; *(Deputy Ray Covin)* Will Geer; *(Sheriff Lynn Early)* Paul Ford; *(Walter)* Jay Silverheels; *(Coroner)* Eddy Waller; *(Parsons)* Will Wright; *(Matron)* Virginia Mullen; *(Ramon Peralta)* Antonio Moreno; *(Ludi)* Arthur Hunnicutt; *(Lucille)* Myrna Dell; *(Luke)* Tom Tyler; *(Mrs. Bannister)* Elspeth Dudgeon; *(Bill Bates)* Paul E. Burns; *(Floyd Buckley)* Hayden Rorke.

Those who have sought the gold buried in the so-called Lost Dutchman mine in Arizona's Superstition Mountains, some 30 miles east of Phoenix, have so far met with failure and, in many cases, tragedy. That was the theme of Barry Storm's book *Thunder Gods Gold,*

which Columbia Pictures purchased and then altered so much in the filming that Storm became furious and sued them. *Lust for Gold,* like those who have tried to find the Lost Dutchman mine, met with little luck, largely because its stars, Glenn Ford and Ida Lupino, played rotten people, as did most of the other actors in this strange, offbeat western. Perhaps it had something to do with the Apache spirit that Arizona legend claims watches over the mine. The Indians feel that the intrusion of the white men in the mine, which they blocked off after it had originally been found by the Spaniards, offends their gods. By the time they got the movie on the market, Columbia executives believed there might be something to the legend.

Lust for Gold, which has almost become a lost film, presents an ironic story of intrigue, murder and frustration, and veers far off the beaten western paths trod into ossified ruts by Hollywood. Problems appeared as soon as the film went into production. The veteran director George Marshall, who had to his credit such fine westerns as *Destry Rides Again* (1939), *When the*

129

Daltons Rode (1940) and *Texas* (1941), walked out after the many script changes and what he thought was lack of focus, and the producer, S. Sylvan Simon, took over as director. Simon had directed two dozen movies, starting in 1938, but after *Lust for Gold,* he never directed again. In fact, he died two years later at the age of 41. He began his Lost Dutchman saga with the idea of using the title of Storm's book, then changed it to *The Secret of Treasure Mountain,* next *For Those Who Dare* and finally *Lust for Gold.* In Hollywood, title changes seldom auger well.

The film begins with Barry Storm (William Prince) seeking the lost mine, said to contain millions of dollars worth of gold ore. Another man, Floyd Buckley (Hayden Rorke), is shot and killed by an unseen assailant while doing the same thing and Storm is accused of the crime. During the questioning, he relates that he is a descendant of Jacob Walz, who owned the mine back in the 1870s. To help clear himself, Storm tells Sheriff Early (Paul Ford) the story of the mine. Flashback—to Storm's encounter with Buckley in the Claims Office in Phoenix. Buckley has an old map showing the mine's location, drawn by Ramon Peralta (Antonio Moreno), the man who first found the site. Storm suggests that he and Buckley become partners, which Buckley rejects, and following Buckley, witnesses his shooting, but without seeing the killer. Later, the sheriff finds on Buckley's body a map with a portion missing.

Myrna Dell, Glenn Ford and players.

130

Glenn Ford and Ida
Lupino.

Gig Young, Paul E. Burns and Glenn Ford.

To further clear himself, Storm takes Deputy Sheriff Ray Covin (Will Geer) back to the mountains to show how he trailed Buckley, and Covin tells Storm that Buckley was the fourth man shot under these circumstances in the past two years. Flashback to the 1840s: Peralta, prospecting for gold, discovers the mine and within a short time great amounts of ore are extracted from the shafts. The miners are attacked by Apaches and all but Peralta are killed, after which the Indians block off the entrance of the mine, which they consider sacred ground. Back to the present: Storm and Covin return to Phoenix, where they visit the aged Mrs. Bannister (Elspeth Dudgeon), who knew Jacob Walz and tells them about him.

Flashback to 1886: Peralta, now a man in late middle age, and his partner, Ludi (Arthur Hunnicutt), set out to find the mine. Walz (Ford), known as The Dutchman, and his companion, Wiser (Edgar Buchanan), follow them. At the mouth of the mine, the two kill Peralta and Ludi, then Walz shoots Wiser, thus gaining total possession of the mine. Walz returns to Phoenix with some of the gold and dazzles the citizens with his talk of a bonanza, while careful not to reveal its location. A scheming woman, Julia Thomas (Lupino), and her wastrel husband, Pete (Gig Young), plot to snare Walz. She hides the fact that she is married and encourages Walz to fall in love with her. He does just that and Julia wheedles the location of the mine from him. Later learning of her duplicity, Walz plans a revenge. When she and her husband arrive at the mine, Walz traps them in a shaft and keeps them there without food or water. In the hope of winning over Walz and promising herself to him, Julia kills her husband. After doing that, an earthquake occurs and Julia is buried in a landslide. Walz escapes the landslide but without food and water, he soon turns mad and dies.

Back again to the present: Storm gathers all his clues and again sets out to find the mine. When he gets there, he finds Covin is ahead of him. Covin admits that he killed Buckley and the others because they had found the mine. He now tries to kill Storm but in the ensuing fight Covin is bitten by a rattlesnake and he falls over a cliff to his death. The final clue to the entrance to the mine involves a shaft of moonlight cutting through a window hewn in a certain rock and striking at a certain time. This is the missing link in the puzzle and the solution can only be found on the anniversary of the night Peralta established the clue. But the question is: what night? what hour? what moment? Storm muses that the earth and the moon are moving objects—and he gives up in complete frustration.

The Lost Dutchman mine has yet to be found, and if *Lust for Gold* is any indication of the problems involved,

Ida Lupino and Gig Young.

132

Ida Lupino and Glenn Ford.

134

it probably never will be found. While *The Treasure of the Sierra Madre* (1948) is generally regarded as the definitive film comment on the perils and futility of avidly seeking gold, *Lust for Gold* is actually a much tougher and more realistic statement. The film has an air of authenticity that heightens its impact. It is grim and bloody and some of its moments of suspense are masterful. Producer-director Simon pulled no punches in probing the unsavory characters in his narrative, which doubtless made the film less appealing to the general public than it might have been had he glamorized it a little. Glenn Ford has never portrayed a less sympathetic character than Jacob Walz and Ida Lupino is superb as the treacherous, sleazy Julia, although the really unsettling performance is given by that fine character actor Will Geer, playing the murderous deputy with an ingratiating, smiling manner that masks his evil soul. Shot on location in Arizona by the masterful Archie Stout, using sepia tones, the film is an expert piece of work.

Lust for Gold was delayed by Columbia in its release due to the bizarre behavior of author Barry Storm. His book had been a documentary account of the lost mine and he ranted that Columbia had turned it into a ripe melodrama without any consultation with him. He charged, and justly so, that the film misrepresented him; he was not related to Jacob Walz in any manner. That was something the producers had invented just to heighten the drama. Storm not only sued Columbia but also wrote and circulated a pamphlet in which he charged the studio with plagiarism and false business practices, and even went so far as to suggest that the writers and producers were part of a communist plot to gain control of the film business. He settled out of court with the studio but remained angry and bitter—to the extent of writing another book about the mine, this time as a novel with fictional elements, presumably as a lesson to Columbia as to how it should have made the picture. The studio was probably sorry it ever undertook to tell the story of the Lost Dutchman mine, which might account for the film being almost as difficult to locate as the mine itself. Such is the strange story of *Lust for Gold*, a fascinating film

THE GUNFIGHTER

20th CENTURY-FOX, 1950

Produced by Nunnally Johnson. Directed by Henry King. Written by William Bowers and William Sellers, based on a story by Bowers and Andre de Toth. Photographed by Arthur Miller. Music by Alfred Newman. 84 minutes.

CAST:

(*Jimmy Ringo*) Gregory Peck; (*Peggy Walsh*) Helen Westcott; (*Sheriff Mark Strett*) Millard Mitchell; (*Molly*) Jean Parker; (*Mac*) Karl Malden; (*Hunt Bromley*) Skip Homeier; (*Charlie*) Anthony Ross; (*Mrs. Pennyfeather*) Verna Felton; (*Mrs. Devlin*) Ellen Corby; (*Eddie*) Richard Jaeckel; (*First Brother*) Alan Hale, Jr.; (*Second Brother*) David Clarke; (*Third Brother*) John Pickard; (*Jimmie*) B. G. Norman.

The old, or more to the point, middle-aged, lightning-fast gunfighter hounded to his death by a reputation from which he would like to escape in order to live out his life peaceably has become a solid western cliché. But that was not the case in 1950, when *The Gunfighter* impressed critics and public alike with its almost Grecian tragic account of Johnny Ringo—and doing it so

well it set the cliché on the way to formation. As limned by Gregory Peck in a manner melancholy, Ringo is not only a man past his prime but now a man living in a West, presumably that of the 1890s, in which he is no longer welcome. Even old friends, after greeting him affably and chatting about the past, expect him not to linger but to move along, lest his presence invites trouble, as it always does. In reviewing the film for *The New York Times,* the esteemed Bosley Crowther referred to it as "a caustic and wholesome anodyne to the fever of six-gun heroics that is shot in most western films."

Gregory Peck was not the actor William Bowers and director Andre de Toth had in mind when they wrote their story. They wanted John Wayne, which was a problem because Columbia had picked up an option on the script, and Columbia was a studio at which Wayne would not set foot as long as Harry Cohn was in command. Wayne held a grudge against Cohn for the manner in which he was treated during his (Wayne's) year at Columbia, 1931, in which he felt he was

Richard Jaeckel, Harry Shannon and Gregory Peck.

sloughed off with bit parts and then dumped. It was a bad time for Wayne, who was trying to pick himself up after having played the lead in the poorly-received epic *The Big Trail*. With Wayne not interested, Columbia dropped its option and the authors took the story to Nunnally Johnson at 20th Century-Fox, who was looking for something in which to star Peck in the wake of his great success in *Twelve O'Clock High*, made under the direction of the venerable Henry King. Johnson felt that Wayne would not be able to give the Ringo role the needed poignancy and that the tough de Toth was not the man to get that poignancy out of Peck. De Toth backed off and Bowers was hired to get his script into shooting form with William Sellers.

Darryl F. Zanuck, who had not in the first place been in favor of making *The Ox-Bow Incident*, was nonetheless aware of the prestige it had gradually gained, and he was in the mood for another western that might go down as a classic. There was no question in his mind that Henry King was the man to direct it and Arthur

Miller was the man to photograph it. As it turned out, it was the last of 56 films Miller (1895-1970) shot at Fox. Referred to as "the master" by other cinematographers, Miller started with Fox in 1932 and made his name with interior rather than exterior material. He photographed *The Ox-Bow Incident*, very much an interior western, as is *The Gunfighter*, the dramatic effectiveness of which owes a lot to Miller's intense, moody, black-and-white settings, an intensity that might be severly altered if colorized.

The Gunfighter is among the best of the films directed by King (1888-1982), who joined Fox in 1930 to direct *Lightin'*, starring Will Rogers and giving young Joel McCrea one of his first parts. He stayed with that studio until 1961 and retired after directing *Tender Is the Night*. Most of the Fox box office winners during those 30 years were directed by King, who was the style-founder at that studio in the same way that Michael Curtiz was the house director at Warners during the same years. King specialized in Americana but his

Millard Mitchell, Helen Westcott and Gregory Peck.

B. G. Norman and Gregory Peck.

only western prior to *The Gunfighter* was *Jesse James* (1939), which appealed to him because it was filmed on location in Missouri. *The Gunfighter* attracted Gregory Peck because it was, like the air force general who has a nervous breakdown in *Twelve O'Clock High,* a story about a man trapped by his fate.

At 34, Peck was not really old enough to play Johnny Ringo. In order to make the character seem older, he not only acquired a handle-bar moustache, the droop of which added to the aura of melancholy, but also submitted to a haircut that looked as if it had been made by placing a bowl over his head, and dressed in a dark, drab suit with a plain gunbelt. In this guise, Peck was much different from the men he had played in his two previous westerns—Selznick's epic piece of western kitsch *Duel in the Sun* (1946), with Peck as the charming but amoral Lewt McCanles, and William Wellman's fine *Yellow Sky* (1948), in which he was a sleek but not entirely dishonorable outlaw.

When first seen, Ringo is riding across to the desert on his way to Cayenne, where his estranged wife and small son live. He stops off in a saloon for a drink and there runs into a brash young gunslinger, Eddie (Richard Jaeckel), who recognizes him and taunts him into a gunfight. Before the boy can clear his gun from its holster, he is felled by the notorious Ringo, who has long grown weary of young men anxious to make a name for themselves by outdrawing him. The men in the saloon are sympathetic but advise him to be on his way because Eddie has three brothers, who doubtless will want vengeance. He arrives in Cayenne and goes into another saloon. The bartender, Mac (Karl Malden), is an old friend who tells him that Mark Strett (Millard Mitchell), another colleague from the long gone bank robbing days, is now the town marshal. Ringo goes to see him and is greeted warmly, but it soon becomes apparent that Strett is a dedicated lawman and that he cannot let Ringo stay in Cayenne.

Through Strett, Ringo arranges a meeting with his wife, a schoolteacher going under the name Peggy Walsh (Helen Westcott). He tells her that he wants to find a new, quiet life and settle down with his family.

Gregory Peck, Karl Malden and Skip Homeier.

The dying gunfighter, surrounded by Karl Malden, Jean Parker and Millard Mitchell. Killer Skip Homeier stands looking down at his victim.

She replies that she would be willing if it were not for their son Jimmie (B. G. Norman), who is happy with his life and unaware that his father is an infamous gunman. She agrees, however, to let him see the boy. In the meantime, the whole town has heard of Ringo's presence and everyone demands of the marshal that he get the outlaw to move on. His presence also comes to the attention of another young would-be gunslinger out to make his name as the killer of Johnny Ringo. Hunt Bromley (Skip Homeier) strides up to Ringo in the saloon and challenges him. Ringo, sitting at a table with his hands under the cover, tells Bromley he has a gun aimed right at his stomach. The boy angrily backs off. After he leaves, Ringo brings up his hands and all he has in them is a pipe and tobacco. He has long known how to bluff.

Ringo meets his son but does not reveal his identity, and the boy asks him if he has ever met Johnny Ringo, the fastest gun in the West. Allowing that he has, Ringo plays down the glory and the excitement of being an outlaw and champions the much better road to be followed with law and order. He realizes that the youngster should stay with his mother and agrees with Strett

140

that it is best for him to leave before sundown. But now the three brothers of Eddie arrive in town. In order for Ringo's departure to be an inconspicuous as possible, Strett sneaks him out the back of the saloon. The brothers, having overheard Strett's plan, wait in a barn behind the saloon but are discovered and disarmed. Just as Ringo is about to leave, surly Hunt Bromley jumps out from behind a corner of the barn and yells at Ringo, but drawing his guns and shooting before Ringo can possibly reach for his own weapon. He falls, mortally wounded. With raging sorrow, Strett pummels Bromley and threatens to see he is tried and hanged. The dying Ringo asks Strett to let Bromley go and also let it be known that he drew first. He wants Bromley to know the burden of being a notorious gunman, "In every town you go there will be someone itching to kill the man who got Johnny Ringo." Eventually the incident is bound to repeat itself and Ringo understands that this probability is fitting punishment.

The Gunfighter remains the finest movie yet made about the fate of the western gunslinger in the days when the West ceased to be wild and tried to calm itself into civilization. The effectiveness of the film lies with Peck's playing of the sad, doomed Ringo—with a lot of help from old pros Henry King and Arthur Miller. In 1958, Peck and King teamed again to make King's only other western, *The Bravados,* in which Peck plays a man tracking the quartet he believes raped and killed his wife. He catches them one by one, but after killing three of them he learns from the fourth that they were not responsible for the crime. Like *The Gunfighter,* it is a bitter commentary on western life and morality in the late 19th century, although it does not state its case with quite the same finality.

Ironically, John Wayne, who was passed over at Fox as not the actor to play Johnny Ringo, ended his film career playing just such a character in *The Shootist,* a dying gunman unable to escape the past.

Robert Taylor and Bruce Cowling.

DEVIL'S DOORWAY

M G M , 1 9 5 0

Produced by Nicholas Nayfack. Directed by Anthony Mann. Written by Guy Trosper. Photographed by John Alton. Music by Daniele Amfitheatrof. 84 minutes.

CAST:

(*Lance Poole*) Robert Taylor; (*Verne Coolan*) Louis Calhern; (*Orrie Masters*) Paula Raymond; (*Rod MacDougall*) Marshall Thompson; (*Red Rock*) James Mitchell; (*Zeke Carmody*) Spring Byington; (*Scotty MacDougall*) Rhys Williams; (*Ike Stapleton*) James Millican; (*Lt. Grimes*) Bruce Cowling; (*Mr. Poole*) Fritz Leiber; (*Dr. C. O. MacQuillan*) Harry Antrim; (*Thundercloud*) Chief John Big Tree.

Broken Arrow (1950) is generally regarded as the first Hollywood film to deal fairly and compassionately with the American Indian. It certainly marked a major turning point in depicting the treatment the Indians had received not only historically but as film figures. It was not, however, the first to regard the native Americans as more than simple savages standing in the way of westward migration. In 1925, Paramount starred Ri-

chard Dix in a major production based on Zane Grey's novel *The Vanishing American,* playing a warrior who returns from heroic military service in World War I to find his people still being cheated by a crooked government official. The film received wide attention and four years later Dix played a Navajo in *Redskin,* telling the tale of a tribesman's conflict with racial prejudice at college and the resentment of his own people when he acts like a paleface—until he strikes oil and makes the tribe wealthy. In 1932, Tim McCoy struck a blow for his Indian friends with *End of the Trail,* but it was largely lost in a decade swamped with stock movie Indians attacking wagon trains and being shot from their horses with relative ease.

George Armstrong Custer was an obvious hero in the romanticized *They Died With Their Boots On* (1941), but the film paid tribute to both the bravery of the Indians and the raw deal they received with broken treaties. Similar respect was paid by John Ford in *Fort Apache* (1948) and his cavalry epics. However, it was *Broken Arrow* that caught the public's fancy, with its tale of a white man who took it upon himself to make peace with Cochise and the Chiricahua Apaches. 20th Century-Fox began production of *Broken Arrow* with James Stewart in June of 1949 but they did not release it until August of 1950, one month after Universal had released Stewart's subsequent *Winchester '73*. With the immediate success of the Universal film, which established Stewart as a plausible western character, Fox felt more secure releasing its own Indian tribute, a box office winner. This in turn gave MGM sufficient confidence to release its account of Indian bravery and maltreatment, *Devil's Doorway,* which had sat on the shelf for almost a year.

Devil's Doorway, however, did not catch the public fancy to nearly the same extent as the less tough, less poignant *Broken Arrow*. Its quality lies with the director, Anthony Mann, and the star, Robert Taylor, who gave his finest performance to this point in his long MGM career. It was the first of 11 exceptional westerns directed by Mann, five of which starred James Stewart. Mann (1906-1967) was a tough, no-nonsense

kind of director who was drawn to stories of basically honorable men caught in conflict with adversity. There was an undercurrent of psychological intensity in all his films, and in his westerns he made conspicuous use of the landscapes to heighten the drama. This is especially true of *Devil's Doorway,* where the magnificent Wyoming settings are in sharp contrast to the grief forced on its Indian dwellers.

Most critics commented upon "Indian" Robert Taylor's obvious Anglo appearance, even with dark make-up and black hair, while at the same time praising the sincerity of his work. Taylor at MGM faced a problem similar to Tyrone Power at 20th Century-Fox—both were extremely handsome young actors whose looks were capital gain for their employers and each for years was limited by those same looks. It was not until both men returned from the war, with a few lines in their faces, that they eventually managed to get more mature roles and prove their worth as actors. Taylor, more than Power, loved horses and operated a small ranch of his own. His first western was *Stand Up and Fight*

Robert Taylor and Paula Raymond.

(1939), as a railroad man slugging it out with beefy Wallace Beery, and two years later he was *Billy the Kid* in an MGM Technicolor fantasy about the celebrated young outlaw. Taylor glowered as best he could but the studio was still selling his looks. He was not seen in another western until the 1950 *Ambush,* as a frontier scout, and he went directly from that into *Devil's Doorway.*

Whereas *Broken Arrow* softened its message of Indian prejudice with a love story between the Stewart character and the beautiful Indian girl played by Debra Paget, the MGM film pulls no punches. Taylor is Lance Poole, returning from the Civil War, a sergeant in the Third Pennsylvania Cavalry and the winner of the Congressional Medal of Honor. He hopes to return to a life of peace in Sweet Meadows, a rich grazing area near Medicine Bow, Wyoming, but the end of the war has resulted in white settlers moving into the valley in which his ranch and property lies. The newly-levied Homestead Act is used by an ambitious lawyer, Verne Coolan (Louis Calhern), to persuade the homesteaders that they are entitled to the Indian lands, especially the sheep farmers who need these thick, grassy meadows. Poole finds that his fertile fields are like a magnet to the desperate sheepmen, who have driven their flocks from drought-stricken Nebraska. They are decent people misled by Coolan, who truly believes the Indians are inferiors and not entitled to property in favor of whites.

The feelings against Poole starts to grow. His father dies when a doctor refuses to answer a call for help, and a gunslinger tries to humiliate him in a saloon, causing a brawl in which the furious Poole thrashes the man. He turns for help to Orrie Masters (Paula Raymond), a lawyer who is sympathetic but explains that the new laws make it possible for the whites to move in on Indian lands. Although they become drawn to each other, they know the situation does not allow for an extended relationship.

Poole does his best to protect his property and his people, which enables Coolan to stir up resentment, leading to an attack of settlers and townspeople on Poole's ranch. With the skill learned in his military service, Poole directs his men in tactics that almost win the battle for him. It is a long, drawn-out battle, with the Indians riding down the hillsides, leaping onto whites, and tossing sticks of dynamite into the wagons. The swirling, noisy fight is made the more bizarre by the frightened bleating of the sheep caught in the conflict. But the skill and bravery of the Indians are not enough in the face of superior numbers. The cavalry arrives, having been summoned by Orrie when she realized Coolan was about to lead an attack, and Poole, whose home has now been reduced to ruins, offers to

surrender if the women and children will be granted safe conduct to a reservation. This is agreed upon. Now Poole, mortally wounded, dresses in his be-medaled uniform and walks toward the commander of the cavalry. he salutes, the salute is returned, and then falls and dies.

A largely neglected film, *Devil's Doorway* is a superb piece of movie making, well photographed, edited and acted, and directed with a clear sense of determination by Anthony Mann. While convinced of the message he

Marshall Thompson, Paula Raymond and Robert Taylor.

was sending about the brutal injustice of the story, Mann also knew he was making a piece of entertainment. The film moves swiftly and the battle sequence remains a masterpiece of its kind. And together with *Broken Arrow*, it did indeed open the door for more thoughtful films about the American Indian. Among the best were *The Savage* (1952), *Apache* (1954), *Drum Beat* (1954), *White Feather* (1955) and *Run of the Arrow* (1957). Never again would the Indian on the screen be just a dumb, animalistic savage, devoid of culture,

Paula Raymond and Robert Taylor.

although there were also films in which Indians were overly glamorized, such as Chuck Connors martyr-like *Geronimo* (1962) and the absurd *Little Big Man* (1971), in which Custer appears as a cowardly, gibbering idiot.

For Robert Taylor, the failure of *Devil's Doorway* to find greater acceptance was a personal disappointment. He had begged MGM to let him play the role of the Shoshone war hero, feeling it not only had something to say but also was a chance to broaden his scope as an actor. It did, however, lead to more westerns, although in each case, Taylor insisted that the parts be better than the usual heroic cliche. He was the misogynistic wagon train guide in *Westward the Women* (1953), a Mexican bandit in *Ride, Vaquero!* (1953), and the Indian-

James Mitchell and Robert Taylor.

hating buffalo hunter in Richard Brooks' fine *The Last Hunt* (1956). The remaining Taylor westerns tended to be somewhat more conventional. He was a retired gunman turned rancher in *Saddle the Wind* (1958), a former outlaw turned marshal in *The Law and Jake Wade* (1958), a rancher trying to hang onto his own in *Cattle King* (1964), and finally, in 1967, two years before his death from cancer at 58, Taylor was a man tracking the murderers of an old friend in the made-for-television *Return of the Gunfighter*. Not a bad track record for an actor who started his career with the label 'pretty boy' and constant drubbings from the critics as a lightweight talent.

ROCKY MOUNTAIN

WARNER BROS., 1950

Produced by William Jacobs. Directed by William Keighley. Written by Winston Miller and Alan LeMay, based on an original story by LeMay. Photographed by Ted McCord. Music by Max Steiner. 83 minutes.

CAST:

(*Lafe Barstow*) Errol Flynn; (*Johanna Carter*) Patrice Wymore; (*Lt. Rickey*) Scott Forbes; (*Pap Dennison*) Guinn 'Big Boy' Williams; (*Jim Wheat*) Dick Jones; (*Cole Smith*) Howard Petrie; (*Plank*) Slim Pickens; (*Gil Craigie*) Chubby Johnson; (*Kip Waterson*) Buzz Henry; (*Kay Rawlins*) Sheb Wooley; (*Pierre Duchesne*) Peter Coe; (*Jonas*) Rush Williams; (*Ash*) Steve Dunhill; (*Barnes*) Alex Sharp; (*Ryan*) Yakima Canutt; (*Man Dog*) Nakai Snez.

Errol Flynn starred in eight westerns, most of which brought great profit to Warner Bros. That he was successful in this kind of film somewhat puzzled Flynn and he joked about himself as "the rich man's Roy Rogers." It is less a puzzle to students of film, who clearly see the image of heroism personified by Flynn

in his peak years as well suited to the mythological nature of Hollywood's super westerns. His gentlemanly British speech and manner may have seemed a little out of place at first but British gentlemen were not uncommon in the real West, so there is no reason why they should not be a part of the film West. In point of fact, Hollywood might have made more of the co-mingling of nationalities and ethnic types in the western migration.

In his first years of stardom, the Tasmanian-born, Australian-parented Flynn was claimed by Warners, with obvious complicity on his part, to be an Irishman, and it is as such that he appears in his first western, the Technicolored romp *Dodge City* (1939). In this, he is Wade Hatton, an Irish adventurer with service in the British Army and the Confederate cavalry—in Jeb Stuart's cavalry, of course. Such a man as Wade would doubtless have served under the dashing Virginian prince of cavalry. The film did so well that a sequel was inevitable, although in *Virginia City* (1940) Flynn is transported back to the Civil War, as a Union officer involved in thwarting Confederate ambitions in the

West. In *Sante Fe Trail* (1940), Flynn actually played J. E. B. Stuart, even though his accent clearly was not Virginian. But by this time, Flynn was so entrenched as a film hero that no accounting for his accent was deemed necessary, as it was not the following year when he played George Armstrong Custer in *They Died With Their Boots On,* one of his most memorable performances. Despite the accent, Flynn was a good choice for Custer; both men were by nature charming cavaliers and laws unto themselves. *Boots* was set to be directed by Michael Curtiz, who had done the first three Flynn westerns, but at this point Flynn rebeled against a man he considered a brutal taskmaster and Raoul Walsh was assigned. Flynn and Walsh had a good rapport and the actor's work became more confidant as a result.

Flynn did not go West again until 1945 with *San Antonio,* another Technicolored shoot-'em-up but a rather empty one, directed like the pumped-up B western it was by the pedestrian David Butler. In 1948,

Scott Forbes, Errol Flynn and Patrice Wymore.

Errol Flynn, Patrice Wymore and Howard Petrie.

Walsh made another western with Flynn, *Silver River,* but it failed to make a killing at the box office although it revealed Flynn for the first time as an actor of greater range than previously suspected. It was also the first time he had played a not entirely admirable character, a cashiered Army officer who heartlessly builds an empire for himself in the West. Now in his 40th year, Flynn was no longer the dashing swashbuckler. The years of high living, the drinking and the drugs produced an air of *weltschmerz,* something remotely melancholy, and which made him a more credible actor. However, there was nothing credible about his next western, the mundane *Montana* (1950), which he simply walked through as an Australian sheep rancher with no attempt at an Aussie accent. Then came *Rocky Mountain,* a venture of much greater substance.

Flynn was a more sensitive actor than his gallivanting ways led people to suspect and he responded to direction, if he felt comfortable with the director. He respected the gentlemanly William Keighley, who had once been an actor and with whom he had made *The Prince and the Pauper* in 1937. Keighley was assigned to direct Flynn in *The Adventures of Robin Hood* that same year, but after shooting several scenes he was replaced by the more vigorous Curtiz. The opportunity to work again with Keighley did not come up until 1950, and even then fortuitously. Warners had bought Alan LeMay's story *Ghost Mountain*—the studio might well have stuck with that title—for Ronald Reagan, who had nagged the studio for years to let him do a western. Reagan, though, was held on location in England longer than expected doing *The Hasty Heart* and Warners, with

Errol Flynn and Patrice Wymore.

Howard Petrie, Peter Coe, Dick Jones, Errol Flynn, Guinn 'Big Boy' Williams, Buzz Henry, Sheb Wooley, Rush Williams and Slim Pickens.

nothing else on hand for Flynn, decided to go ahead with him. The first Reagan heard about the switch was when he read about it in *Variety*.

Rocky Mountain is a tragic western, dealing as it does with the last and most futile effort of the Confederacy to win support in the West. The story is based on an actual incident and the film begins with a view of the marker which places the time and location—in Nevada, near the California line. The time is late March of 1865, only a month or so from the ending of the Civil War. A Confederate patrol of eight men, commanded by Lafe Barstow (Flynn), arrives at a rendezvous to meet a band of California outlaws who will aid them in attempting to win the territory for the South. The men settle at the base of a vast, gaunt rock formation, where they are met by California Beal (Howard Petrie), who tells Barstow that the large forces of Cole Smith will soon arrive. While waiting, Barstow and his men ride to the aid of a stagecoach under Indian attack. Only the driver and a young woman, Johanna Carter (Patrice Wymore), survive and Barstow takes them to his encampment. Johanna is on her way to meet her fiance, Union Army Lieutenant Rickey (Scott Forbes), who turns up the

next morning with two troopers, searching for her, and is taken prisoner by Barstow. Accompanying Rickey are three Indians, a father and two sons.

Rickey identifies Beal as being Cole Smith and warns Barstow that any alliance with such a scalawag is doomed, which Barstow has already begun to suspect. However, he allows Smith to leave on the promise of returning with reenforcements. That night, the Indians try to flee and the two younger ones are killed, with the father escaping. Rickey asks Barstow to let him proceed to his garrison 60 miles away and take Johanna. Barstow refuses but Rickey manages to get away. The following day, Smith's riderless horse is found and Barstow realizes that the situation is dire, a fact made the more obvious by the sight of smoke signals and the sound of Indian war drums.

Barstow decides to make a run for it in order to allow Johanna, the coach driver and the one surviving soldier—the other died while trying to escape with Rickey—to get away and ride to the garrison. She and the men ride only a few miles before running into Rickey and a company of cavalry, who now ride to the rescue of the Confederates. Barstow and his seven

153

men gallop across the flat expanse followed by Indians but ride into a box canyon and realize there is no escape. They turn, deploy themselves in line and charge in cavalry fashion toward the Indians. Fighting furiously but futilely, they are all killed. As the Union cavalry approaches, the Indians retreat and Rickey gives the Confederates a military funeral, placing their battle flag, tied to a rifle, on a high point overlooking the graves.

Rocky Mountain was filmed in its entirety—there are no interior shots of any kind—in New Mexico and not the less spectacular Nevada setting of the story. Keighley took a cast and crew of over 100 people to the area just northeast of Gallop, in the vicinity of the Chaco Canyon National Monument, where the rock formations are indeed dramatically impressive. The photography of the veteran Ted McCord is one of the film's major assets. Another is the pervading sense of doom that Keighley gives the story, with Flynn excellent as a southern gentleman who knows in his heart that the cause is lost and the mission hopeless. So do his battle-hardened men, who do not hesitate to follow him.

The story is slight but the setting, the sad spirit of the picture and the sense of fatalism about it make *Rocky Mountain* an unusual western. The horsemanship is remarkably good, particularly from ex-rodeo champion Slim Pickens, here making one of his first film appearances. On a more nostalgic note the film includes Guinn 'Big Boy' Williams, who had appeared with Flynn in *Dodge City, Virginia City* and *Sante Fe Trail,* although here a grizzled and solemn old soldier rather than the jovial buffoon of the previous films. And unlike so many westerns in which Indians are often played by whites, in *Rocky Mountain* they are all genuine Navajos, recruited from the reservations in the areas around Gallop. The authenticity makes a difference.

For Flynn, it would be the end of his screen image as a westerner but the beginning of a new marriage. Patrice Wymore, who had previously appeared in only one film, *Tea for Two,* was given co-star billing to boost her promising career. She played in a few films but her main role thereafter was as Mrs. Flynn, which ended when she became his widow in 1959. They were difficult years for her, as Flynn's career and health declined. The man who so spiritedly played Robin Hood, George Armstrong Custer and Gentleman Jim Corbett finally burned himself out at 50.

Errol Flynn

154

Tom Tyler, Jack Buetel, John Archer, Lawrence Tierney, Walter Brennan, Bruce Cabot and Robert Ryan.

BEST OF THE BADMEN

RKO, 1951

Produced by Herman Schlom. Directed by William D. Russell. Written by Robert Hardy Andrews and John Twist. Photographed in Technicolor by Edward Cronjager. Music by Paul Sawtell. 83 minutes.

CAST:

(*Jeff Clanton*) Robert Ryan; (*Lily*) Claire Trevor; (*Bob Younger*) Jack Buetel; (*Matthew Fowler*) Robert Preston; (*Doc Butcher*) Walter Brennan; (*Cole Younger*) Bruce Cabot; (*Curley Ringo*) John Archer; (*Jesse James*) Lawrence Tierney; (*Joad*) Barton MacLane; (*Frank James*) Tom Tyler; (*Jim Younger*) Bob Wilke; (*John Younger*) John Cliff; (*Lieutenant*) Lee MacGregor; (*Oscar*) Emmett Lynn; (*Wilson*) Carleton Young.

Like all tall, ruggedly handsome leading men, Robert Ryan was required to spend time riding around the Hollywood West. In his case, he had to mount up almost as soon as he appeared before the cameras, playing bit parts in two 1940 super westerns, *Northwest Mounted Police* and *Texas Rangers Ride Again.* Progress in films

was slow for Ryan, who decided to go back to the stage where good notices enabled him to return to Hollywood and be taken more seriously. He began playing supporting roles in 1943, until a year later he joined the Marines. Four years later, under contract to RKO, Ryan began his film career in earnest, appearing with Randolph Scott in *Trail Street,* which displayed Scott as the legendary lawman Bat Masterson and Ryan as a decent businessman in conflict with the bad guys.

The much underrated Ryan (1909-1973) was a Chicagoan who attended Dartmouth College and became its heavyweight boxing champion. He majored in dramatic literature and set out to be a journalist, but these were the years of the Depression and he ended up doing a variety of manual labors, including work as a sand hog, a ship's stoker and a ranch hand. A family investment paid off and enabled him to take tuition in Los Angeles with the great Viennese impresario Max Reinhardt, making him the only Reinhardt pupil ever to star in westerns. However, it would not be in westerns that Ryan would make his greatest impact; he distin-

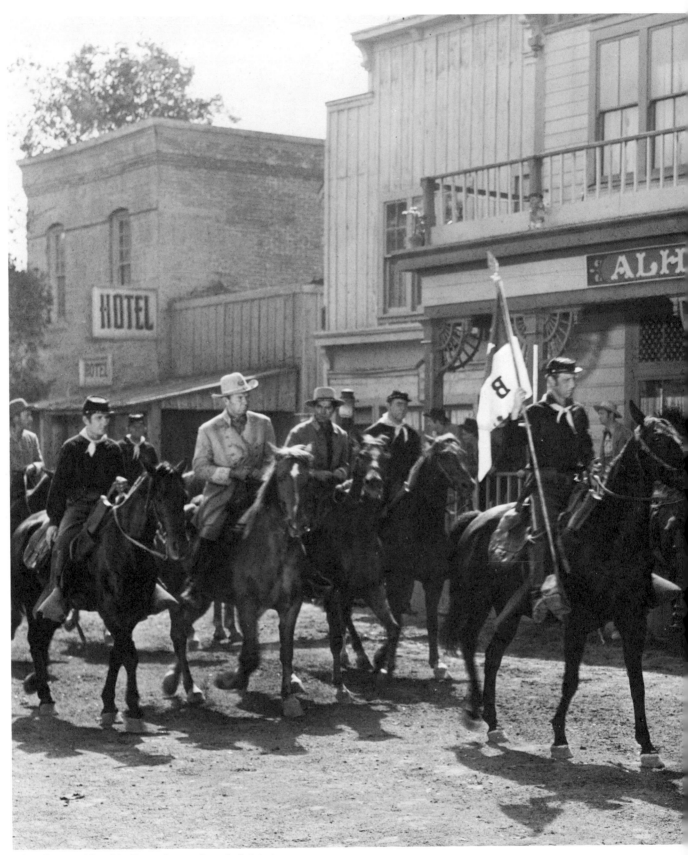

Robert Ryan and Lee MacGregor brings the rebels into town.

156

Barton MacLane, Robert Preston and Carlton Young.

guished himself playing a racial bigot in *Crossfire* (1947), a washed-up boxer in *The Set-Up* (1949), a bitter, brutal cop in *On Dangerous Ground* (1951), a demented, murderous handyman in *Beware, My Lovely* (1952), and several other frightening characters, culminating with the most frightening of them all, the evil Claggart in *Billy Budd* (1962). In person, the gentle Ryan smiled somewhat ruefully at the darker side of his screen image, "I have been in films pretty well everything I am dedicated to fighting against."

Following *Trail Street*, Ryan's next western also teamed him with Randolph Scott, *Return of the Badmen* (1948), this time as the famed outlaw The Sundance Kid, although in a much meaner version than the one played by Robert Redford opposite Paul Newman's Butch Cassidy in 1969. In this piece of fiction, Scott is the retired marshal who returns to gun business to put down the gang organized by Sundance, which includes the Younger Brothers, the Daltons and Billy the Kid. A similar outlaw round-up concept was used by RKO for Ryan's next western outing, *Best of the Badmen*, which unites the Youngers with the James Brothers as ex-Confederate guerrillas struggling to stay alive after the Civil War.

The post-Civil War period in Missouri has been one of Hollywood's richest sources of western material. The number of films made about Frank and Jesse James, the Youngers, the Daltons and sundry other bandits and outlaws runs into dozens. The reasons are obvious: Missouri, both during and after the war, was rife with divided loyalties and many brutal conflicts. It was also the state that raised more guerrilla fighters than any others, due mainly to William Clarke Quantrill, who was only 28 when he was killed in 1865, and Bloody Bill Anderson, a character dealt with in some detail in Clint Eastwood's *The Outlaw Josey Wales*. Such was the brutality of the Missouri guerrillas that, unlike regular Confederate soldiers, they were denied amnesty and returned to their home ground as outlaws. This fact is reversed by scenarists Robert Hardy Andrews and John Twist in their script for *Best of the Badmen*, which begins with a company of former Quantrill raiders making their way home and being caught up with by a Union cavalry force under Major Jeff Clanton (Ryan).

Clanton, a Missourian who chose the blue instead of the grey, is familiar with many of the Confederates, including their leader, Cole Younger (Bruce Cabot), his young brother Bob (Jack Buetel), Jesse James (Lawrence Tierney), Frank James (Tom Tyler), old Doc Butcher (Walter Brennan) and the treacherous Curley Ringo (John Archer). Clanton advises them that there is no point in resisting and promises them amnesty if they will return with him to the Army post at Breckenridge and take the oath of loyalty to the Union. As the

Bob Wilke, Robert Ryan, Walter Brennan, Lawrence Tierney, Tom Tyler, Claire
Trevor, Bruce Cabot, Jack Buetel and John Cliff.

Jack Buetel, Bruce Cabot and Bob Wilke.

men ride through the streets of the town, they come to the attention of Matthew Fowler (Robert Preston), who runs a detective agency and sees the opportunity for picking up rewards for men like the Youngers and the Jameses. Fowler stirs up a group of townspeople, who mill outside the Army gates and demand that the outlaws be turned over. In the struggle to hold the people back, one of them is shot and killed. Clanton administers the oath and the former Quantrill raiders leave. A few days later, Clanton, now a civilian, is arrested as he is about to leave town, charged with murder, and in a trial rigged by Fowler, convicted and sentenced to be hanged. Aid now appears from a surprising source; Lily (Claire Trevor), Fowler's estranged wife, visits Clanton in jail and slips him a gun. She is disgusted with her carpetbagger husband and his plans to commandeer the area. She describes him as "a filthy gunman trying to be a gentleman."

Clanton is pursued by Fowler's men and recaptured, but rescued by Doc and Bob Younger, who take him to the town of Quinto, in what has become known as the Badman's Territory of Oklahoma. There he again comes across Lily, making her living as a saloon hostess. She encourages him to proceed with his plans to stop Fowler, who has been pinning all his own crimes on Clanton. The plans go awry when Curley Ringo sides with Fowler and informs him of an intended raid, and Lily is among those wounded in an ambush—and also reclaimed by her husband and taken back to Breckenridge. Clanton now resorts to his military skill and uses the ex-Confederates for their similar ability. Knowing this, Fowler places men in waiting at various points in the town. All is quiet until the middle of the night, when a stagecoach comes down the main street.

The coach is loaded with dynamite and the men in it throw sticks at the Fowler positions. Clanton and Doc slip off the coach in the darkness and head for Fowler's home. The Confederates keep the Fowler men busy and Clanton makes his way into the house. There the two men fight, ending up on the balcony overlooking

162

the street. Seeing one of the men about to aim at him, Clanton grabs Fowler and swings him around, causing Fowler to take the bullet in the back. Then, with the battle over, Clanton surrenders to the authorities, knowing Lily will wait for him and that the facts will clear him.

Best of the Badmen is a solid piece of western entertainment, typical of its time, a time in which the facts of history were regarded merely as points of departure. What makes this one acceptable is the quality of the acting. For Claire Trevor, who had made her role in *Stagecoach* (1939) so touching, it was a

Robert Ryan and Walter Brennan rob the stage coach.

163

chance to play a somewhat unusual part for a woman in a western, an estranged wife trying to bring down a venal husband. For Robert Preston, that was a role on his actor's path toward increasing screen villany in the postwar years, before hitting his true image as *The Music Man*. But the real value of *Best of the Badmen* is Robert Ryan, for whom an unconvincing role was seemingly impossible. No matter what he played, Ryan was without a flaw and it might be argued that of all American film actors a true appreciation has yet to be made.

Ryan received top billing in only two westerns, this one and *Horizons West* (1952), in which he was directed by Budd Boetticher, although it was far from being one of that remarkable actor's best works. That, too, was a post Civil War story, with Ryan as a man who has enjoyed the danger of battle and who plans a western empire, knowing it will bring him into conflict with the law and his honest brother (Rock Hudson). But Ryan's best work in westerns now came as a supporting actor, as the cunning outlaw goading his captor (James Stewart) in *The Naked Spur* (1953); as yet another would-be empire builder, this time opposed by Clark Gable, in *The Tall Men* (1955); as one of the mercenary adventurers in *The Professionals* (1966); as the cold blooded Ike Clanton in *Hour of the Gun* (1967), trying to murder Wyatt Earp (James Garner); as a gold-hungry deserter in *Custer of the West* (1968); and finally as the outlaw hired to pursue a former colleague in *The Wild Bunch* (1969)—all of them the work of a master actor.

SPRINGFIELD RIFLE

WARNER BROS., 1952

Produced by Louis F. Edelman. Directed by Andre de Toth. Written by Charles Marquis Warren and Frank Davis, based on a story by Sloan Nibley. Photographed in WarnerColor by Edwin Du Par. Music by Max Steiner. 93 minutes.

CAST:

(*Major Alex Kearny*) Gary Cooper; (*Erin Kearny*) Phyllis Thaxter; (*Austin McCool*) David Brian; (*Lt. Col. John Hudson*) Paul Kelly; (*Captain Tennick*) Philip Carey; (*Elm*) Lon Chaney; (*Matthew Quint*) James Millican; (*Olie Larsen*) Martin Milner; (*Sergeant Snow*) Guinn 'Big Boy' Williams; (*Lt. Evans*) Jerry O'Sullivan; (*Pvt. Ferguson*) James Brown; (*Sims*) Jack Woody; (*Mizzell*) Alan Hale, Jr.; (*Cook*) Vince Barnett; (*Jim Randolph*) Fess Parker; (*Colonel Sharpe*) Wilton Graff; (*Sergeant Poole*) Ned Young; (*Corporal Ramsey*) William Fawcett; (*General Halleck*) Richard Hale.

The common denominator in all the many tributes paid Gary Cooper following his death from cancer on May 13, 1961, just six days after his 60th birthday, was the view that he was the American Everyman, an idealization of the way Americans like to see themselves—honest, straightforward, likable and devoid of intellectual conceit. Cooper was quiet and modest and strong. On the legitimate stage, he would probably have been lost, but on film he had a magic presence. John Barrymore once said of him, "He can do, with no effort, what the rest of us spent years trying to learn—to be perfectly natural."

A third of Cooper's 90 films were westerns or dealt with some aspect of frontier life. Despite his quintessential American persona, he was born of English parents, although in a quintessentially American place—Montana, where his father was a state supreme court judge and a part-time rancher. He showed an early flair as an artist, and while attending Grinnell College in Iowa, his cartoons and caricatures started to appear in the school paper and in his hometown paper, the *Helena Independent*. During his summers, he worked on his father's ranch and learned the life of a cowboy, a knowledge that would soon be of great advantage to him. His parents retired to California and,

Gary Cooper—cashiered.

Philip Carey and Wilton Graff conspire with Cooper.

while visiting them in late 1924, he made the decision to stay in the state and find work as a newspaper illustrator. Cooper failed to get any work of that kind but he ran into some Montana friends in Los Angeles and found they were making a living as extras in westerns, getting ten dollars a day for riding around on horses and more if they fell off. Cooper was soon similarly engaged. Years later he said, "On my third picture, a Tom Mix western called *The Lucky Horseshoe,* I saw Mix act and was told he got $17,500 a week. I figured I could do that kind of acting, too."

After a year and a half of riding around in westerns, Cooper was given a small role in Ronald Colman's *The Winning of Barbara Worth.* "Cooper," *Variety* noted, "is a youth who will be heard of on the screen and possibly blossom out as an ace lead." Following a few more supporting roles, he was given the lead in *Arizona Bound* in late 1927, and he was then a star for his remaining 33 years. Under contract to Paramount, he was used in several more westerns, the most memorable being *The Virginian* (1929), and he then developed in a variety of mostly romantic pictures, of which *Morocco* (1930), opposite Marlene Dietrich, was a major winner.

It was Cecil B. DeMille who brought Cooper to the world of the super western, giving him the part of Wild Bill Hickok opposite Jean Arthur's Calamity Jane in *The Plainsman*. With that success, it was obvious there would be more westerns, although Cooper was cautious about typecasting. In 1940, he became *The Westerner* for Samuel Goldwyn, and five years later, when Cooper made his first film as a producer, he played it safe in a cowboy role in *Along Came Jones*. As he grew older, the western identity grew stronger, reaching a note of genuine distinction in 1952 with *High Noon*, for which he won his second Oscar, the first being for *Sergeant York* (1941). Ironically, Gregory Peck turned down *High Noon*, feeling the role was somewhat similar to his previous *The Gunfighter*.

As an aging lawman left to defend himself against a group of vengeful outlaws and virtually deserted by the frightened townspeople, Cooper was poignant and painful. The film was hugely successful but it did not pass without some criticism from the western traditionalists. John Wayne, in particular, felt that the townspeople's cowardice was not an accurate depiction of the true West and that far too much socio-political comment was being made on contemporary America. No such criti-

167

cism could be leveled at *Springfield Rifle,* the western Cooper chose to make immediately after. It was set in an era that had always paid off well for Hollywood—the western sector of the Civil War.

In *Springfield Rifle,* Cooper is Major Alex Kearny of the Army's newly formed military intelligence service and an officer who believes that counterespionage is needed to solve the problems faced by the Army in its failure to ship horses from the West. All efforts in 1864 to obtain sufficient horses have failed because raiders and Confederate sympathizers have intercepted every herd on its way to railroad shipment at Fort Hedley. A similar fate is about to rob Kearny of a herd under his command; surrounded by bandits in mountainous, snow-covered country, Kearny informs his second in command, Captain Tennick (Philip Carey), that he intends to give up without a fight. Back at the fort, Tennick places charges of cowardice against Kearny in his report to the commandant, Lt. Col. John Hudson (Paul Kelly), who initiates a court martial, at which Kearny is stripped of rank and drummed out. Tennick taunts him, causing a fight (witnessed by many), but it is all a ruse. Kearny proceeds to a meeting of those who are involved in supporting the Union cause and Tennick is among them, and explains the tactics he will take to find out how and why the horses are being lost. Later, told by Hudson that his wife Erin (Phyllis Thaxter) has arrived, Kearny goes to a hotel to meet her and tell her he cannot do as she wishes and return East, although she begs him and pleads that their son needs his attention. She cannot understand his decision to remain after the disgrace and he cannot tell her why.

Hudson makes a deal with rancher Austin McCool (David Brian) for all the horses he can supply and Tennick is given command of the shipment. Tennick fails in the assignment and once back at the fort he is treated with contempt by Kearny, provoking a fight that ends with the latter being thrown in the guardhouse. There he makes plans for escape with Mizzell (Alan Hale, Jr.) and Sims (Jack Woody), the two men Tennick has captured and brought in. After breaking out, Kearny finds that McCool has been doubling dealing, accepting Union money and then having his men raid the herds and sell them to the Confederates. Kearny joins Mc-Cool, pretending to be an angry turncoat but at the same reporting to his Union associates, and they agree that McCool must be killed during the next raid. Tennick leads the next shipment and, though mortally wounded when it is attacked, manages to kill McCool.

After McCool's death, the raiders think it best to disband but Kearny persuades them otherwise, saying he will take over, necessitating making contract with the man in charge of the Confederate rustling operation. To Kearny's astonishment, this turns out to be

Hudson, who has never resigned his Union Army rank even though a dedicated southerner. The two decide to work together, with Kearny reporting the situation to his superior, Colonel Sharpe (Wilton Graff), and learning that his runaway son has been found. He tells his Erin, who mentions it to Hudson, a longtime family friend. Hudson now realizes the situation and arrests Kearny as a southern spy, with a death sentence to be carried out the following morning. Sergeant Snow (Guinn 'Big Boy' Williams), aware of Kearny's actual status, arranges for his escape. Hudson realizes it is time for him to flee on his own, and joins the bandits who are about to stage another raid. This time, the bandits are unsuccessful because Kearny has armed the soldiers with the new, quick-firing, repeating Springfield rifle, allowing for greater speed and accuracy. Hudson rides off but Kearny catches up with him and brings him in to be court-martialed. At a ceremony at the fort some time later, General Halleck (Richard

Springfield Rifle was far from being the last Gary Cooper western, although the next three, *Blowing Wild* (1953), *Garden of Evil* (1954) and *Vera Cruz* (1954) would all be set in Mexico. There would be three more after that. *Man of the West* (1958), doubtlessly the most brutal of all his western pictures, *The Hanging Tree* (1959) and *They Came to Cordura* (1959), in which he seemed more tired and older than his years. He was in fact a dying man, although unaware. His doctors kept the presence of cancer away from him until near the end. With his death, an Italian newspaper, *Corriere Della Sera,* made a good point: "Perhaps with him there is ended a certain America . . . that of the frontier and of innocence which had or was believed to have an exact sense of the dividing line between good and evil."

Hale) commends the now reinstated Kearny on his use of counterintelligence and on proving the worth of the new rifle.

Springfield Rifle, filmed by Warners in the California Sierras partly in the wintertime, is a handsome western with an interesting Civil War twist. Its main strength is the dignified Cooper, playing a dedicated officer subjected to humiliations but rising above them. But the more difficult role is that of the traitorous Hudson, played with quiet skill by Paul Kelly. Hudson is a desperate man but not a true villain, simply a man serving a cause as he sees fit. Kearny's cat-and-mouse scenes with Hudson are superbly played, a credit to director Andre de Toth. The Hungarian-born de Toth was a tough, unsentimental director, whose westerns often dealt with unstable, treacherous human relationships. *Ramrod* (1947) is a case in point, as are *Man in the Saddle* (1951) and *The Stranger Wore a Gun* (1953), both with Randolph Scott.

Gary Cooper and Paul Kelly.

169

MAN WITHOUT A STAR

UNIVERSAL, 1955

Produced by Aaron Rosenberg. Directed by King Vidor. Written by Borden Chase and D. D. Beauchamp, based on the novel by Dee Linford. Photographed in Technicolor by Russell Metty. Music by Joseph Gershenson. 89 minutes.

CAST:

(*Dempsey Rae*) Kirk Douglas; (*Reed Bowman*) Jeanne Crain; (*Idonee*) Claire Trevor; (*Jeff Jimson*) William Campbell; (*Steve Miles*) Richard Boone; (*Strap Davis*) Jay C. Flippen; (*Tess Cassidy*) Myrna Hansen; (*Moccasin Mary*) Mara Corday; (*Tom Cassidy*) Eddy C. Waller; (*Latigo*) Sheb Wooley; (*Tom Carter*) George Wallace; (*Little Waco*) Frank Chase; (*Mark Tolliver*) Paul Birch; (*Sheriff Olson*) Roy Barcroft; (*Cookie*) William Phillips.

It took a while for Kirk Douglas to feel at home in the movie West. In his first western, Raoul Walsh's *Along the Great Divide* (1951), he still seemed like an easterner serving a western apprenticeship. However, by now the forceful Douglas screen persona had gelled—he had been the ambitious, driving boxer of

Champion, the compulsive musician of *Young Man With a Horn* and the heartless newspaperman of *Ace in the Hole.* No one expected Kirk Douglas to play a wimp. With *The Big Trees* and *The Big Sky,* both released in 1952, he cut deeper into his western claim, in the former as a hard timber baron and in the latter as a tough frontiersman. By 1955, he was ready to play a westerner with absolute conviction, and with Douglas, being convincing has always been a passion. Universal signed him to do *Man Without a Star,* which happily brought him into contact with a master director, King Vidor.

Vidor made his first western in 1930, *Billy the Kid,* which he filmed in Lincoln County, New Mexico, the site of the conflict between the Kid and Sheriff Pat Garrett, and in which he used young Johnny Mack Brown in the title role. Six years later, he did the rollicking *The Texas Rangers,* with a big Paramount budget, and then in 1939, MGM put him in command of their expensive attempt to capture Kenneth Roberts' *Northwest Passage* on film. The attempt may have fallen short of the mark but Vidor put enormous effort and skill into the spectacular location sequences. More of the same was required when David O. Selnick hired him to direct *Duel in the Sun,* the legendary producer's bid to make a western *Gone With the Wind,* which would also fall short of the mark and cause Vidor to several times walk away in exasperation with his interfering boss. Be that as it may, some of the action sequences in *Duel in the Sun,* particularly cattle baron Lionel Barrymore's rounding up of all his cowboys to try to stop the railroad, are among the finest ever filmed. With *Man Without a Star,* Vidor did not have the budget or the scope but his shots of cattle stampedes are the work of a master film craftsman.

Man Without a Star touches upon an aspect of western history rarely seen in Hollywood's account of the West, the fact that many of the biggest ranches were run by owners who lived in the East, as well as in England and Europe. These absentee owners allowed managers and foremen to run their spreads, often with

Jeanne Crain and Kirk Douglas.

171

few questions asked. By the 1890s the open range factor had become a major contention, causing smaller ranchers to used barbed wire to mark their property lines. And barbed wire is what this film is about, especially its disturbing meaning for the main character, a charming drifter and rugged individualist named Dempsey Rae (Douglas).

Dempsey is a Texas cowpoke on his way north, a carefree man always looking for new horizons. Riding a railroad boxcar, he strikes up a friendship with a young farmhand, Jeff Jimson (William Campbell), who has a hankering to be a cowboy. The men are riding illegally, along with a group of others, and a guard is knifed as he tries to throw them off. When the trail pulls into a

William Campbell,
Kirk Douglas and
Jeanne Crain.

station, Sheriff Olson (Roy Barcroft) arrests Jeff, who had been seen to scuffle with the guard, but Dempsey points out the real killer and picks up a reward of 50 dollars, which he splits with Jeff. In town, Dempsey meets an old friend, Idonee (Claire Trevor), who runs a bordello, and the two celebrate their reunion in the saloon. Jeff, now duded up in flashy western clothes, is jeered at and goaded into a gunfight, again running afoul of Sheriff Olson but released when ranch foreman Strap Davis (Jay C. Flippen) backs up Dempsey's claim that Jeff acted in self defense.

Strap offers Dempsey and Jeff jobs on the Triangle Ranch, which is owned by someone back East named Reed Bowman. But the owner shows up and the hands

173

Kirk Douglas—quick-draw banjo player. Leaning on the piano is Claire Trevor—leaning on the bar is Jay C. Flippen.

The humiliating beating.

are surprised to find Reed Bowman is a beautiful woman (Jeanne Crain). The cheeky Dempsey tries to charm her, angering top hand Latigo (Sheb Wooley), who tries to assert his superiority by getting rid of Dempsey. Instead, Dempsey beats him senseless and wins the top hand job for himself. Reed does not spurn Dempsey's amorous advances and for a time he imagines he has found the perfect job. In the meantime, he coaches Jeff in the crafts of the cowboy and dazzles the impresionable lad with his dexterity with a gun. Dempsey quick draws, twirls the pistol, flips it in and out of his holster and back and forth over his elbows. Then he tells Jeff, "That's all hogwash. What matters is that you get the gun out and point it."

176

Dempsey's idyl comes to an end when he realizes that Reed has no interest in ranching, that she has no concern for the other ranchers on whose ground she allows her cattle to graze, and that it is simply her intention to make a killing and get out. She offers to make Dempsey foreman but he declines and walks out. When she asks, "What about your pay?" he looks at her and replies with contempt, "I've had it." The footloose Dempsey is a man with his own code of conduct. She replaces him with another Texan, Steve Miles (Richard Boone), whom Dempsey knows to be tough and unscrupulous, "Steve Miles is your kind of man—he'll do your killing for you."

After enjoying himself in the saloon and announcing

177

his intention to drift on, Dempsey is severely beaten in the street by Miles and his men, who rope him and leave him tied up. Humiliated, Dempsey now decides to help the opposition. He joins the smaller ranchers, led by Tom Cassidy (Eddy C. Waller), in helping them string barbed wire fences across their properties to keep out the Bowman cattle. This is traumatic for Dempsey, who has a fear of barbed wire, having been once dragged through it and badly scarred. But he knows it has to be done. Miles' solution is to stampede large herds of cattle at the fences, what he calls "Texas style." Dempsey's tactic is to deploy his cowboys and turn the herds, causing many of Miles' men to be killed. When he catches up with Miles, the two men fight savagely and Dempsey leaves him hanging on the barbed wire fence.

The ranchers offer Dempsey a place of his own if he will stay but he declines. He is a drifter by nature, a man who has yet to find a star to follow, a happy wanderer who feels he must move further and further west in order to escape the fences. When Jeff asks if he can come along, Dempsey refuses. He is a loner and

Retribution—Kirk thrashes Richard Boone.

he tells his young friend to stay and settle down. And off he drifts into a hazy future.

The theme of *Man Without a Star* is the gradual disappearance of freedom in the West, as ranching settled down to organized business, requiring the fencing off of investments. The kind of loner played by Douglas, admirable as he might be, was on the way out, as was the kind of ranch owner played by Crain. The film is an unusual one in having its lovely co-star as a lady who loses both the game of sex and her ambition to run a ranch with no regard for others. In no other western has a beautiful woman of property offered herself so blatantly and in no other has the hero walked away from it all so disgustedly. He may be a man without a star but not without ethics. (Fourteen years later, Universal remade the film as *A Man Called Gannon,* with Tony Franciosa in the lead.)

His success with *Man Without a Star* now opened up the film West for Kirk Douglas. He immediately followed it with *The Indian Fighter,* the maiden film of his own Bryna Productions, playing a frontier scout in the Oregon of 1870. In 1957, Douglas went west again,

this time as the legendary Doc Holliday, playing opposite the Wyatt Earp of Burt Lancaster in *Gunfight at the O. K. Corral,* a solid winner at the box office corrals. Producer Hal B. Wallis and director John Sturges managed to get Douglas back two years later for *Last Train From Gun Hill,* in which the actor trod more unusual western turf as a white man with an Indian wife. In *The Last Sunset* (1961), he became almost incestuous by falling in love with a young girl he did not know to be his daughter.

The theme of the West's transition was never more poignantly touched upon than with Douglas in *Lonely Are the Brave* (1962), set in modern times and dealing with a cowboy who cannot adjust. Like Dempsey Rae, the Jack Burns of this film is a man trying to live by his own standards, in fact he might well be Dempsey Rae several generations later. Burns tries not to buckle down to civilization but is eventually beaten by it, dying when he and his horse are knocked over by a truck as they cross a highway at night. *Man Without a Star* and *Lonely Are the Brave*—two high points in the career of an actor-producer who is himself a maverick. Like the heroes of these two films, Douglas is a man who has yet to knuckle under to any system.

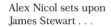
Alex Nicol sets upon
James Stewart . . .

THE MAN FROM LARAMIE

COLUMBIA, 1955

Produced by William Goetz. Directed by Anthony Mann. Written by Philip Yordan and Frank Burt, based on a story by Thomas T. Flynn. Photographed in Technicolor by Charles Lang. Music by George Duning. 101 minutes.

CAST:

(*Will Lockhart*) James Stewart; (*Vic Hansboro*) Arthur Kennedy; (*Alec Waggoman*) Donald Crisp; (*Barbara Waggoman*) Cathy O'Donnell; (*Dave Waggoman*) Alex Nicol; (*Kate Canadray*) Aline MacMahon; (*Charley O'Leary*) Wallace Ford; (*Chris Bolt*) Jack Elam; (*Frank Darrah*) John War Eagle; (*Tom Quigby*) James Millican; (*Fritz*) Greg Barton; (*Spud Oxton*) Boyd Stockman; (*Padre*) Frank de Kova.

Despite the esteem in which it is now held, Frank Capra's *It's a Wonderful Life* was not a great success when it first appeared at the end of 1946 and it left James Stewart wondering about being able to recapture the popularity he had enjoyed before going off to war for five years. The charmingly awkward, gangling persona with which he had made his name now seemed passé. He needed a change of image. The first director to spot Stewart as a more subtle and complex actor than he seemed was Anthony Mann, who in 1949 hired him to play the driven Lin McAdam in Universal's *Winchester '73*. With this tough western, Stewart established his ability to display anger, neurosis and ferocity, underneath a mostly calm exterior. It began an association with Mann that resulted in seven more films together, four of them westerns and forming of body of work that is among the best achieved in the genre. As an actor-director relationship in westerns, it ranks second only to that of John Wayne and John Ford. (Tyrone Power and Henry King made 10 films together, but only one western.)

The second Stewart-Mann western was Universal's *Bend of the River* (1952), which again presented the actor as a quiet man with an edginess about him, one who erupts in rage if leaned upon too heavily. This persona was even more sharp the following year with MGM's *The Naked Spur*, in which Stewart played a vengeful bounty hunter, desperate to earn money and

. . . and beats him and drags him through a campfire. The old fellow looking on is Wallace Ford.

regain the property out of which he has been cheated. *The Far Country* (1955) presented a less complex Stewart, as a hard-bitten cowboy with his own interest at heart, but with *The Man From Laramie,* Mann brought the actor back to bitter vengeance. Mann had often spoken of his interest in doing a western version of *King Lear* and his *Laramie* is a bold step in that Shakespearean direction, particularly so in having Donald Crisp as a Lear-like cattle baron whose ambitions bring about his death. His Alec Waggoman rules over a section of New Mexico as if it were a feudal kingdom, his one weakness being his smothering love for his wayward son Dave (Alex Nicol).

Into this kingdom rides a man from Laramie, Wyoming, Will Lockhart (Stewart), who poses as a freighter but who is actually an Army officer seeking those who sold guns to the Indians and indirectly caused the death of his younger brother, also an Army officer. En route he stops at the site of the massacre and muses on the scene, wondering how his brother might have died. In the county town of Coronado, he meets Barbara Waggoman (Cathy O'Donnell), a niece of Alec Waggoman, whom Lockhart rightly sums up as being the dominant man in the area. After unloading his merchandise, Lockhart rides out for more supplies and stops on some salt flats, assuming them to be open ground. He is attacked by Dave and his henchmen, who shoot Lockhart's mules, burn his wagon and brutally beat him. When he asks the identity of his assailants, the hot-headed Dave points to a horse brand and tells him it is all he needs to know. Dave, a cheerful sadist, rides off with his men, leaving the exhausted Lockhart, who is saved from death by Vic Hansboro (Arthur Kennedy), Waggoman's foreman and foster son.

Back in town, Lockhart again meets Hansboro and finds him friendly. He next meets old Waggoman himself, who offers to compensate him for his losses but advises him to get out of town. The wealthy land baron is a civilized, educated man but guarded about any intrusion in his little empire. Lockhart declines the advice, partly because he finds Barbara appealing but mostly due to a job offer by rancher Kate Canaday (Aline MacMahon), which enables him to stay in the area while seeking to avenge his brother's killing. Lockhart's friendship with Hansboro becomes strained when Hansboro realizes that because of the vicious Dave he is not likely to get his share of the empire when the old man dies. Hansboro becomes increasingly surly and is no longer friendly toward anyone. Even though he knows his son is a weakling, Waggoman names Dave as his sole inheritor, and Hansboro's disgust increases when he witnesses a gunfight between Dave and Lockhart. Lockhart gets the best of the younger man one on one but is punished when Dave has some of his men pin Lockhart down while he pumps a bullet into the stranger's right hand. In agony Lockhart screams, "You scum!"

When Lockhart recovers from the wound, he pursues his investigation even more heatedly. However, it is old man Waggoman himself who discovers that it was Dave and Hansboro who sold guns to the Indians. When he faces Hansboro with the facts, the embittered foster son forces the old man off a cliff and leaves him for dead. He lives long enough to tell Lockhart, who finds him lying in a gully, all he knows about the sins committed by his sons, who are about to face each other in hatred. Hansboro kills Dave in the showdown and tries unsuccessfully to pin the blame on Lockhart, who tracks him down and kills him in a shootout.

By 1955 standards, *The Man From Laramie* was a

James Stewart thrashes Arthur Kennedy, and Aline MacMahon keeps Alex Nicol covered.

183

notably brutal western. Nothing quite so severe as the torture of Stewart or his being dragged by a villain on horseback had been seen in such a film. In terms of life in the Old West, shooting a man in the hand and incapacitating him was almost like castration. It is a film with many fine performances, particularly those by Stewart, by the ever reliable Arthur Kennedy as a scalawag not entirely without compassion, and by the then 73-year-old Scotsman, Donald Crisp, as the hard landowner, blinded by the love of a psychotic son. His is an almost Shakespearean character—an old man, gradually going blind, who in the end tries to atone for his sins by telling the truth. In one scene, Crisp tells Stewart about his nightmares, and it is a memorable piece of acting by an actor who had by that time been in films for 40 years.

Cathy O'Donnell, Arthur Kennedy, Frank de Kova and James Stewart.

Donald Crisp and James Stewart.

The primary credit for the film belongs to Anthony Mann, who took his cast and crew to New Mexico and filmed on various locations within a hundred miles of Santa Fe. As with all 11 of his westerns, Mann used his landscapes to sharpen his dramatic points, characterizations and action. Few directors did this more effec-tively than Mann, for whom *Laramie* would unfortunately be the final collaboration with Stewart. The two men had planned to make another western together, *Night Passage* in 1957, but Mann backed off, claiming the script by Borden Chase, with whom he had worked on *Winchester '73, Bend of the River* and *The Far*

Arthur Kennedy and James Stewart.

Country was below the standards they had set. Mann turned instead to *The Tin Star,* which had a fine script by Dudley Nichols and starred Henry Fonda as one of a number of ambiguous men in conflict—the kind of dramatic situation Mann looked for. Stewart stubbornly decided to go ahead with *Night Passage* and gave photographer James Neilson his first crack at being a director. The film did only moderate business, proving Mann's instincts to be correct but sadly causing a rift with Stewart. Aside from their five westerns they also had made *Thunder Bay* (1953), *The Glenn Miller Story* (1954) and *Strategic Air Command* (1955), adding up to one of Hollywood's most successful star-director collaborations.

Despite their professional estrangement, Mann never stopped paying tribute to Stewart as an intensely dedicated actor who worked hard to make their westerns as realistic as possible. According to Mann, Stewart was willing to subject himself to hard and rough work. In *Laramie,* he rode his horse down a steep slope and allowed himself to be nearly trampled under the hooves of horses during a brawl, as well as being dragged through a camp fire. Stewart considered all this as part of the job of giving a credible performance, an attitude that made him one of the most important actors in westerns. John Wayne, Joel McCrea and Randolph Scott were all superb movie westerners but none had Stewart's dramatic range.

The Man From Laramie was Stewart's last major western starring vehicle but far from his last work in the genre. In 1961 no less than the master himself, John Ford, called the actor back to the saddle with *Two Rode Together,* as a crusty, venal sheriff, immediately followed by the masterly *The Man Who Shot Liberty Valance,* as an idealistic lawyer-politician in a film that centered on the melancholy gunman played by John Wayne. For Ford, Stewart did a humorous cameo as Wyatt Earp in *Cheyenne Autumn* (1964). Then he was the tough patriarch in the Civil War *Shenandoah* (1965), a battered old cowboy in *The Rare Breed* (1966), a village sheriff in *Firecreek* (1968), an outlaw in *Bandolero!* (1968), an aging cowpoke who inherits a brothel in *The Cheyenne Social Club* (1970) and finally the doctor who tells John Wayne he has little time left in *The Shootist* (1976). The easterner who spent his first dozen years playing mostly affable, idealistic young men in business suits ended up with one of the best western portfolios of any film actor—thanks to a transition largely brought about by Anthony Mann.

A MAN ALONE

REPUBLIC, 1955

Produced by Herbert J. Yates. Directed by Ray Milland. Written by John Tucker Battle, based on a story by Mort Briskin. Photographed in TruColor by Lionel Lindon. Music by Victor Young. 96 minutes.

CAST:

(*Wes Steele*) Ray Milland; (*Nadine Corrigan*) Mary Murphy; (*Gil Corrigan*) Ward Bond; (*Stanley*) Raymond Burr; (*Dr. Mason*) Arthur Space; (*Clantin*) Lee Van Cleef; (*Anderson*) Alan Hale, Jr.; (*Slocum*) Douglas Spencer; (*Maybanks*) Thomas B. Henry; (*Luke Joyner*) Grandon Rhodes; (*Ortega*) Martin Garralaga; (*Sam Hall*) Kim Spaulding; (*Wilson*) Howard J. Negley; (*Tio Rubio*) Julian Rivero; (*Higgs*) Lee Roberts; (*Mrs. Maule*) Minerva Urecal; (*Roy*) Thorpe Whiteman; (*Kincaid*) Dick Rich; (*Dorfman*) Frank Hagney.

Ray Milland was a classy Welshman whose real name was Reginald Truscott-Jones. He first made a name for himself in the movies as a debonair leading man in romantic fare. With a fine speaking voice that was well paced in mid-Atlantic, he hardly seemed like an actor who would ever appear in westerns—except for two things. First, he spent three of his early years in the elite Royal Horse Guards of the Household Cavalry, and second, he became one of the British Army's top marksmen during that time. Milland was 26 when he arrived in Hollywood in 1931, following his appearances in a few British pictures. He made a nice living with his dapper image but gradually grew tired of the lightness of his material and sought stronger roles. In 1945, he won an Oscar as the pitiful alcoholic of *The Lost Weekend*, after which he was better able to manage the course of his career, that included a hankering to do westerns.

The 1946 Paramount outdoor epic, *California*, gave Milland his first chance to ride the Hollywood range, as a soldier of fortune in the period before the territory became a state in 1850, challenging those trying to keep it an independent province for their own ambitions. *Copper Canyon* (1950) was his next trip West, as a southern gentleman involved in the Union-Confederacy conflict during the Civil War and the attempts of both sides to gain control of copper supplies. Milland later admitted *Copper Canyon* was not a film he enjoyed making, mostly because he disliked working with Hedy Lamarr. In 1952, he starred in something more to his taste, playing a cashiered cavalry officer in *Bugles in the Afternoon,* bent on settling the score with the brother officer who brought about his disgrace.

Milland starred in only one more western, by far his best, and one which he directed himself. He may have reasoned that had he failed with *A Man Alone,* his attempt at direction might not have been as conspicuous as with a non-western. Fortunately, the film brought him good critical comment and he went on to direct several other films and a good amount of television. The lone man of this unusual western is Wesley Steele, a middle-aged gunslinger of some repute, who is on his way to nowhere in particular. He rides through a windstorm in the desert and has to destroy his horse when it stumbles and breaks its leg. He trudges along and comes across an abandoned stagecoach, its driver and four passengers dead. The blasted lock on a strongbox points to robbery. Steele unharnesses the four horses,

Alan Hale, Jr. and Ray Milland.

sets three loose and mounts one for himself. The three horses gallop back to the point from which they started, the town of Mesa, arriving in the middle of the stormy night and puzzling the men playing cards in the saloon. One of them is Deputy Sheriff Anderson (Alan Hale, Jr.), who goes outside and spots Steele arriving on the other horse. He creeps up on the dismounted Steele, but Steele senses his presence, turns and shoots the deputy, lightly wounding him. The men in the saloon come out, see what has happened, and go after Steele, who eludes them by stepping into a business building.

As he waits in the dark, Steele overhears a conversation in the next room. A group of men are reporting to a businessman named Stanley (Raymond Burr) about the stagecoach robbery and the haul of $63,000. Stanley's partner, Luke Joyner (Grandon Rhodes), tries to disassociate himself from the robbery and killings, whereupon Stanley shoots him down. Steele accidently makes a noise and the men come after him. He escapes into a cellar but when Stanley is told of the wounding of the deputy and the arrival of the gunman on one of the stagecoach horses, he says, "He couldn't have come at a better time," and schemes to pin the stagecoach massacre on Steele.

Mary Murphy and Ray Milland.

Ward Bond being dragged out to be hanged.

In the morning, Steele discovers that a beautiful young girl, Nadine Corrigan (Mary Murphy), has come down to attend to her cat and ruminate over the things in her hope chest. Steele stays hidden, but in trying to sneak out of the house, is spotted by Nadine. He is surprised that she recognizes his name, until she tells him she is the sheriff's daughter and familiar with the resumés of wanted men. Steele has another surprise coming—her father, Gil Corrigan (Ward Bond), has yellow fever and the house is under quarantine. Having some knowledge of yellow fever, Steele helps Nadine nurse her father and tells her of his life and how tired he is with his notoriety. "A reputation can get to be too big to live with."

Steele leaves the house to escape problems his staying will cause for the now sympathetic Nadine and makes his way to the church, where Stanley is eulogizing the people whose deaths he has caused. Standing alone, staring at the coffins, Stanley becomes aware of someone in the shadows. "Who are you?" "I'm the man you're looking for." The frightened Stanley offers to let him escape but Steele refuses. In the fight that ensues, Steele believes he has beaten Stanley to death. In leaving the church, he is shot by one of Stanley's men and makes his way back to Nadine. When the men come for Steele, she refuses to give him up and shoots one who tries to enter. She calls for a doctor (Arthur Space), who promises not to hand over Steele to a mob and assumes that the now-recovered Sheriff Corrigan will handle the matter.

Corrigan is now faced with several problems—holding off a mob, accepting the fact that his daughter has fallen in love with an outlaw, and being told by her that he himself is a crook. Nadine has examined the family accounts and realizes that her father has much more money stashed away than his salary would have provided. He has been taking money from Stanley, which he justifies because of having lost his wife when Nadine was a baby and also having lost his herds to drought. "This is hard country. I had to sit there and watch her die . . . I didn't want that for you. Back East, they all talk about how wonderful the West is . . . how a man can get rich overnight. Folks who tell you that have never seen the West, at least they've never seen what I've seen. I had to live. You were only two when your mother died. I promised myself right then that you'd never know a hungry day or a cold night. So far, I've kept that promise."

To win over his daughter, Corrigan gives Steele his gun and tells him he is free to leave. He escorts Steele out of town and points to a trail by which he can make his way with little detection. When the townspeople learn of this, they come to try to lynch their sheriff. The doctor unsuccessfully appeals to Stanley to intercede but is told that the sheriff appears to be in cahoots

Ward Bond, Mary Murphy and Ray Milland.

with Steele. As Corrigan is about to be hanged, Steele appears, pulls a gun, warns the crowd to stop, and calls on Stanley to admit that he is the man behind the massacre. Stanley refuses but one of his men, fed up with his venal boss' actions, runs into the street and yells to the crowd that what Steele has said is true. Stanley guns him down but is then overpowered by the townspeople.

Partly vindicated by helping to bring Stanley to justice but humiliated by his own part in it, Corrigan tells

194

his daughter she is free to leave town with Steele. "There's no life for you here, this is a rotten town. Wherever he takes you has got to be better than this." Replies Steele, "She's not going anywhere with me because I'm not leaving. Who knows if this place is any worse than the next one I'd hit? From the way things look now, it's got a good chance of being better."

A Man Alone is a modestly-scaled western, much more an interior work than an exterior one, and a credit to Ray Milland. His Wes Steele is yet another infamous gunman trying to escape the past, but the characterization of that of a man of some intelligence and a possible background of some class. As producer, director and star, Milland could easily have gone wrong had he tried to be pretentious. Instead, the style is straightforward, with no artistic indulgences in telling a story of somewhat complicated morality. The scene in which Ward Bond as the sheriff justifies his compromises with the law is touching and plausible, made more so by an actor who mostly stood as a bastion of western values.

THE TALL T

COLUMBIA, 1957

Produced by Harry Joe Brown. Directed by Budd Boetticher. Written by Burt Kennedy, based on a story by Elmore Leonard. Photographed in Technicolor by Charles Lawton, Jr. Music by Heinz Roemheld. 77 minutes.

CAST:

(*Pat Brennan*) Randolph Scott; (*Frank Usher*) Richard Boone; (*Doretta Mims*) Maureen O'Sullivan; (*Ed Rintoon*) Arthur Hunnicutt; (*Billy Jack*) Skip Homeier; (*Chink*) Henry Silva; (*Willard Mims*) John Hubbard; (*Tenvoorde*) Richard Burton; (*Jace*) Robert Anderson; (*Hank Parker*) Fred E. Sherman; (*Jeff*) Chris Olsen.

Randolph Scott, the most astute businessman ever to become a film actor, made a decision in 1948—to go West and stay there. After *Albuquerque,* released in February of that year, his next 34 films, made in the remaining 14 years of his career, were westerns, with most of them involving him as producer as well as star. Well aware of the boundaries of his talent, he said, "I believe in letting well enough alone. I'm not looking for new fields to conquer." Scott formed two production companies, one with Nat Holt and the other with Harry Joe Brown, and most of his films between 1948 and 1962 were produced by either one or the other, with Scott very much concerned about the choice of material. These films form the strongest body of work in westerns to be achieved by any one actor, and seven of them, directed by Budd Boetticher, form a particularly interesting chapter in the annals of western film.

Boetticher's career is an odd one. The strength of his talent would indicate a man who might have become a major director rather than the cult figure he became. After making *Comanche Station* in 1960, his seventh film with Scott, he disappeared for eight years and then emerged with a film he had made about bullfighting in Mexico, *Arruza,* the sport being the major fascination of his life. Subsequently, he directed *A Time for Dying* for producer Audie Murphy, a film released after Murphy's death. Little has been heard of Boetticher since then. Born in Chicago in 1916, Boetticher initially went to Mexico to recover from football injuries sustained in

196

Randolph Scott, Maureen O'Sullivan and John Hubbard.

college and decided to become a matador. His first job in Hollywood was as an advisor on the Tyrone Power bullfight picture, *Blood and Sand* (1941), after which he became an assistant director, graduating to full director in 1944. Seven years later, with the blessing of producer John Wayne, he finally got the chance to make a movie about his passion, *The Bullfighter and the Lady,* starring Robert Stack as a Boetticher-like American enthralled with the bullring. In 1955, Boetticher came up with an even more impressive treatment of his theme, *The Magnificent Matador,* with Anthony Quinn. Boetticher's first western was *The Cimarron Kid* (1951), with Audie Murphy, followed by half a dozen others, of which the best is *The Man From the Alamo* (1953), with Glenn Ford.

In 1956, Boetticher was hired by John Wayne to direct him in *Seven Men From Now,* to be made by Wayne's company, Batjac. Wayne at the time was tied up with John Ford on *The Searchers,* the production of which lasted longer than expected, and after that he was further committed to Ford to make *The Wings of Eagles.* Wayne was not about to pull away from patriarch Ford even for his own company and asked Randolph Scott if he would like to take over the role in

Richard Boone and Randolph Scott.

197

Skip Homeier, Henry Silva, Randolph Scott and Richard Boone.

Seven Men From Now. One reading of the Burt Kennedy script was enough for Scott to make up his mind, and after filming it, he was determined to hire Boetticher and Kennedy for his own company to make *The Tall T.*

All seven of the Scott-Boetticher westerns are notable for tight, compact structure, with none of them running more than 77 minutes. The style in each case is that of *machismo,* a masculine sense of pride and honor that has both strengths and weaknesses, and is obviously a style affected by Boetticher's love of the bullring. There is a core of fatality, morality and serenity in these films that sets them apart from anything else accomplished with the western film. In each, Scott is an unbending figure, best summarized by Kennedy's line, "There are some things a man just can't ride around," or as his ex-boss says about him in *The Tall T,* "A man can turn his back when you're around."

In *Seven Men From Now,* Scott is Ben Stride, out to avenge the killing of his wife. In *The Tall T* he is Pat Brennan, a man who has left his job as the ramrod of a big ranch to strike out on his own. Running a place all by himself, he needs a seed bull to start a herd and he gambles his horse in a contest to win the bull. He loses and has to walk back to his ranch. On the way, he is

198

Henry Silva, Richard Boone, Randolph Scott and Maureen
O'Sullivan.

given a lift by his old friend, Rintoon (Arthur Hunnicutt), who operates a stagecoach. The coach has been chartered by Willard Mims (John Hubbard), who is taking his bride, Doretta (Maureen O'Sullivan), on a trip. Rintoon has a low opinion of Mims, who has married Doretta for the family fortune. As the coach pulls into a relay station, three outlaws, led by Frank Usher (Richard Boone), assume it to be the regular mail coach.

Usher and his vicious young thugs, Chink (Henry Silva) and Billy Jack (Skip Homeier), have killed the two station men and dumped their bodies down a well. When Rintoon reaches for his gun, they kill him too and order Brennan to do the same with the body. He refuses, saying it is not a fit ending for such a man.

Mims quickly reveals his cowardice by volunteering that his wife is the daughter of a rich man, who will surely pay a handsome reward for her return. Usher tells him to proceed with Chink and return with $50,000. Keeping Brennan and Doretta as hostages, Usher fixes a point in the desert as a rendezvous. While the others are gone, Usher tells Brennan he admires the kind of man he is and that he rides with his young gunmen only because he must. When Mims returns to report that the money will be waiting for Usher at a certain point, he shows no interest in the welfare of his wife and accepts Usher's offer to leave, but gets only a short distance before the contemptuous Usher has Chink gun him down.

When Usher leaves, Brennan comforts Doretta in the

Randolph Scott and Maureen O'Sullivan.

cave in which they have been placed and assures her that her husband is no loss. He advises Chink that his boss is not to be trusted and that he had best ride after Usher to make sure he returns. Brennan then instructs Doretta to entice the sexually repressed Billy Jack into her presence by unbuttoning her blouse. Thus distracted Billy Jack is overpowered and killed by Brennan. Hearing the shot, Chink rides back, where further maneuvering by Brennan and Doretta bring about his end. When Usher returns with the money, Brennan easily gets the drop on him from behind but Usher refuses to turn around to face him, confident that he will not be shot in the back. Dropping the money, Usher proceeds to his horse and slowly rides off, but when he gets a distance away, he stops to make a decision. For his own sense of pride, he must either kill Brennan or die in the attempt. He turns, draws his rifle and charges toward Brennan, who shoots him out of the saddle. Brennan puts his arm around Doretta, "It's all over. Come on now, it's gonna be a nice day."

The Tall T is as free from padding as a marble statue. It is a straightforward treatise about the difference between pride and honor, and the necessity of making choices. The hero and the villain are, as in all the Boetticher pictures, men of strength and courage, and differing mainly because one is guided by morality and the other is not. With Scott and Boone, he could not have had finer personifications. Scott by this time in his life appeared like a man chiseled from the granite of a mesa and Boone was an actor of subtle craft, one who specialized in complex characters. The success of working with Boetticher on this film was not lost on the shrewd Scott, who after fulfilling a commitment to Warners to do *Shoot-Out at Medicine Bend,* contracted Boetticher to direct him in *Decision at Sundown* and the several other westerns with which Scott decided to conclude his career.

In *Decision at Sundown* (1957), Scott is Bart Allison, in pursuit of the man who had an affair with his wife and caused her suicide. In *Buchanan Rides Alone* (1958), he is the title character, riding into Agrytown and finding it dominated by a single corrupt family, which almost costs him his life. In *Ride Lonesome* (1959), Scott is Ben Brigade, another man seeking vengence for the murder of his wife, and in *Westbound* (1959), he is John Hayes, a Union cavalry officer engaged in shipping gold from the West to finance the war against the Confederacy. In the last of his films with Boetticher, *Comanche Station* (1960), Scott is Jefferson Cody, hired by a rich man to rescue his young wife from the Comanches and hunted by outlaws who want the reward money.

With *Comanche Station,* Randolph Scott fully intended to retire from films. He had been in it for some 30 years and two-thirds of his 90 movies had been westerns, by far the largest number for any major actor. In Budd Boetticher he found someone with whom he was able to summarize all he had learned and to virtually crystalize his persona in the western arena. He felt he had said all he had to say—until Sam Peckinpah's *Ride the High Country* came his way, an offer he just could not refuse.

3:10 TO YUMA

COLUMBIA, 1957

Produced by David Heilwell. Directed by Delmer Daves. Written by Halsted Wells, based on a story by Elmore Leonard. Photographed by Charles Lawton, Jr. Music by George Duning. 92 minutes.

CAST:

(*Ben Wade*) Glenn Ford; (*Dan Evans*) Van Heflin; (*Emmy*) Felicia Farr; (*Alice Evans*) Leora Dana; (*Alex Potter*) Henry Jones; (*Charlie Prince*) Richard Jaeckel; (*Mr. Butterfield*) Robert Emhardt; (*Bob Moons*) Sheridan Comerate; (*Bartender*) George Mitchell; (*Ernie Collins*) Robert Ellenstein; (*Marshall*) Ford Rainey; (*Matthew*) Barry Curtis; (*Mark*) Jerry Hartleben.

Aside from being a film that marked a more compassionate regard for the American Indian, *Broken Arrow* was the first western of Delmer Daves (1904-1977), a man with not only strong interest in western history but personal ties. His grandfather had been a Pony Express rider and several immediate ancestors had crossed the country in covered wagons. Whatever he learned from his family he augmented with further study, all of which resulted in his western films having a credibility beyond the norm. Daves made another fine account of Indian history with Alan Ladd's *Drum Beat* (1954), dealing with the Modoc Indian wars in northern California in the early 1870s, with Charles Bronson as the legendary Modoc leader Captain Jack. Two years later, he directed *Jubal*, with Glenn Ford as a cowboy caught up in an adulterous, murderous affair. The actor impressed Daves so much that he used him for *3:10 to Yuma*, as well as for *Cowboy* (1958), which co-starred Jack Lemmon as a tenderfoot learning the facts of cowboy life from trail boss Ford.

Daves' fascination with western lore was also apparent in *The Last Wagon* (1956), with Richard Widmark as a trapper who avenges the murder of his Indian wife; *The Badlanders* (1958), featuring Alan Ladd and Ernest Borgnine as rival gold robbers (a western remake of *The Asphalt Jungle*); and *The Hanging Tree* (1959), set in the mining area of Montana, with Gary Cooper as a doctor dogged by a gunman past. But of all the Delmer

Felicia Farr and Glenn Ford.

Daves westerns, the one that is held in highest regard is *3:10 to Yuma,* the moral and emotional nature of which is inevitably compared with *High Noon* (1952), dealing as it does with the dilemma of a single courageous man in a town short on collective courage.

The film in the main is a study of two men, a quiet, amiable outlaw, Ben Wade (Ford), and a rancher, Dan Evans (Van Heflin), who runs a small spread with his wife Alice (Leora Dana) and two small sons. Evans is having a hard time of it in a period of drought and no funds. Riding across his property, he finds that his small herd of cattle is being used to stop the Butterfield stagecoach. Wade rides up and advises Evans not to get involved lest it prove dangerous for his accompanying sons. Back at the coach, whose owner (Robert Emhardt) protests the stealing of a gold shipment and threatens action, Wade kills the driver who tries to stop the hold-up, and then steals the horses of Evans and his boys so they cannot ride into town and inform the law.

Wade and his men proceed to Bisbee, Arizona, on their escape route to the Mexican border, and there he becomes interested in a pretty barmaid, Emmy (Felicia Farr), a girl who has gone West for her health and whom Wade recalls having seen once before in another

town. She is as taken with him as he with her, and he dallies, against the advice of his chief henchman, Charlie (Richard Jaeckel). In the meantime, Butterfield rallies a posse, including Evans, and they track Wade to Bisbee. Wade, who has told his men to go ahead without him, now pays the price for the romantic daliance. He is captured and taken back to Contention City. En route, Evans takes him to his home, where Wade is invited to sit at the family table for a meal. His manners and his appreciation make Evans feel all the more uneasy. In town, Butterfield offers Evans $200 to guard Wade for the period between mid-morning and ten minutes after three, when the train will leave for Yuma and the state penitentiary. Although it is a job he does not want, Evans accepts because he badly needs the money to feed his cattle.

Wade is taken to the hotel and placed in a second floor room, with Evans, shotgun in hand, guarding him. With more than four hours to pass, Wade now begins to taunt Evans in several ways. He alludes to Evans' hard lot and bad financial luck and offers to double the money put up by Butterfield to let him escape. Evans refuses and continues to do so as the offer increases. The strain becomes far greater when Charlie rides by and lets it be known that he is aware of Wade's presence in the hotel and that he intends to bring help. On the other hand, the apprehensive Evans' resolve to go through with the job increases with the anger he feels when the funeral procession for the murdered stagecoach driver passes in the street. After the burial, the slain driver's furious brother bursts into the hotel room and tries to kill Wade, and it is only Evans' efforts that save the life of the outlaw.

When Charlie arrives in Contention City with his gunmen, the situation quickly changes. The members of the posse who have gathered in the hotel lobby to escort Wade and Evans to the train now find reasons for leaving, "I didn't figure on a big gun fight," "We've got families," and "Everybody wants to live." Charlie taunts them, "What do you think you're gonna die for—Butterfield's gold?" His men shoot and hang one of the men in the hotel lobby. Now Butterfield himself starts to crack, telling Evans he is releasing him from the obligation and promises him $200 if he will let Wade go. Evans believes he must go through with his original deal, even though his wife now asks him to change his mind.

A few minutes before the arrival of the train, Evans takes Wade out the back door of the hotel, despite the route to the station being covered by Wade's men. Taking advantage of whatever cover he can, such as passing cattle and horses, Evans manages to get to the station. There, in a cloud of steam from the shunting engine, Wade advises Evans to jump with him into a

Glenn Ford and Van Heflin

cattle car, "You're gonna have to trust me this time." As the train gathers speed, Wade explains, "I don't like to owe anybody any favors. You saved my life back at the hotel." Then he adds as he sees the look of astonishment on Evans' face, "It's alright, I've broken out of Yuma before." Evans waves at his wife from the train. It starts to rain. His ordeal is over.

3:10 to Yuma is a taunt piece of filmmaking, compact and believable in its comment on human nature. The outlaw is not entirely without character and the rancher is a basically decent man who finds just enough courage to do what he thinks must be done. Director Daves derived his tension not with gunplay but with the conflict of character between his two main figures. He was a director who literally mapped out his cues and set-ups, drawing sketches of the camera movements on the pages of his scripts and notations for his cast and crew. Everyone in a Daves film knew exactly what he or she was required to do. Among the assets of *3:10 to Yuma* is the subdued music score by George Duning, which differs from the more forceful style used in most

204

Glenn Ford, Robert Emhardt and Van Heflin.

Glenn Ford and Van Heflin.

previous western epics by composers like Max Steiner and Dimitri Tiomkin. For this film, Duning wrote a poignant main theme, which, with lyrics by Ned Washington, was sung over the credits by Frankie Laine—a device successfully established by Washington and Tiomkin in *High Noon,* for which they won the 1952 Best Song Oscar. Although practically every score is written after a film's completion, in the case of *3:10 to Yuma,* Daves asked Duning to write the principle themes prior to shooting. He then used playbacks of the music to establish moods and timings in some of the scenes.

3:10 to Yuma is a highlight in the career of an actor whose contributions to the western genre are many. Glenn Ford was never a cowboy but he enjoyed making westerns and he rode particularly well. His laconic acting style served him well in his first western, *Texas* in 1941, co-starring with William Holden as a pair of young drifters who wind up on opposite sides of the law, Ford the good guy, but with the roles reversed when Ford and Holden made *The Man From Colorado* seven years later. Ford picked up some tips playing

with Randolph Scott in *The Desperadoes* (1943) and turned totally villainous for *Lust for Gold* (1949). He was *The Man From the Alamo* (1953), directed by Budd Boetticher, and he was one of *The Violent Men* (1955), a settler standing firm against maniacal tycoon rancher Edward G. Robinson. Ford starred in Anthony Mann's big-budgeted but disappointing *Cimarron* (1960) and stayed out of the saddle for five years before making *The Rounders,* a fine contemporary western with Henry Fonda. In 1967, with his career winding down, Ford turned more and more to westerns, starting with *The Last Challenge,* followed by *Day of the Evil Gun* (1968),

Heaven With a Gun (1968), *Smith* (1969), and finally doing a contemporary western series for television in 1971, *Cade's County*. The best westerns Glenn Ford made remain those he did for Delmer Daves—*Jubal, 3:10 to Yuma* and *Cowboy*.

Glenn Ford and Van Heflin

Audrey Hepburn, June Walker, Charles Bickford, Lillian Gish, Audie Murphy and Burt Lancaster.

THE UNFORGIVEN

UNITED ARTISTS, 1960

Produced by James Hill. Directed by John Huston. Written by Ben Maddow, based on the novel by Alan LeMay. Photographed in Technicolor by Franz Planer. Music by Dimitri Tiomkin. 123 minutes.

CAST:

(*Ben Zachary*) Burt Lancaster; (*Rachel Zachary*) Audrey Hepburn; (*Cash Zachary*) Audie Murphy; (*Johnny Portugal*) John Saxon; (*Zeb Rawlins*) Charles Bickford; (*Mattilda Zachary*) Lillian Gish; (*Charlie Rawlins*) Albert Salmi; (*Abe Kelsey*) Joseph Wiseman; (*Hagar Rawlins*) June Walker; (*Georgia Rawlins*) Kipp Hamilton; (*Jude Rawlins*) Arnold Merritt; (*Lost Bird*) Carlos Rivas; (*Andy Zachary*) Doug McClure.

As with his friend and fellow easterner Kirk Douglas, it was only a matter of time before Hollywood found a saddle for Burt Lancaster, and like Douglas it would take a film or two before Lancaster would look at home in the saddle. In his western debut, *Vengeance Valley* (1951), Lancaster moved with the grace of an athlete rather than the less graceful gait of a cowboy. In *Apache* (1954), he played Massai, the proud Indian chieftain who refused to surrender with Geronimo, and the earnestness of his playing almost overcame his clearly non-Indian looks. But he followed it with a western in which his looks and his physique were perfect—*Vera Cruz,* as a bandit bouncing with energy and unbounding charm, a grinning animal of a man, in sharp contrast to the slow, quiet demeanor of co-star Gary Cooper. Then came an interesting piece of early frontier Americana, *The Kentuckian,* which Lancaster himself directed. He turned away from the West for a couple of years and then turned up as a very sober Wyatt Earp in the box office winner, *Gunfight at the O. K. Corral,* with Kirk Douglas as Doc Holliday. By now, Lancaster was an actor very much at home on the range.

John Huston's *The Unforgiven* was Lancaster's 32nd film in the 14 years he had been in Hollywood with a reputation as an actor for not willingly settling for ordinary roles. With pictures like *Come Back, Little*

Sheba (1952), *The Rose Tatoo* (1955) and *Sweet Smell of Success* (1957), he had made it clear that merely being a handsome, athletic hero was not enough. He had a need to stretch himself as an actor, and producers found that the best way to get Lancaster interested in a film was to offer him roles as complicated men facing the dilemmas of life. Such a man is Ben Zachary, the strong head of household on a ranch in the Texas Panhandle of the 1850s. Living in their adobe home, the back of which is built into the side of a hillock, are the mother, Mattilda (Lillian Gish), brother Cash (Audie Murphy), much younger brother Andy (Doug McClure) and adopted sister Rachel (Audrey Hepburn). Rachel has always believed that her parents were wagon train immigrants killed in an Indian attack. A different story now begins to emerge.

While out riding, Rachel meets a strange old man, who wears a sword and claims he is a carrier of God's truth. She tells her mother of the meeting and from the description Mattilda knows it is Kelsey (Joseph Wise-

Burt Lancaster and Charles Bickford.

209

Audrey Hepburn and Audie Murphy.

210

man), a demented religious fanatic seeking vengeance for the loss of a son to the Indians many years ago. Mattilda tries to make light of it, but then a Kiowa chieftain comes to the house and claims that Rachel is his sister. He wants her but Ben denies him and the Indians retreat. Feelings against the Kiowas are strong, especially in hot-headed Cash, who seethes with hatred for them and who resents Ben's having hired an Indian, Johnny Portugal (John Saxon), as a top hand. But it is Johnny, with his tracking skill, who captures Kelsey and brings him to the crowd gathered at the home of Ben's ranching partner, Zeb Rawlins (Charles Bickford). Raw-

Lillian Gish and Audrey Hepburn.

Audie Murphy and Kipp Hamilton.

lins has just lost his son, Charlie (Albert Salmi), to the Kiowas and he wants the truth about Rachel, who had planned to marry Charlie.

As Kelsey sits with a rope about his neck on a horse beneath a tree, he claims that Rachel was found in an Indian encampment that he and others tried to wipe out. The baby had been spared and taken to Mattilda, who had just lost a child in birth. Charlie's mother (June Walker), grief stricken and furious with anger, shouts that Rachel should be turned over to the Kiowas. Mattilda, also angered but denying the story just heard, hits the horse with a stick, causing Kelsey to be hanged before he can say more. Ben leads his family away, warned by Rawlins that if Ben stands by Rachel it will mean the end of their partnership. With 6000 head of cattle ready to be driven to market, Rawlins thinks Ben may change his stand. But Ben is deeply attached to Rachel and he is prepared to make any sacrifice for her.

Back at their home, Mattilda confesses that what Kelsey said was true and that she loves Rachel as if the girl were her own. The revelation makes some difference to Ben, who has always loved her and can now do so beyond the bounds of supposed brotherhood. It makes a vast difference to the Indian-loathing Cash,

who storms out and drinks himself into a stupor. He returns to the Rawlins ranch, to the arms of the eager Georgia (Kipp Hamilton), who wants him to marry her. Waking up the next morning, Cash is disturbed by the distant sound of gunfire and he leaves to go back to his home.

The Kiowas attack the Zachary home to take Rachel. Ben directs the defense skillfully but when the Indians drive a herd of cattle onto the roof of the building, he builds a fire on the roof to clear them off. The family

Burt Lancaster, with Audrey Hepburn and Doug McClure in the background.

212

retreats to the cellar, with Ben going outside to shoot at the Indians as Cash arrives to help out. The Indian claiming to be Rachel's brother gets into the cellar, where Rachel, pistol in hand, looks at him, deliberates and then fires. She has made her choice. Mattilda dies in the attack and, standing in the ruins of their home, the Zacharys know they must in some manner continue their lives, but with Ben now morally free to love Rachel more than simply as a brother.

The Unforgiven, well directed by the estimable John Huston, failed to find great public favor. It was perhaps a little too grim and offbeat for the average western buff, although the depiction of the harsh frontier life is more exact than in most films of its kind. It is a somberly poetic film, dealing with a fierce brand of racial prejudice and hinting toward an unusually strong attachment between a brother and sister. Unfortunately, the casting of the delightful Audrey Hepburn works against the film. It is impossible to accept her as a blood Kiowa. Here she is a misplaced Dresden doll,

her patrician features and cultured accent undermining the intensity of the acting. Lancaster, however, is perfect as the unbending brother, holding his family together and restraining his feelings for Rachel. It is Lancaster at his best, giving a shaded portrayal of a tough, leathery man who lives by a simple code of honesty, who will not compromise, and whose seemingly unemotional nature hides a streak of tenderness. This is a classic figure in American film and Lancaster always performed it with conviction.

The Unforgiven also marks the highlight in the modest career of Audie Murphy, whose 44 films were mostly westerns. Born into poverty in East Texas in 1924, Murphy became the most decorated soldier of World War II. His boyish looks masked a seemingly tortured soul and he was never quite able to cope with his celebrity as either soldier or actor. He had little interest in acting initially but a girlfriend sent a photo of him to producer William Cagney and suggested he might be good in the movies. Cagney was intrigued by the idea and gave Murphy a bit part as a West Point cadet in Alan Ladd's *Beyond Glory* (1948). Ironically, Murphy had applied to West Point after the war and had been turned down because of his wartime injuries. In 1950, Universal put him under contract and assigned him to a series of modestly budgeted westerns. With his soft Texas accent and his obvious skill with guns, he did well in the minor movie league but despaired of anything better.

Murphy's chances to do better things failed. Luck was not with him. John Huston borrowed him in 1951 to play the lead in *The Red Badge of Courage,* in the classic Stephen Crane story of the young soldier who overcomes cowardice in battle. Murphy was the perfect choice, touching and sad in Huston's brilliant handling of the material. But MGM, sure that there was no market for such a film, butchered it in the editing, reducing it to little more than an hour and sent it out as the bottom of a double bill. Murphy's luck was not much better when he played James Stewart's young outlaw brother in *Night Passage* (1957), one of the least successful of Stewart's westerns. Huston knew that Murphy was right for the tormented Cash in *The Unforgiven* but again the film's lack of wide acceptance worked against Murphy. He was not a man with much confidence and he was heard to say, "I'm working with a great handicap—I have no talent." In truth his playing in *The Unforgiven* is so strong he almost steals the film from Lancaster. The highlight of his career came, in fact, when he starred in *To Hell and Back* (1955), the story of his own life—the casting, at least, was perfect.

By the mid-'60s, the western trail had run out for Murphy. He said, "I've made the same western about 40 times. I don't mind being an actor so long as I don't have to live up to a reputation I don't have." Murphy went into a number of business enterprises, including being the producer of the film *A Time for Dying,* in which he played a cameo as Jesse James. The title proved tragically prophetic. By the time it was released, Murphy was dead. He was killed in an air crash on May 28, 1971, three weeks short of his 47th birthday.

RIDE THE HIGH COUNTRY

MGM, 1961

Produced by Richard E. Lyons. Directed By Sam Peckinpah. Written by N. B. Stone, Jr. Photographed in Metrocolor by Lucien Ballard. Music by George Bassman. 93 minutes.

CAST:

(*Gil Westrum*) Randolph Scott; (*Steve Judd*) Joel McCrea; (*Heck Longtree*) Ronald Starr; (*Elsa Knudsen*) Mariette Hartley; (*Billy Hammond*) James Drury; (*Joshua Knudsen*) R. G. Armstrong; (*Judge Tolliver*) Edgar Buchanan; (*Kate*) Jennie Jackson; (*Elder Hammond*) John Anderson; (*Sylvus Hammond*) L. Q. Jones; (*Henry Hammond*) Warren Oates; (*Jimmy Hammond*) John Davis Chandler.

After making *The Gunfight at Dodge City* in 1959, Joel McCrea decided the time had come to retire from the movies. A few months later, with the completion of *Comanche Station*, Randolph Scott came to the same conclusion. Wealthy and with other business interests, neither man had any reason to labor any longer in front of cameras, especially with television now almost glutting the airwaves with western fare. But then Burt Kennedy, who had written four of the films Scott had made with Budd Boetticher, including *Comanche Station*, sent the actor a script he had found fascinating—*Guns in the Afternoon* by N. B. Stone, Jr. The story of a pair of impoverished, over-the-hill former lawmen getting together on a job appealed to Scott. It had an elegiac quality to it, dealing with men past their prime and their time, the one man honorbound and the other embittered and pragmatic. Scott agreed to do it if producer Richard E. Lyons could get McCrea.

McCrea liked the idea of the film and of making it with Scott but he felt uneasy about Lyons' request that he play Gil Westrum, the man who sees a chance to make some easy money, even if it means turning on the unbending, moral Steve Judd. "Lyons thought I was a little subtler than Randy and that it would be a little more deceptive if I would turn and double-cross him. But I told him that if I was going to do one more picture, I wasn't going to destroy my image with it. My

Randolph Scott

216

image was Steve Judd. He's the guy who, through his integrity, will get the job done. I asked Lyons not to say anything to Randy because he was the guy who came up with the project and ought to have his choice about which man he'd play. But if he chose Judd, I'd back out. We all had lunch at the Brown Derby, along with Sam Peckinpah, who was going to direct, and I put it to Randy. He said he'd play either one but if he had his choice he'd prefer Westrum. He said, 'I've played the straight, honest guy so damn long and so much that this would be interesting.' I told him that was fine by me because I wanted to play Judd."

When MGM released *Ride the High Country* (the original title *Guns in the Afternoon* was used for the British release), it did so with no promotion, thinking it too offbeat a western to win much of an audience. To the studio's amazement film critics lavished praise upon it. *Newsweek* named it as the best film of 1962, as did the editor of the prestigious *Film Quarterly,* and it won

a prize at the Venice Film Festival. Since then, it has appeared on the favored list of just about every western film buff. Even without Scott and McCrea it would be an interesting story; with them it is a special film in which two giants of the genre appear to summarize their long association with the film West. Both had been on the screen since 1929 and both had appeared in many of the best examples of this kind of movie.

Ride the High Country is about a pair of cowboys washed aside by civilization in the turn-of-the-century West, once heroic men now reduced to picking up a living as best they can. Judd rides into the town of Hornitos to take a job as a bank guard escorting gold from the mining community of Coarse Gold. He does his best to hide his frayed shirtcuffs and he goes to the men's room to read his contract so that the banker cannot see his need for glasses. He needs an assistant in order to do the job, and in walking around town, bumps into an old friend, Westrum, who is now making

Mariette Hartley, Ronald Starr, Joel McCrea and Randolph Scott.

Joel McCrea, John Anderson, John Davis Chandler, James Drury and Warren Oates.

his living as a sideshow sharpshooter and spouting Buffalo Bill nonsense about the Wild West. Westrum agrees to come in with Judd but insists on bringing in his young, scrap-happy friend, Heck Longtree (Ronald Starr). Despite their long friendship and their work together as lawmen, Judd and Westrum are different kinds of men. Judd is a moral Rock of Gibraltar with an ironclad code of honor, whereas the embittered Westrum sees the job as a chance to steal gold as recompense for all his years of underpaid law service.

On their way through the mountains—the film was shot in the California Sierras in the area of Lake Mammoth—the men stop at the home of Joshua Knudsen (R. G. Armstrong), a farmer and religious fanatic. Heck takes a shine to Knudsen's repressed daughter Elsa (Mariette Hartley, in her film debut) who, to escape home, has accepted a proposal from miner Billy Hammond (James Drury), one of five brothers living in Coarse Gold. Judd and Westrum reluctantly take Elsa with them, but when she gets to her intended husband, she is disgusted to find the Hammonds a wild and filthy bunch living in squalor. Elsa reluctantly goes through with the wedding, which takes place in a saloon-bordello, but then, with Billy drunk, she has to fight off his brothers, who regard her as community property. Realizing the situation in which the girl has placed herself, Judd and Westrum agree to take her back to her father. The Hammonds, wanting both the girl and the gold, now track the group, only retreating to lick their wounds after two of the brothers are killed. For Judd though, the problem is not simply the remaining Hammonds but Westrum, who makes it known he intends to take the gold. Reluctantly, Judd ties Westrum's hands. Heck, because of his love for Elsa, decides to side with Judd. Westrum escapes during the night, goes back to the scene of the conflict with the Hammonds and finds himself a horse and a gunbelt.

When Judd gets to the Knudsen farm, he finds that the old man has been murdered and that the three Hammonds are in the barn. A gunfight erupts and both Judd and Heck are hit, but Westrum, who has been following from a distance, rides down to join his old pal. As they lie in a ditch, they agree that the best tactic is to challenge the Hammonds to an open fight. Judd calls out to the Hammonds, "You red-necked pecker-woods, you damn dry gulchin' southern trash," which offends them and brings them out. The three Hammonds walk toward the group, blazing away with their rifles. Judd and Westrum stand, carefully aim and bring down the brothers, but Judd takes two more bullets. He knows it is all over for him and he tells Westrum that he does not want Elsa and Heck to see him die, "I'll go it alone." Westrum assures him, "Don't worry about anything, I'll take care of it." Says Judd, "Hell, I know that, I always

Joel McCrea and Randolph Scott.

Joel McCrea, Mariette Hartley and Ronald Starr.

did. You just forgot it for a while, that's all. So long, partner." Then as Westrum, Heck and Elsa ride away, Judd closes his eyes, lies back and dies.

No western has ever dealt with morality more surely than *Ride the High Country*. When Westrum pleads with Judd to join him in taking the gold shipment, saying, "The bankers won't be hurt by the loss," Judd angrily replies, "Not them, only *me!*" And in discussing the rigid morality of her bible-bound father, the puzzled Elsa asks, "My father says there's only right and wrong, good and evil, nothing in between. It isn't that simple, is it?" Judd replies, "No, it isn't. It should be, but it isn't." When Westrum questions Judd's stance he is told, "All I want to do is enter my house justified."

The major assets of *Ride the High Country* are clearly Scott and McCrea, two top-notch actors who set a dignified style of mythic western heroism, but credit also is due director Sam Peckinpah, for whom this was his second feature film. A year previously, he had made the western *The Deadly Companions*, which indicated the tough style that would mark all his wes-

terns. Peckinpah had cut his western teeth with his writing and directing of television series like *Gunsmoke, The Westerner* and *The Rifleman*, and by the time of his death in 1986, he had established an indelible reputation, albeit one of a difficult, hard-drinking man constantly at odds with studio management. About *Ride the High Country* he said, "MGM saw it as a low-budget quickie they could throw away in the summer double-features, and if I'd tried to talk to them about the basic theme, which was salvation and loneliness, they'd have fired me on the spot. Even so, they hated what I had done and threw me out before I could finish cutting, dubbing and scoring."

For Randolph Scott, the film marked complete retirement and he hung up his saddle. In the remaining 25 years of his life he showed no further interest in movies and played no part in Hollywood society, not that he ever had been much a part of it. He was the only actor accepted as a member of the elite Los Angeles Country Club, which rightly regarded him as an astute business tycoon and one of the unpublicized sponsors of the

222

Mayo Clinic. Joel McCrea also had intended that *Ride the High Country* would be his last film, but eight years later, his son Jody persuaded him to play a bit in the latter's *Cry Blood, Apache,* and four years after that, McCrea was intrigued enough to go to Canada to play an old cowboy in *Mustang Country,* a small but charming picture that never received the attention it deserves. Since then no one has managed to get Joel McCrea back before the cameras. At this writing, he and wife Frances Dee are still living on their ranch in Calabasas, where he says, "I intend to just sit around and dream about the old days."

Joel McCrea, Randolph Scott, Ronald Starr and Mariette Hartley.

WILL PENNY

PARAMOUNT, 1968

Produced by Fred Engel and Walter Seltzer. Directed and written by Tom Gries. Photographed in Technicolor by Lucien Ballard. Music by David Raksin. 108 minutes.

CAST:

(Will Penny) Charlton Heston; *(Catherine Allen)* Joan Hackett; *(Preacher Quint)* Donald Pleasance; *(Blue)* Lee Majors; *(Rafe Quint)* Bruce Dern; *(Alex)* Ben Johnson; *(Ike Wallerstein)* Slim Pickens; *(Catron)* Clifton James; *(Dutchy)* Anthony Zerbe; *(Boetius Sullivan)* Roy Jenson; *(Anse Howard)* G. D. Spradlin; *(Jennie)* Quentin Dean; *(Dr. Fraker)*; William Schallert; *(Mrs. Fraker)* Lydia Clarke; *(Shem Bodine)* Robert Luster; *(Sambo)* Dal Jenkins; *(Romulus)* Matt Clark; *(Foxy)* Luke Askew; *(Bigfoot)* Anthony Costello; *(Rufus Quint)* Gene Rutherford.

No working man has been more romanticized than the cowboy, who is, when all is said and done, simply a manual laborer on horseback. His job is to tend cattle, to round them up and to get them to market. It is difficult to think of such work as romantic; the hours are long and tedious, the security is minimal and the pay, particularly in the days of the Wild West, is poor. Few films have managed to convey this bleak picture better than *Will Penny,* although doing it amid beautiful western scenery photographed by the masterly Lucien Ballard, whose previous work in the wide open spaces included *Buchanan Rides Alone, Ride the High Country* and John Wayne's *The Sons of Katie Elder* (1965). After *Will Penny,* Ballard shot *The Wild Bunch, True Grit* (1969), the film that brought Wayne his Oscar, and yet another Sam Peckinpah homage to the passing of the Old West, *The Ballad of Cable Hogue* (1970). As to why the work of the cowboy has emerged on the screen as romantic, the most apparent reason is that it has been filmed with artistry and imagination by men like Lucien Ballard.

To play the illiterate title character of *Will Penny,* writer-director Tom Gries chose Charlton Heston, a far from obvious choice in view of Heston having distinguished himself playing Andrew Jackson, Moses, Ben-Hur, El Cid, John the Baptist and Michelangelo. On the other hand, the rugged actor, a star from his first day

Charlton Heston.

The brawling cowboy.

Charlton Heston and Donald Pleasance.

before the cameras in 1950, had served enough time in the saddle to qualify him as a working cowpoke in any account of the West. In his first western, *The Savage* (1952), he was a white man brought up as a Sioux, and in his second, *Pony Express* (1953) he was no less than Buffalo Bill Cody. In *The Far Horizons* (1955), Heston played William Clark, helping Fred MacMurray as Meriwether Lewis open up the West. He was a quarrelsome ranch owner in Rudolph Maté's *Three Violent People* (1957), a tough ranch foreman in William Wyler's super western *The Big Country* (1958), and Sam Peckinpah's obsessive cavalryman *Major Dundee* (1965). But now, having served as a commanding and imposing figure in so many movies, Heston was required to be a lonesome cowboy, unable to read or write.

When first seen, Penny is a tired, dirt-caked cowpoke on the last day of a trail drive. Now in middle age, he wonders where the next job might come from. He and his buddies, Blue (Lee Majors) and Dutchy (Anthony Zerbe), pick up their pay and ride off to nowhere in particular. The next morning, they shoot an elk for food but come into conflict with a wild-eyed old coot, Preacher Quint (Donald Pleasance), and his three sons, who claim the carcass. One of the Quint boys is shot and killed, and Quint gallops off vowing vengeance. Dutchy is wounded in the fracas and his buddies load him into a wagon. They come to a ranch, where a woman, Catherine Allen (Joan Hackett), offers to help, although offended by the men's rough manners and their apparent primary interest—drinking. When they

Charlton Heston and Joan Hackett.

228

arrive in the village of Alfred, they deposit Dutchy with the doctor and then head off, Blue in one direction and Penny in another.

While following a trail, Penny comes across a dead cowboy, lying near his horse. He puts the body on the horse and proceeds to the nearby Flatiron Ranch, where the foreman, Alex (Ben Johnson), suspects, as do some of the other hands, that Penny has killed the man in order to get his job. But Alex needs another hand and hires Penny as a border guard, requiring him to spend the winter in a shack in the hills, looking out for stray cattle and rustlers. On the way to the shack he is spotted and followed by Quint and the two remaining sons, Rafe (Bruce Dern) and Rufus (Gene Rutherford). At the shack, he finds it already occupied by Catherine and her son Horace (Jon Francis). She explains that they are en route to California to join her husband and that they have been deserted by their guide. He tells her she cannot stay, except for the few days he has to go out on the trail rounding up strays. The first night out, he is attacked by the Quints, who knife him, take his clothes and leave him to freeze to death. Penny summons his strength and manages to find his way back to the shack.

Catherine and the boy nurse him back to health, and with time, she and Penny become fond of each other, giving him the problem of knowing he is breaking company rules by allowing her to stay. At Christmas, they have a small celebration, which is shattered by the arrival of the Quints, who tie up Penny and assault Catherine. Quint tell her she must marry either one or the other of his sons. The next day, Penny is put to work cleaning up the property, during which time he advises Catherine to invite both the Quint sons to meet her behind the shack in the evening so that she can decide which one of them she would prefer as her husband, but not to tell either the other has been invited at the same time. At the meeting the brothers start to quarrel and fight, which causes Quint to stop guarding Penny and check into the commotion. Penny gets into a wagon and takes off, pursued by the Quint boys, but, as they are about to catch up with him, Blue and Dutchy happen along and turn the tide of battle. The Quints retreat to the shack, where Penny and his

229

buddies mount an attack. Penny drops sulphur down the chimney and, as the Quints emerge, they are shot down.

Alex and some of his ranch hands soon arrive, figuring that something was wrong when the cattle were found straying unattended. Accepting Penny's explanation, Alex says he has no course but to fire him. Penny must now make a decision. He and Catherine love each other but he knows he has nothing to offer. "I'm damn near 50 years old. What am I good for?" She suggests that they could start a farm together. "A farm? I don't know nothin' about farmin'. We'd starve. And all the time I'd be thinkin' how I took you from your husband and the boy from his father. I couldn't face it, Cath." She can say nothing to hold him. Regretfully, he gets on his horse and heads off, with Dutchy and Blue, the three continuing their bleak lives as aging cowpokes looking for work, with each passing year becoming harder and harder.

Will Penny is about an honest a film about cowboy life as has ever been made and Heston was able to communicate the simple, honest nature of a man who knows the severe limitations of his life. It is a melancholy performance, made the more touching by the grandeur of the settings and the portrayal of Joan Hackett as a woman who also knows the terms on which she must live. There is a dignity to both the man and the woman, and an intelligence in the way Gries scripts and directs his story. Unfortunately, the film did not do well at the box office, its honesty about cowboy life perhaps being a little too stark for western buffs, and the shabbiness of the title character maybe not what his admirers expected of Heston. However, the fans of Donald Pleasance, an English actor who has specialized in demented, scummy villains, doubtlessly enjoyed his playing of Preacher Quint, a scavenging rawhider, filthy in appearance and sadistically enthusiastic in the act of beating and killing.

In a small role as the wife of the local doctor is Lydia Clarke, an up-and-coming one-time actress who gave up her career to become Mrs. Charlton Heston.

Filmed by Ballard in the Sierras, not far from Lone Pine, and taking advantage of winter, the scenery is indeed beautiful. It gives more than a little indication of the source of cowboy strength, the sense of loneliness that breeds the spirit of individualism and a certain kind of idealism that sustains a man like Will Penny. The film also gives a graphic account of what it is like to work on the range, to eat and sleep on it, to herd cattle and to keep company with simple men in bunkhouses and saloons. In short, *Will Penny* is the definitive story about a cowboy.

Ernest Borgnine, Warren Oates, William Holden and Ben Johnson.

THE WILD BUNCH

WARNER BROS., 1969

Produced by Phil Feldman. Directed by Sam Peckinpah. Written by Walon Green and Sam Peckinpah, based on a story by Green and Roy N. Sickner. Photographed in Technicolor by Lucien Ballard. Music by Jerry Fielding. 145 minutes.

CAST:

(*Pike Bishop*) William Holden; (*Dutch Engstrom*) Ernest Borgnine; (*Deke Thornton*) Robert Ryan; (*Sykes*) Edmond O'Brien; (*Lyle Gorch*) Warren Oates; (*Angel*) Jaime Sanchez; (*Tector Gorch*) Ben Johnson; (*Mapache*) Emilio Fernandez; (*Coffer*) Strother Martin; (*T.C.*) L. Q. Jones; (*Pat Harrigan*) Albert Dekker; (*Crazy Lee*) Bo Hopkins; (*Mayor Wainscoat*) Dub Taylor; (*Herrera*) Alfonso Arrou.

With *Ride the High Country,* Sam Peckinpah directed a film that ruefully and romantically noted the passing of the Old West. With *The Wild Bunch,* he noted the same transition with stark tragedy and a visual violence bordering on the surreal. The first film deals with morality and codes of honor, the second, set in Texas in 1913, is devoid of morality and the only honor touched upon is that of the main character, a hardened outlaw named Pike Bishop (William Holden) who believes that "when you side with a man, you stay with him . . . if you can't do that you're worse than some animal." Other than that there is little to be said for Pike and his gang, who are simply old fashioned outlaws trying to survive in a West that is now better organized against crime. And yet it is clear that Peckinpah, himself a maverick, regards Pike with more than a little affection. Pike may be a man severely at odds with society but he does not lack for backbone; he may be a loser but he goes out fighting. Sam Peckinpah, who never made a film that did not find him at odds with his employers, drowned his regrets in alcohol and died in 1984 at the age of 58.

The bitter tone of the film is set at the start as Pike and his men ride into town dressed as an Army unit and set on robbing a bank. On the way in, Pike notices a group of children amusing themselves by dropping a scorpion into a seething nest of red ants. Later, they further amuse themselves by placing straw around the

231

nest and setting fire to it. Something similar is about to happen to the Pike gang, who have been betrayed by Pike's former friend, Deke Thornton (Robert Ryan), now in the employ of railroad executive Pat Harrigan (Albert Dekker). Thornton, captured in a previous raid on railroad property, is promised parole by Harrigan if he will help bring in Pike. Having been flogged in the Yuma Penitentiary, Thornton reluctantly takes sides against Pike, all the while complaining about the low caliber of the men Harrigan has hired for the job. Halfway through the bank robbery, Pike becomes aware that he and his men are surrounded; a parade through the street by a group of temperance believers provide some cover for the escape, during which many townsfolk and a few of Pike's men are killed.

When they pull up and make camp after crossing the border into Mexico, they realize just how much of a failure the attempted robbery has been—the bags contain metal washers instead of gold. For Pike and his steadfast friend Dutch (Ernest Borgnine), it is a bitter failure because they had hoped this would have been the final caper. "One good score and we'll back off." Angel (Jaime Sanchez), the youngest of the half-dozen survivors, takes them to his village to recuperate and relax. While there, they learn of the pillage and carnage caused by General Mapache (Emilio Fernandez), one of revolutionist Pancho Villa's deadly rivals in the upheavals now wracking Mexico. Pike decides to stay in Mexico, thinking he will not be pursued. He is wrong. Harrigan sends Thornton after him. Thorton warns his men they are up against the best, "He never got caught."

Pike and his men run into Mapache in the next town they visit. The crude, drunken general hires Pike to raid an munitions train in Texas and bring the guns and ammunition to him in return for gold. The train, guarded by soldiers, also carries Thornton and his men, who are bound for the point at which they will cross into Mexico. Pike sees this as another chance, "This is our last go-round, Dutch. This time we do it right." When the train stops at a watering station, Pike and his men take over the engine and uncouple the carriages

William Holden and Ernest Borgnine.

that follow the open car containing the crates of munitions. Getting the cache across the border, they are closely followed by the Thornton group, who are blown up as they cross into Mexico over a bridge that Angel had wired with dynamite. Thornton and three others survive the explosion and push on in the pursuit, driven by the determined Thornton, who knows he must catch Pike in order to be a free man. He looks with contempt at his men, whom he considers scum, "We're after *men*—and I wish to God I was one of them."

Pike now faces an unexpected problem—Angel brings in his own men to take the munitions in support of the revolution and to wipe out corrupt warlords like Mapache. But the wily Mapache has anticipated trouble and sends his forces to surround both the Pike group and Angel's men. Pike goes through with the deal, delivering the guns and ammunition in batches in order to get paid and not wiped out, but he cannot save Angel from being taken by Mapache. The besotted warlord amuses himself by brutally torturing Angel and dragging him around on a rope behind his car. Pike, Dutch and

the remaining survivors, the Gorch brothers, Lyle (Warren Oates) and Tector (Ben Johnson), stay in the village occupied by Mapache in order to avoid Thornton but become disgusted with the behavior of Mapache and his men. No amount of drinking and whoring can make them leave Angel in this hellish situation. Early one morning, Dutch says, "I'm tired of being hunted." Pike looks at him and then at the others, "Let's go." They know what he means. They walk up to Mapache and ask for Angel. Mapache seems ready to comply. He pulls the barely alive Angel to his feet, cuts his ropes but then slits his throat as he pushes Angel toward Pike. Pike pulls his pistol and kills Mapache, triggering a ferocious battle with the hundred or so troops around him. Using the machine guns and automatic rifles they brought to Mapache, Pike and his men slaughter the troops while taking shot after shot themselves. Finally Pike and his men lie in grotesque positions of death, surrounded by piles of dead and wounded men and women.

Thornton and his group soon arrive and the bodies of

Ben Johnson and William Holden

William Holden.

Pike, Dutch and the Gorches are tied on horses to be taken back to Harrigan. Thornton sits down against a wall, sad and disgusted, knowing that no one other than Pike brought about his own death. Pike made his choice and now Thornton will make his. He gets up and gives a rueful smile to old bandit Sykes (Edmond O'Brien), a former member of the Pike gang but now ready to throw in his lot with Thornton. Laughing, Sykes says that life goes on, it may not be what it used to be but it is better than nothing.

The Wild Bunch did well at the box office but critics fell over themselves intellectualizing about its meaning and about its almost balletic use of graphic violence and its seemingly absurdist heroism. Peckinpah claimed only that he was telling a story about violent men in a violent time, and about a time in which values were changing and erupting. This he felt applied as much to

1969 as to 1913. He was disappointed to hear himself referred to as a man glorifying violence, claiming that what he was doing was showing violence as the painful, bloody thing it really is, and that the best way to get across that message is with passion and excess. Among those who had doubts about his message was Warner Bros., which denied him the final edit on his proposed 150 minute version and came out with several versions running as much as 20 minutes less. However, he still fared better with *The Wild Bunch* than he did with his previous picture, *Major Dundee* (1964), which Charlton Heston and others who worked on it claim was muti-

Ben Johnson, Warren Oates, William Holden and Ernest Borgnine.

234

lated by Columbia. That one, for all the editing, remains a remarkable film and one of the best to portray the Army-versus-Indians warfare.

It is easy to regard Peckinpah as a later day John Ford, since both were western devotees and both liked to work with a stock company of players. Many of the actors who played in *Ride the High Country* and *Major Dundee* appear in *The Wild Bunch* and would appear in later Peckinpah films, most of which dealt with the West. Ben Johnson was a spillover from the Ford bunch to the Peckinpah crew; a former cowboy and stuntman, Johnson became an increasingly fine actor, and sur-

prised even himself by winning an Oscar in 1971, playing a dignified, graying cowboy in *The Last Picture Show*. Two Peckinpah actors since have died, Warren Oates and Strother Martin. In *The Wild Bunch,* Oates is the dumb Lyle Gorch, devoted to Pike, and Martin is Coffer, the scavenger working for Thornton and despised by him. Both actors played with an intensity that was riveting.

The Wild Bunch is a reminder that not only Peckinpah, Oates and Martin are gone but so are William Holden, Robert Ryan and Edmond O'Brien, all actors of remarkable film presence. Especially sad is Holden, who like Tyrone Power and Robert Taylor, was given a beauty of face that made him feel uncomfortable. More than Power and Taylor, Holden could hardly wait to get lines and splotches in his face, until in the end it was disturbing to look at him and remember the young Holden. There was a troubled spirit inside him which led to excessive drinking, until the day in 1981 when he fell over in a stupor, struck his head on a coffee table in his apartment and died alone. In playing the driven, fatalistic outlaw of *The Wild Bunch,* Holden gave one of his many fine performances, and possibly one he understood more than most actors.

Ernest Borgnine and William Holden.

235

Foreground: John Pascal, Bruce Davison, Richard Jaeckel and Jorge Luke. Background: Tex Armstrong, Hal Maguire, Nick Cravat, Ted Markland, Dick Farnsworth and Burt Lancaster.

ULZANA'S RAID

UNIVERSAL, 1973

Produced by Carter De Haven. Directed by Robert Aldrich. Written by Alan Sharp. Photographed in Technicolor by Joseph Biroc. Music by Frank DeVol. 103 minutes.

CAST:

(*McIntosh*) Burt Lancaster; (*Lt. Garnett DeBuin*) Bruce Davison; (*Ke-Ni-Tay*) Jorge Luke; (*Sergeant*) Richard Jaeckel; (*Ulzana*) Joaquin Martinez; (*Captain Gates*) Lloyd Bochner; (*Rukeyser*) Karl Swenson; (*Major Cartwright*) Douglas Watson; (*Mrs. Riordan*) Dran Hamilton; (*Corporal*) John Pearce; (*Mrs. Rukeyser*) Gladys Holland; (*Mrs. Ginsford*) Margaret Fairchild; (*Indian Woman*) Aimee Eccles; (*Ginsford*) Richard Bull; (*Steegmeyer*) Otto Reichow; (*Horowitz*) Dean Smith; (*Mulkearn*) Larry Randles.

On November 2, 1970, Burt Lancaster reached his 57th birthday, still a major film actor but no longer the dashing athlete of his early films, as could hardly be expected. Neither could he be expected at this time in his career to make three westerns in a row. That he did so was due to the nature of the parts offered him in those westerns, parts which let him present complex men faced with difficult choices. Producers had learned that, in order to get Lancaster for a film, he had to be given a role that intrigued him. In *Valdez Is Coming,* he is an aging half-breed constable living in a town near the Mexican border and running up against racial prejudice in addition to crime. He is expected to do his job but keep his place, and there is little aid for him when he gets into trouble. Neither is there much appreciation when he brings justice to bear.

Lancaster chose something a little more conventional for *Lawman,* produced and directed by Englishman Michael Winner in Mexico and clearly influenced in its brutality by the Sergio Leone school of spaghetti westerns. In it, Lancaster is the marshal relentlessly tracking the men who smashed up his town. He finds them in another town, where the weary sheriff (Robert Ryan) advises against action because the men work for the local land baron (Lee J. Cobb). The advice goes unheeded and by the end of the film all the men have paid with their lives, including the tycoon, who commits suicide when he sees the marshal gun down his son.

Of these three Lancaster westerns, the most fully realized is *Ulzana's Raid,* which deals with Apache warfare in Arizona in the 1880s and tributes both their bravery and their brutality. After *Broken Arrow* and *Devil's Doorway* in 1950, Hollywood tended to go overboard in righting its previous screen wrongs about portraying the Indians as savages without culture. Many films now leaned too heavily upon their culture and supposed nobility. Among them was *Apache* (1954), in which Robert Aldrich directed Lancaster as an Indian who refused to give in to white law. Despite the intensity of his playing, Lancaster was not an ideal choice to play an Apache, but now, 18 years later, Aldrich and Lancaster were working together again on a film in which the casting was letter perfect. Here Lancaster is a grizzled old Army scout named McIntosh, a man with great knowledge of the Apaches, along with respect for their skill as fighters as well as their cruelty. That cruelty was part of their culture and no film conveys that truth better than this one.

Ulzana (Joaquin Martinez) is a renegade who raids the San Carlos Indian Reservation and steals a herd of horses. When the raid is reported to Major Cartwright (Douglas Watson), the commandant of Fort Lowell, he calls in McIntosh to lead Lieutenant Garnett DeBuin (Bruce Davison) on a campaign to capture Ulzana. Newly arrived from West Point and the son of a minister, DeBuin speaks of treating the Indians with Christian charity, a view that he will modify in the days ahead. Cartwright, long tired of his posting, reminds the greenhorn lieutenant of a comment made by General Grant, "If I owned hell and Arizona, I'd live in hell and rent out Arizona." McIntosh warns him that he is up against an enemy who burns, rapes, tortures and maims, and "Half of what he says is lies, the other half isn't true." DeBuin is soon exposed to evidence. On the first morning of the expedition, he and his men come across the body of a woman who has been shot in the head by a soldier to spare her the treatment she would suffer if captured alive by the Indians. The soldier has himself committed suicide for the same reasons, which does not stop the Apaches from cutting out his heart. The woman's husband, Rukeyser (Karl Swenson), had sent her away to Fort Lowell for safety, knowing his farm will be attacked by Ulzana. It is. He puts up a good fight and comes out of his barricaded house when he hears a cavalry bugle call. The call is made by an Indian, and when McIntosh finds Rukeyser, the farmer has been bound to a tree and burned to death.

Karl Swenson and Burt Lancaster.

DeBuin asks McIntosh's Apache guide, Ke-Ni-Tay (Jorge Luke), why his people are so cruel. The stoic Indian is puzzled by the question, "That's how they are, they've always been that way. The man who kills takes power from the man he kills. Here in this land a man must know about power." When DeBuin asks why Ulzana did not kill Rukeyser's young son, Ke-Ni-Tay explains, "A man cannot take power from a boy." With the native skill of Ke-Ni-Tay and his own scouting knowledge, McIntosh combats the tactics of the crafty Ulzana in cutting back and forth across the land. "The problem with fighting Apaches is knowing what they'll

Jorge Luke and Burt Lancaster.

238

do next." When DeBuin quotes the Bible in regard to compassion toward the enemy, McIntosh tells him, "Christ never had to deal with the Apaches."

McIntosh, DeBuin and the company of cavalry come across the scene of another massacre. At a small ranch they find the owner tied upside down over a fence and burned to death. In a wagon lies his wife, groaning in agony, having been brutally raped. DeBuin orders part of his company to escort the woman back to the fort, but McIntosh advises him that this is exactly what Ulzana is counting upon. Usually women are raped to death. This one has been allowed to live for a purpose.

DeBuin, who has now come to respect the old scout, accepts the suggestion to seemingly divide the command, but with the second group later turning and following the first. Ulzana lies waiting for McIntosh, DeBuin and their soldiers but the attack is even more ferocious and effective than expected. Most of the troops are killed and McIntosh is mortally wounded. It remains for Ke-Ni-Tay to go after Ulzana, who has also lost most of his men in the fight. Only an Apache can catch an Apache. When he is trapped by Ke-Ni-Tay, Ulzana submits to his fate. He drops to his knees and sings his death chant. Ke-Ni-Tay stands behind him and shoots him in the back of the neck.

DeBuin prepares to pick up the wounded McIntosh, paralyzed with a bullet in his spine, but the old man tells him he wants to be left to die. Says the officer, "It's not Christian." McIntosh looks up at him, "That's right, lieutenant, it's not." When DeBuin, who has learned a great deal about fighting Apaches on his first campaign, offers two men to stay with him, McIntosh again refuses, "I don't want to spend my last hours sitting with grave diggers." DeBuin gives in, and then

Jorge Luke, Bruce Davison and Burt Lancaster.

tells Ke-Ni-Tay to bury the body of Ulzana. The proud young guide demands the honor of returning with the body to the fort. Again DeBuin gives in, and moves off, leaving the exhausted McIntosh lighting a cigarette.

Filmed for the most part in southern Arizona, near Nogales and the Mexican border, as well as in the Coronado State Park with its cactus forests, *Ulzana's Raid* gives an authentic version of its subjects, with the stark and harsh beauty of the Arizona landscapes providing the exact setting for the story of Apache courage and primitive savagery. With this film, Lancaster and Robert Aldrich help set straight Indian history, bringing back into focus the somewhat glamorized and overly liberal concept of the American Indian that they themselves had been party to with their *Apache*. In 1972, some critics made points about *Ulzana's Raid* being a veiled comment upon America's painful mission in Vi-

240

In 1980, Lancaster played notorious bandit Bill Doolin in *Cattle Annie and Little Britches,* a light-hearted romp about a pair of adolescent girls in search of the kind of western adventure they have read about in the Ned Buntline kind of dime novels. The relatively little seen film failed to amuse and marked Lancaster's final foray into the cinematic West, until he reteamed with old pal Kirk Douglas as over-the-hill train robbers in the delightful modern day western, *Tough Guys,* half a dozen years later. In the long run, Lancaster need have no regrets about his work in western film. His 15 entries may not have all been winners at the box office but they represent the widest variety of such material attempted by any major film actor, an actor for whom the box office has never been the primary driving force.

etnam, but those views now seem more than a little forced.

Ulzana's Raid is the high water mark in Burt Lancaster's catalogue of westerns. In 1976, he undertook, as a supporting actor, the role of western impressario Ned Buntline in Robert Altman's bitterly satirical and unsuccessful *Buffalo Bill and the Indians,* with Paul Newman playing Cody. Buntline was the man who almost single-handedly started the merchandizing of the Wild West, persuading Cody to restage his adventures for the public in colorful exhibitions and to write about them in paperback novels. The mythology of the West begins with Buntline but Altman's overly schematic and cynical film comes close to being a guilt trip, possibly proving that it is better to leave well enough alone. It is difficult to prove false something that makes no bones about being false.

Bruce Davison and Burt Lancaster.

241

THE OUTLAW JOSEY WALES

WARNER BROS., 1976

Produced by Robert Daley. Directed by Clint Eastwood.
Written by Philip Kaufman and Sonia Chernus, based on the
book *Gone to Texas* by Forrest Carter. Photographed in
DeLuxe Color by Bruce Surtees. Music by Jerry Fielding.
135 minutes.

CAST:

(*Josey Wales*) Clint Eastwood; (*Lone Watie*) Chief Dan George;
(*Laura Lee*) Sondra Locke; (*Terrill*) Bill McKinney; (*Fletcher*)
John Vernon; (*Grandma Sarah*) Paula Trueman; (*Jamie*) Sam
Bottoms; (*Little Moonlight*) Geraldine Keams; (*Carpetbagger*)
Woodrow Parfrey; (*Rose*) Joyce Jameson; (*Cobb*) Sheb Wooley;
(*Ten Spot*) Royal Dano; (*Kelly*) Matt Clark; (*Chato*) John
Verros; (*Ten Bears*) Will Sampson; (*Carstairs*) William O'Con-
nell.

Clint Eastwood may turn out to be the last important
movie star to be a major figure of western film. In
1985, he tried to revive his early success in westerns
with his own production of *Pale Rider,* but the box office
returns were disappointing. Why? It might be that the
western form has long said all it has to say. *Pale Rider*
had nothing new to say. Eastwood was again the mysterious, righteous avenger, although in a film that
seemed like a blend of *Shane* and *Paint Your Wagon.*
But 1985 was also the year of *Silverado,* whose producers spent $20-million to make a spanking, lusty, old
fashioned horse opera and found it a dubious investment. Since then Hollywood's only westerns have been
for television, where the ratings have also been disappointing, especially so with dismal remakes of *Stagecoach* and *Red River,* among others. It might be that
like the glorious days of the musical, the glorious days
of the western are in the past—a past with which we
cannot compete.

Eastwood was involved in the two factors that
changed the western—television and the sagebrush
sagas made by Italy's Sergio Leone. Born in San Francisco, Eastwood did not start out with the idea of being
an actor, let alone a westerner. It all happened by
chance. He had been a fine athlete in school, and while
serving in the Army, an actor friend, David Janssen,

Clint Eastwood and Chief Dan George.

suggested he afterwards try getting work in the movies. Eastwood managed to do that, and after work as an extra, he was signed by Universal, which started giving him bit parts in 1955. His career seemed to be going nowhere in particular when a television producer invited him to test for the role of a cowboy in a proposed series called *Rawhide*. It was his seven years playing Rowdy Yates that made an international favorite of Clint Eastwood. While vacationing in Europe in the summer of 1964, Eastwood was contacted by Leone, an admitted western devotee, who offered him the lead in *A Fistful of Dollars*, explaining that he could pay only $15,000 and that both Charles Bronson and James Coburn had turned him down. The idea of making a western on location in Europe, mostly Spain, amused not-yet-star Eastwood—and thus came about the oddity known as the spaghetti western.

A Fistful of Dollars, with Eastwood as a poncho-clad, mysterious mercenary with no apparent name and very little dialogue, was a surprise international success and the following year Eastwood went back to Leone to do *For a Few Dollars More*, which resulted in far more than a few dollars more for the actor. His third Leone western was *The Good, the Bad and the Ugly* (1966), which ended Eastwood's adventures making westerns in Europe but which inspired a good many others of this strange ilk, all of them more bizarre than anything done on the home turf until that time. The success of the spaghetti westerns, however, was not lost on Hollywood, or on Eastwood, who set up his own company,

Malpaso, and produced *Hang 'Em High* in 1968. It was every bit as fanciful and gory as those he had made with Leone. He turned director in 1971 with *Play Misty for Me* and he did his first western as both star and director a year later with *High Plains Drifter*, revealing a style that showed obvious Leone influences. Again he played the mystical avenger, and the tone of the film bordered on the surreal.

Everything that Eastwood had learned about making westerns, from the admirable *Rawhide*, one of the more realistic television treatments of the West, to the extreme flights of violent fancy concocted by Leone, came together in *The Outlaw Josey Wales*, Eastwood's 26th film. It is a magnificent piece of work, with a fine sense of style and an equally fine understanding of the times in which the story is set—the final years of the Civil War in Missouri and the bitter, cruel ones that followed. Many have been the films made about that era and setting but none have ever shown the misery and the desperation so vividly.

Josey Wales is a farmer. One day while plowing his fields, he notices smoke arising from the direction of his home. There he finds a band of Union Army guerrillas, led by a man named Terrill (Bill McKinney), firing and ransacking his property and raping his wife. Terrill fells him with a rifle blow to his face. When Wales awakens his home is a smoldering ruin, in which his young son has been trapped. He buries his family, and soon afterwards joins a band of Confederate guerrilla fighters. With the war over, the leader of the Confed-

erates, Fletcher (John Vernon), persuades his men to lay down their arms and take the oath of allegiance to the Union. All do, except Wales. At the surrender, Fletcher, who has been accepting money for getting Confederates to give up, is stunned to see his men shot down with gattling guns. Wales witnesses the slaughter and rides to attack, killing many of the soldiers and managing to rescue one wounded boy, Jamie (Sam Bottoms). Fletcher is now instructed to go after Wales, which he knows he must do to keep Wales quiet. The man really responsible for the massacre, however, is Terrill, now a captain, who also realizes he must pursue Wales in order to save his own life.

Jamie dies from his wounds but Wales, now a hunted man, picks up another traveling companion, Lone Watie (Chief Dan George), an old Indian, who is sardonic in his exceptance of Indian defeat in the wake of white supremacy. As a posted outlaw with $5000 on his head, Wales is hounded by men for whom even one dollar is a prize. Only his calmness, his shrewdness and his skill with his pistols keep him alive. He and Lone Watie make their way to Texas and Terrill observes, "He's not a hard man to track—he leaves dead men wherever he goes." En route, Wales saves a small band of Kansas

migrants from the deprivations of a gang of savage outlaws, all of whom he kills, and travels with them to an abandoned ranch house, which they decide to make their home. Among the migrants is a young girl, Laura Lee (Sondra Locke), whose love for Wales slowly makes an impression on him and brings back the warmth that he has lost in the years of obsessive hatred.

The Comanches prepare to attack the settlers but Wales rides to meet their leader and talks him into peace. He makes a plausible bid for living side by side and sharing whatever the land has to offer. No such logic prevails the day Terrill and his band of guerrillas turn up. The smile of satisfaction leaves Terrill's face when he finds that Wales has not forgotten the military skill learned in the war. Terrill lines his men up to face the lone Wales in front of the ranch. Wales unbuckles his gunbelt but it is a signal for all the windows in the house to open and rifles to appear. The handful of settlers blast away and shoot Terrill's men from their horses. The wounded Terrill flees with Wales in pursuit, cornering him in an old building. There Wales walks toward him firing his pistols but on empty chambers, prolonging the expected death. Out of ammunition

246

himself, Terrill draws his sword, which Wales slowly turns on him.

A pair of Texas Rangers later arrive to investigate. Wales is introduced as "Mr. Wilson," with everyone ready to swear that the real Wales is dead. The rangers doubtlessly know who he is, but they also know the nature of Terrill and his bloody guerrillas. The time has come to put an end to the war. The rangers ask one of the men to sign an affidavit to the effect that Wales is dead and then they move on. With them is another man, his face hidden in shadow. He moves forward—Fletcher. In the street, he and Wales face each other, with Fletcher looking Wales in the eye and talking about all the death they have lived through. Wales thinks for a moment and says, "I guess we all died a little in that damn war," and walks away. He goes back to his settler friends and Laura Lee.

Unlike the Leone westerns, the hard and bitter man intent on revenge in *The Outlaw Josey Wales* is relieved of his burden of hatred. He will never forget the agony of his losses and his experiences but he has the humanity to move on. He is not consumed by revenge. Clint Eastwood, a kind of latter day Gary Cooper but harder, has not fared well with the critics as an actor. They find him wooden. It is an unfair estimate, particularly in regard to his Josey Wales, which is a believable portrait

Bill McKinney and Clint Eastwood.

of a tormented man, possessed with contained fury. It is hard to fault the scene in which he breaks down when burying his family.

It is a film that takes its time, a full two and a quarter hours, to tell its story and its director shows a keen sense of pacing. The visual effects and the intensity of the acting makes it hard to realize that the principle actor is also the director (having taken over from Philip Kaufman). In its early sequences, *Josey Wales* contains some of the truest Civil War material ever filmed. It has none of the romantic notions that often well up in dealing with the war between the Blue and the Gray. These scenes are as dismal in their shabbiness as they are sad in their ferocity, and Bruce Surtees' photography is admirable in its intelligence. He uses muted color in the war sequences, none of which glamorize the action, and his shooting of landscapes and changing seasons is a counterpoint to the grungy nature of so many of the characters in the story. Eastwood may or may not make another western but with *Josey Wales* he can be credited with a masterpiece.

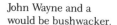
John Wayne and a would be bushwacker.

THE SHOOTIST

PARAMOUNT, 1976

Produced by M. J. Frankovich and William Self. Directed by Don Siegel. Written by Miles Hood Swarthout and Scott Hale. Based on the novel by Glendon Swarthout. Photographed in color by Bruce Surtees. Music by Elmer Bernstein. 100 minutes.

CAST:

(John Bernard Books) John Wayne; *(Bond Rogers)* Lauren Bacall; *(Gillom Rogers)* Ron Howard; *(Dr. Hostetler)* James Stewart; *(Mike Sweeney)* Richard Boone; *(Pulford)* Hugh O'Brian; *(Cobb)* Bill McKinney; *(Marshal Thibido)* Harry Morgan; *(Beckum)* John Carradine; *(Serepta)* Sheree North; *(Sam Dobkins)* Richard Lenz; *(Moses)* Scatman Crothers; *(Burly Man)* Gregg Palmer; *(Barber)* Alfred Dennis; *(Streetcar Driver)* Dick Winslow; *(Schoolteacher)* Kathleen O'Malley.

John Wayne received an Oscar on the evening of April 7, 1970, as Best Actor of 1969, for his performance as the fat, bellicose, one-eyed curmudgeon sheriff Rooster Cogburn in *True Grit.* He seemed genuinely surprised to have beaten out the likes of Richard Burton, Peter

O'Toole, Dustin Hoffman and Jon Voight, but it was less of a surprise to the Hollywood community, which was rewarding him not so much for a single performance but for his 40 years in the movies, a good half of which had seen him consistently on the highest level of popularity. Wayne had been nominated two decades earlier as Best Actor for *Sands of Iwo Jima* but his chances of winning at that time were slight. It was after the age of 40 that Wayne gradually emerged as an American icon—and in terms of western film, a kind of Rock of Gibraltar on horseback. As he aged, he looked more and more like a man created by painter Frederick Remington.

Wayne was never a cowboy and he had no interest in ranching, yet he became a virtual personification of the American West. Critics seldom fell over themselves praising his talent as an actor and yet it would be hard to think of performances more fitting than Wayne's Thomas Dunston in Howard Hawks' *Red River* (1948) or his Ethan Edwards in John Ford's *The Searchers* (1956), which Wayne considered his best work as an actor. Both Dunston and Edwards are complicated men, quiet by nature but harboring resentments against life. There is nothing quiet or complicated about Rooster Cogburn, who rails like a banshee when pursuing villains and gets roaring drunk in his off hours. Such was the success of *True Grit* that more of the same was sheer business logic. In its wake came *The Undefeated* (1969), *Chisum* (1970), *Rio Lobo* (1970), *Big Jake* (1971), *The Cowboys* (1972), *The Train Robbers* (1972), *Cahill, United States Marshal* (1973) and a grand reprise, *Rooster Cogburn* (1975), with no less than Katharine Hepburn as his co-star. But finally came *The Shootist*, a horse, so to speak, of a different color.

No film is more of a valedictory than *The Shootist*, which is the story of an old westerner dying of cancer, made by an old player of westerners who was himself dying of cancer. Wayne was found to be suffering from lung cancer in 1962 but after the removal of a lung he was considered cured. He had licked the Big C—until it came back. In the films made after *True Grit*, it was obvious that he was straining to appear relaxed on horseback. His weight increased and action sequences were carefully photographed and edited. There is little action in *The Shootist*, but action is not what the film is about. It is about a man coming to terms with life and choosing his manner of exit. John Bernard Books is a man who has made his career as a gunman, reputedly the killer of 30 men, sometimes for the law and often as a hired hand for less than lawful causes. He is a loner with his own code of honor, "I won't be wronged, I won't be insulted and I won't be laid a hand on. I don't do these things to other people and I require the same from them."

Books arrives in Carson City, Nevada, on January 22, 1901, there to visit an old acquaintance, Dr. Hostetler (James Stewart) and find out why he is wracked with pain in his lower back. "You have a cancer." Books wants to know how much time he has. "Two months—six weeks—less—no way to tell." He needs somewhere to stay, and Hostetler steers him to the widow Rogers (Lauren Bacall), who takes in lodgers. She does not take to his gruff, out-spoken manner but when he explains his situation she becomes sympathetic. Her teenage son, Gillom (Ron Howard), is greatly impressed by having the celebrated gunman in his home, as are others for different reasons. The town marshal, Thibido (Harry Morgan), tells Books he must move on but allows him to stay after hearing the news, which he greets with pleasure while advising Books to not take too long about dying. His promise to keep the news to himself is not kept, resulting in Books coming to the kind of attention he was hoping to avoid.

A young newspaperman, Dobkins (Richard Lenz), tries to persuade Books to cooperate on the writing of

a book about his life, but Books kicks him out. A day or so later an old love, Serepta (Sheree North), comes to pay a visit and ask him to marry her, so she will benefit from his name. She brings up the business of the book and admits Dobkins would ghost write it for her. He refuses and she leaves in disgust. His pains increasing, Books goes back to Hostetler, who gives him an awful-tasting, pain-killing medicine and jokes about it being addictive. Books wants to know what is going to happen to him. Hostetler cringes when he explains that there will be more pain in the lower spine and groin. "If you're lucky you'll lose consciousness." Then, as Books leaves, the doctor adds, "One more thing. I would not die the death I've just described—not if I had your courage."

The old gunfighter moves to put his affairs in order, especially following a night attack by two men who break into his room and try to kill him. Both meet their own end. Books gives the eager Gillom some lessons about gunplay but tries to disillusion him about the glories of being a western badman. He wins the friend-

John Wayne and James Stewart.

John Wayne and Richard Lenz.

ship of Mrs. Rogers and takes her riding in the country-side. On the way back into town they bump into another of his old acquaintances, Sweeney (Richard Boone), whose brother was killed by Books. Sweeney implies he is in town and willing for another meeting. Similar messages come from Cobb (Bill McKinney), a rough-neck milkman for whom Gillom works, and Pulford (Hugh O'Brian), an elegantly attired gambler, who works at the Metropole Casino and is noted for being a skilled gunman. All three are men who would like to be known as the killer of John Bernard Books.

Books agrees to a rendezvous. He walks into the Metropole early one morning. Inside are just four men—Pulford, Cobb and Sweeney, and the bartender, who leaves after serving Books a drink. Cobb is the first to make a play and Books easily disposes of him. Sweeney charges from behind a small table but Books' bullets smash through it and kill him, although not until Books himself has taken two slugs. The cool, accurate Pulford now fires and hits Books, who retreats behind the counter. Books tricks Pulford into revealing his position and kills him. He then pulls himself up and staggers toward the door. The bartender reappears with a shotgun and fires into Books' back. Gillom comes into the casino in time to see this, picks up Books' pistol and fires three shots at the bartender. Then, disheartened at what he has done, he slings the pistol across the room. Books looks up at him and with his

Lauren Bacall and John Wayne

Ron Howard and
John Wayne

dying strength gives the young man a small nod of approval. The career of a famed gunman has come to an end and Gillom will not follow in his footsteps.

The Shootist was not intended by John Wayne to be his final film—indeed he had a whole roster of projects at his disposal—but as a final film it would be difficult to think of anything more fitting. It is a contemplative movie, the story of a courageous, dignified man whose time has come and gone. No actor was more qualified to play John Bernard Books than Wayne, himself a man of quite some courage and dignity, as well as one whose time was up. If *The Shootist* is a valedictory, it is sadly also Wayne's film epitaph. Did western film die with him? There is an emotional temptation to think so, much as one tries to resist it. Certainly nothing filmed since *The Shootist* has met with much favor or success. In fact, even *The Shootist* failed to draw the expected Wayne-size audience. Anyone looking for a slam-bang horse opera was bound to be disappointed; anyone knowing Wayne was bound to find the film unsettling.

I saw Wayne a number of times while he was making *The Shootist*. While it was a Paramount production, the street scenes were shot on the backlot at the Warner studio in Burbank, not far from my home. In those days, I frequently went to the studio to join friends for lunch in the commissary. I first met Wayne when he was making *Hatari!* in 1962 and I was with him on a publicity junket for his controversial *The Green Berets*. I found him easy to talk to, especially in discussing the West and his western pictures. During one lunch at Warners, I kidded him about the fact that once he had gone there would be no replacement. "Well, my group's going pretty fast and I'm surprised they haven't replaced us already. Hell, I'm 68 now and I've always liked good whiskey. Maybe it has something to do with the writers. They always seemed to know what to write for me in the old days. Nobody seems to be writing specifically for anybody any more." The thought seemed to depress him. He looked around. "There isn't the feeling on the set of a closely-knit unit that there used to be." I said something to the effect that there no longer seemed to be any big, hard tough guys like him anymore. "Well, it isn't a case of being hard or tough—those things are written for you, you know

that. I'm not really a killer at heart." "No, but you're a pretty leathery old character though." As he got up to go back to the set he winked at me, "Yeah? Well, don't let this gray hair make a coward out of you."

I did not see Wayne again after that until the evening of April 3, 1979, when he came to the Dorothy Chandler Pavilion of the Los Angeles Music Center to give the Best Film Oscar at the Academy Awards. I was a script writer for that production and it became my job to write Wayne's speech, which turned out to be the last words he ever spoke in public. It was a shock to see him. The huge bulk had gone. He was now thin, gaunt, the face ashen and the eyes those of a dying man. I was tempted to write a lot of copy for him to read but he looked it over and said, "Cut it down." In giving him an introduction, Johnny Carson agreed that all he needed to say was, "Ladies and Gentlemen, John Wayne." The standing ovation was thunderous. The state of his health was well known in the industry and it appeared doubtful that he would be strong enough to do the show. But he had promised producer Jack Haley, Jr., that he would be there. This is what I wrote for him:

"I thank you. Believe me when I tell you how pleased I am to be here. Oscar and I have something in common. Oscar first came on the Hollywood scene in 1928. So did I. We're both a little weatherbeaten but we're both still here. And plan on being around a whole lot longer, I might add.

But my job tonight is to hand out the award for the Outstanding Picture of the Year—so let's 'move 'em out.' "

He then introduced clips from *Coming Home, The Deer Hunter, Heaven Can Wait, Midnight Express* and *An Unmarried Woman,* with the Oscar going to *The Deer Hunter.* It was the end of the show and all the winners trooped onstage and stood around Wayne. Carson said, "Duke, you've added the capper to a most emotional evening, and we're all delighted you could be with us as Oscar begins his second half century. A lot of your friends would like to say hello to you, and I know you join me in congratulating all the winners tonight."

In giving Wayne the line, "And plan on being around a whole lot longer," we all knew that it was a lie happily agreed upon. He died two months later, on June 11, just two weeks after his 71st birthday. His track record was one that may never be equaled—50 years as a star movie actor. Half of his 150 films were westerns and it seems likely that it will always be Wayne the Westerner that first comes to mind at the mention of his name. He epitomized the romantic concept of the Old West, he brought the mythology of it all to life. He was believable as a man who could lead a cavalry charge or a wagon train or a cattle drive. And if the men of the real West did not actually look like John Wayne, then they should have.